ARISTOPHANES

LYSISTRATA, THE WOMEN'S FESTIVAL, AND FROGS

Oklahoma Series in Classical Culture

ARISTOPHANES

LYSISTRATA,
THE WOMEN'S FESTIVAL,
AND FROGS

Translated and with Theatrical Commentaries by
MICHAEL EWANS

UNIVERSITY OF OKLAHOMA PRESS : NORMAN

Also by Michael Ewans

Janáček's Tragic Operas (Faber, 1977)
Wagner and Aeschylus: The Ring *and the* Oresteia (Faber, 1982)
Georg Büchner's Woyzeck (Peter Lang, 1989)
Aeschylus: Oresteia (editor and translator) (J. M. Dent, 1995)
Aeschylus: Suppliants and other Dramas (editor and translator) (J. M. Dent, 1996)
Sophocles: Four Dramas of Maturity (editor and co-translator) (J. M. Dent, 1999)
Sophocles: Three Dramas of Old Age (editor and co-translator) (J. M. Dent, 2000)
Opera from the Greek: Studies in the Poetics of Appropriation (Ashgate, 2007)

Aristophanes: Lysistrata, The Women's Festival, *and* Frogs is Volume 42 in the Oklahoma Series in Classical Culture.

Library of Congress Cataloging-in-Publication Data

Aristophanes.
    [Selections. English. 2011]
    Aristophanes : Lysistrata, The women's festival, and Frogs / [Aristophanes] ; translated and with theatrical commentaries by Michael Ewans.
        p. cm. — (Oklahoma series in classical culture ; v. 42)
    Includes bibliographical references and index.
    ISBN 978-0-8061-4151-0 (pbk. : alk. paper)
    1. Aristophanes—Translations into English. 2. Greek drama (Comedy) — Translations into English. I. Ewans, Michael, 1946– II. Aristophanes. Lysistrata. English. III. Aristophanes. Thesmophoriazusae. English. IV. Aristophanes. Frogs. English. V. Title.

PA3877.A2 2011
882'.01—dc22

                                                          2010015355

Contents

Illustrations

PREFACE

This book presents new, accurate, and actable translations of the three comedies of Aristophanes that survive from the last years of the Peloponnesian War. The principle behind this series is to group plays by the dates of performance, so that theatre practitioners, readers, and students may find in one volume Aristophanes' comic response to a particular phase in the fortunes of his native city. The second volume to appear, *Aristophanes: Acharnians, Knights, and Peace*, will group together three plays from the first years of the war.

While there have been on the one hand some close prose versions of Aristophanes, and on the other a number of free adaptations for the modern stage, there has not been an actable English verse translation of these three plays since the series by Kenneth McLeish. In my view his versions were often too free and left out more of the sense of the original than is acceptable.[1]

This translation of *Frogs* has been workshopped in a replica of the original Greek stage shape, and these translations of *Lysistrata* and *The Women's Festival* were given full productions in the same space. Accordingly it has been possible to provide a firm focus on Aristophanes as a playwright who wrote for performance. This edition provides the study aids needed by those who are primarily interested in Aristophanes' relationship to his social and political context, but in addition I have supplied theatrical commentaries on the plays, discussing the staging issues that each scene and *choros* presents and outlining possible solutions. The commentaries

---

1. McLeish 1993*a* and *b*. They were also based on texts that have been superseded by more recent editions of the Greek (see introduction, Translation).

owe much to the talent, commitment, and sheer hard work of the Newcastle Drama students who voluntarily took part as casts and crews in the workshops and productions, and I take this opportunity to thank them all. Special tribute must be paid to Samantha Fiddes (associate director, choreographer, and Myrrhine in *Lysistrata*), Angela Bobbins (assistant director, choreographer, and Fawn in *The Women's Festival*), and Anne-Marie Adams (Lysistrata and Kritylla).

CHRONOLOGY OF ARISTOPHANES' LIFE AND TIMES

487/86 B.C.E.	First performances of comedy at Festival of Dionysos
c. 447/46	Aristophanes born
c. 442	First performances of comedy at Lenaian Festival
432	Athenian alliance with Kerkyra
431	Peloponnesians invade Attika; outbreak of Peloponnesian War
	Euripides, *Medeia*
430	First outbreak of great plague at Athens
429	Euripides, *Hippolytos*; first version, not performed
	Death of Perikles
428	Euripides, *Hippolytos*; second, less controversial version performed
427	Aristophanes, *Banqueters* [lost]. Produced by Kallistratos. 2nd prize, Lenaia
426	Aristophanes, *Babylonians* [lost]. Produced by Kallistratos. 1st prize(?), Dionysia
425	Aristophanes, *Acharnians*. Produced by Kallistratos. 1st prize, Lenaia
	Kleon becomes Athens's leading politician
424	Aristophanes, *Knights.* Produced by Aristophanes. 1st prize, Lenaia
423	Aristophanes, *Clouds*. Produced by Aristophanes. 3rd prize (surviving text is revised version, c. 418, never performed)

422   Aristophanes, *Wasps*. Produced by
               Philonides. 2nd prize, Lenaia
            Death of Kleon
421   Aristophanes, *Peace*. Produced by Aristo-
               phanes. 2nd prize, Dionysia
            Peace of Nikias between Athens and Sparta
420   Athens/Argos alliance
416   Athenians sack Melos
415   Euripides, *Women of Troy*
            Sicilian expedition; mutilation of Hermai
414   Aristophanes, *Birds*. Produced by Aristo-
               phanes. 2nd prize, Dionysia
            Sparta resumes hostilities against Athens
413   Sicilian expedition destroyed by Syracuse
412   Euripides, *Helen* and *Andromeda*
411   (February) Aristophanes, *Lysistrata*. Pro-
               duced by Kallistratos. Lenaia
            (March) Aristophanes, *The Women's Festival*.
               Produced by Kallistratos. Dionysia
            (May) Right-wing coup; government of the
               "Four Hundred"
            (August) "Four Hundred" expelled and
               replaced by moderate oligarchy of the
               "Five Thousand"
410   Restoration of full democracy at Athens
409   Sophokles, *Philoktetes*
408   Euripides, *Orestes*
408/407   Euripides leaves Athens for the court of
               Archelaos in Makedonia
407   Athenians defeated at sea by Lysandros at
               Notion
406   Deaths of Sophokles and Euripides
            Athenian naval victory at Arginousai
405   Aristophanes, *Frogs*. Produced by
               Philonides. 1st prize, Lenaia
            Crushing defeat of Athenian navy at
               Aigispotamoi

404   (March) Revival of *Frogs*? Dionysia
              (April) Surrender of Athens
              (summer) Sparta imposes the junta of the
                  Thirty Tyrants
403   Democracy restored at Athens; general
                  amnesty
399   Trial and execution of Sokrates
?392   Aristophanes, *Assemblywomen*
388   Aristophanes, *Wealth*
c. 385/80   Death of Aristophanes

ARISTOPHANES

LYSISTRATA,
THE WOMEN'S FESTIVAL,
AND FROGS

Greece c. 424–404 B.C.E. Map by John Gilkes.

Introduction

The Festivals of Dionysos

The Great Festival of the god Dionysos, at the start of the sailing season in March, was a preeminent focus for Athenian life. It was fundamentally an affirmation of several core religious beliefs of this polytheistic society, in particular the complex forces that swirled around the worship of Dionysos himself. This god, though terrifying if rejected and defied, had the power to augment the value of life through attainment by his worshipers, who were also the theater audience and the tragic and comic actors, of a state of *ekstasis*,[1] standing outside one's normal personality. Wine, the celebratory ambience of the festival, and above all the drama performances themselves all contributed to the attainment of Dionysian ecstasy. And this experience was replicated on a less extravagant scale at the smaller festival of the Lenaia, held in January, at which plays were also performed. The Great Festival also gave the Athenians an opportunity to affirm the ideology and display the excellence of their city-state through ceremonies, including the display of tribute from their subject allies and a parade of war orphans who had now come of age and pledged themselves to the military service of the state.[2]

At the festivals, the comic and tragic playwrights enjoyed an almost unparalleled license to use their dramas to critique any aspect they wished of the city's policies and

1. All italicized Greek terms are explained in the glossary of Greek words.
2. Cf. Goldhill 1990 and 1997.

3

values.[3] This freedom of speech was granted because the festivals of Dionysos were detached from the cut-and-thrust of debate in the Assembly and the Council in Athens's extremely vigorous and robust participatory democracy. The Theater of Dionysos nestled under the Akropolis, next to his temple and in his sanctuary. It was sited a substantial distance from the centers of daily political and social life, approximately 1 kilometer from the hill of Pnyx, where the Assemblies of the people were held, and 1.5 kilometers from the Agora, the marketplace where most other civic activities took place. Simply to walk to the theater from the city for the Festival was to detach oneself from day-to-day affairs, and the social and ceremonial ambience of the Festival, as well as the use of masks by the actors in these performances consecrated to the god,[4] ensured a special reception for the ideas presented by the playwrights. P. Wilson expresses the point perfectly:

> The political character of Athenian drama is now generally understood not as if it were a forum for narrow, thinly-veiled political pamphleteering for a particular course of action in the "primary" political arenas of the Assembly or courts; but rather more as an institution in many ways parallel to them, one in which could be raised the more unwieldy, problematic "big questions" of life in the *polis* that underlie it but exceed the terms of its diurnal [everyday] debate.[5]

The playwrights whose dramas were selected for production were entitled to speak out to the *demos*, the citizens of Athens, on any matter that concerned them. In Aristophanes'

3. Though they were not immune from prosecution by aggrieved individual members of the audience. Cf. Sommerstein 2004 on Kleon's reaction to Aristophanes' early comedies.

4. Cf. Wiles 2007, especially 230ff., 245–51, 258, on the sacred role of tragic masks. There is no comparable work on the implications of the fifth-century comic mask.

5. Wilson 2000, 67.

view, they were not only entitled to do this, but had a duty to do so.[6]

Aristophanic Comedy

Our knowledge of Athenian comedy in the late fifth century B.C.E. comes from the nine surviving plays from this period by Aristophanes (who created more than forty comedies between 427 and the late 380s) and from numerous brief fragments of his lost comedies and of those by other playwrights.[7] To judge from the surviving plays, Aristophanic comedy was a formidable combination of a richly exuberant, surreal, and downright zany comic invention with a strong sense of form.

In this respect his medium has an ethos that is, surprisingly, parallel to that of Athenian tragedy; Aischylos, Sophokles, and Euripides disciplined the extremes of emotion in their tragic dramas within a similarly controlled formal structure. Tragedy and comedy were both performed at festivals of the god Dionysos, and in each genre there was the Dionysiac element of *ekstasis*. As the performers, through the act of impersonation, almost literally stood outside their normal selves in a state of heightened realization,[8] the audience, collectively moved to tears or laughter, also reached metaphorical *ekstasis*.[9] Just as actors and audience could explore the most extreme emotions in tragedy, so too the Athenian democracy in the late fifth century gave comedy

6. See below, Comedy and Politics.

7. In addition to the nine plays preserved from the Peloponnesian War period, we also have two Aristophanes comedies from the late 390s and early 380s—*Assemblywomen* and *Wealth*. They are almost a different genre, certainly lacking the vigor and bite of Aristophanes' earlier work.

8. Wiles 2007, 245–47.

9. For the highly emotional response of Athenian audiences to tragedy, see Stanford 1983. Aristophanes frequently shows awareness of his need to entertain his audience and make them laugh. See, for example, the opening lines of *Frogs* and the closing lines of *TWF*.

the license to explore extremes. Aristophanic comedy exhibits a total lack of inhibition—which extends both to sexual and scatological jokes and to a comic universe in which anything is possible, nothing is sacred, and no one, from Zeus to the lowest female slaves—except the city's patron goddess, Athena—is exempt from satire and ridicule.[10] Indeed, in the surviving comedies, Aristophanes satirizes not only individual public figures such as Kleon, Sokrates, and Euripides, but whole classes of society—among them politicians, warmongers, jurymen, sophists, and women. But just as the festival's Dionysiac *ekstasis* was moderated through formal ceremonies and competitions, in which Athenian society celebrated and affirmed the organizing powers of the polis, so too in Aristophanic comedy there is, in creative tension with the liberating element of Dionysiac freedom, the disciplining power of form.[11]

Athenian tragedy and comedy shared many conventions. Both were performed by a small number of solo actors interacting with a *choros*; all actors were masked and played multiple roles;[12] and similar meters and verse forms were used for dialogue and lyric verses. The difference between the two media is not, as has sometimes been supposed,[13] that tragedy is static and comedy dynamic. Performance-based research has revealed that Greek tragedy requires almost as much flexible movement as Aristophanic comedy.[14] Nor was

10. So too in tragedy, Theseus, the legendary founder of Athens, is always portrayed with respect.

11. On the civic values enshrined in the organization of the festival, see Goldhill 1997, 54–67. On the formal elements in Aristophanes, see below. The harnessing power of comic form is especially evident in *TWF*, whose scenes of high farce and tragic parody alternate with solemn choral invocations of the gods.

12. A suggested breakdown of the original doublings of solo roles in these plays is supplied in appendix 2. It was rare for the *choros* to play more than one collective character in one play, but see *Frogs* (Frogs and subsequently Initiates) and Euripides' *Hippolytos* (Huntsmen and subsequently Women).

13. See, for example, McLeish 1980, 48, and Revermann 2006, 3 and 108.

14. See the notes on staging (by Graham Ley, Gregory McCart, and Ewans) in Ewans 1995 and 1996, and Ewans, with Ley and McCart, 1999 and 2000.

it that tragedy is serious and comedy frivolous.[15] The fundamental differences are as follows:

- Tragedy almost never acknowledged that it was performed in a theater,[16] whereas in Aristophanic comedy the presence of the audience, the stage machines (*ekkuklēma* and *mēchanē*), and even, at the start of *Frogs*, the fact that the actors are comedians first and players of roles are all openly acknowledged.
- Tragedy was almost invariably based on myths—legends about the distant, heroic past;[17] comedy could invade this territory and provide mythical pastiche[18] but was more frequently set in (or took its point of departure from) contemporary Athens.
- Comedy was open ended, drawing its subject matter from almost any conceivable aspect of society, with a total freedom both of fantasy and of comic invention and no consistency of character. By contrast, the plots of tragedy were always plausible, and every character had to be credible.

Aristophanes' plays were written in verse—which to the Greeks meant combinations of long and short syllables in varying degrees of intricacy. There were three main types of verse: iambic trimeter, the meter of spoken dialogue; tetrameter, a longer verse used for declamatory "recitative"; and a variety of lyric meters for the sung and danced sections, ranging from the pedestrian anapest to choral lyric meters

15. On the serious elements in Aristophanic comedy, see below, Comedy and Politics.

16. The exception that proves the rule is Athena's address to "our future citizens" (the actual audience in 458 B.C.E.) at Aischylos, *Eumenides* 681ff.

17. Two of the three known exceptions are political plays dealing with the threat of Persia: Phrynichos's lost *Sack of Miletos* and Aischylos's surviving *Persians*. Aristotle records (*Poetics* 51b21) that Agathon wrote a tragedy, *Antheus*, in which all the characters were his own invention.

18. To judge from the titles of lost plays, the comedians often presented pastiches of myth, but no example of this kind of comedy survives.

with the capacity to become far more elevated—and passionate.[19] Aristophanes selected his meters carefully to respond to the nature and tone of each comic situation he created.

In Aristophanes' surviving comedies, there is a typical and recurrent pattern:[20] a lead character who is highly motivated (usually because he or she finds something unacceptable about the current state of the polis) embarks on a fantastic plan that in real life would be impossible but in the world of the play is treated as totally achievable. The playwright then creates a series of episodes, each given form by a tightly knit structure and timed to last precisely as long as its humorous content can bear. This structure in its basic form (seen most clearly in *Acharnians*, *Peace*, and *Birds*) is:

- introductory scene: the protagonist's dissatisfaction leads to a heroic resolve;
- *parodos* (entry of the *choros*): usually a spectacular scene;[21]
- episodes: might include an *agōn* (contest);
- achievement of the hero's goal;
- *parabasis* (usually halfway through the play): the *choros* addresses the audience, in character but outside the play, and often in the earlier plays speaking overtly on behalf of the playwright;
- further episodes, in which conflict occurs (the hero is often confronted by freeloaders, who seek either to undermine or to cash in on his or her achievement);[22]
- a *kōmos* of fulfillment (a final scene of revelry and festivity): celebration of the hero's triumph.

19. For the strategies I use to translate each of these styles of verse, see below, Translation. In these translations, all chanted (anapestic) and sung (lyric) passages are double indented to distinguish them from spoken dialogue and recitative.

20. See especially *Acharnians, Peace, Birds, Lysistrata, Frogs,* and *Assemblywomen.*

21. *TWF* is unique among the surviving comedies in that the *choros* enters in silence: 280ff.

22. An *agōn* may occur here too, as, for example, in *Knights, Clouds,* and *Frogs.*

It should be emphasized that this simplified pattern does not fit all the surviving plays. *Acharnians, Peace,* and *Birds* conform closely, but elsewhere Aristophanes experimented with form. For example, he placed the *parabasis* well before the midpoint in *Clouds* and well after it in *Wasps;* he created conflict between Dionysos and assorted boastful characters throughout the first half and reserved the only (and very important) *agōn* in *Frogs* for the second half; and he ended *Clouds* and *The Women's Festival* without a celebratory *kōmos,* and virtually abolished the *parabasis* in *Lysistrata* by leaving the *choros* as two hostile half *choroses* of Old Men and Old Women until late in the play—who therefore cannot speak with a united voice at the midpoint.[23] We should also note that the plays sometimes include causality-free episodes that, like the *parabasis,* do nothing to advance the plot.[24]

Aristophanic comedy was performed before a very large audience in an open-air *theatron.*[25] These performance conditions—and the fact that the comedies were played by masked actors in grotesquely padded costumes and (when playing male parts) long artificial phalluses—make the original experience very remote from most modern experience of theater. As a result, all too often modern productions of these plays use free adaptations rather than close translations of the text. The aim of this book is to try to place students, readers, and theater practitioners inside Aristophanes' own comic world.

Getting inside Aristophanic comedy demands a knowledge of the sociopolitical context of each individual comedy (each having been created for one performance at one specific

23. See Theatrical Commentary, *Lysistrata* choros 3.
24. See Silk 2000, 264–65.
25. Estimates of the seating capacity are normally between thirteen thousand and seventeen thousand. Revermann (2006, 168) adopts a more conservative position in light of the findings of recent excavations, for which see Goette 2007.

festival) and a knowledge of Athenian performance conventions. It also requires the ability to understand how accurate translations of these comedies might work effectively in modern performance. That in turn requires practice-based research, in which the disciplines of the workshop and the rehearsal room are applied to the draft script. This process produces translations that have been road tested for actability and modified where specific passages failed to work in rehearsal. The process also makes possible the unique feature of this edition, the theatrical commentary, which deals with staging issues both from the point of view of Aristophanes and/or his producers and from the perspective of those striving to reclaim these dramas by realizing their comic power in modern performance. The book's commentaries span the range of issues involved in performance—among them the acting style; the spatial dynamics of performance in the original stage shape; the use of stage machinery, set, props, and costumes; and proven ways in which modern productions can respond to the forms and styles of Aristophanic comedy.

Aristophanes and the Athenians

Aristophanes grew up as Athens was reaching the apex of its power, which the city had been consolidating steadily since the 460s, when it turned the Delian League (founded in 478 B.C.E. as a defensive alliance against Persia) into an empire of tribute-paying states. He began to write comedies as a young man, four years after Sparta and its allies declared war on Athens. Aristophanes blamed the Peloponnesian War no more on the Spartans than on the Athenians,[26] whose leaders, following the untimely death of Perikles, had made serious mistakes. Among these was Kleon, whom

26. *Acharnians* 509ff.

Aristophanes regarded as a corrupt warmonger and whom
he criticized stridently in *Acharnians* and attacked with
venom in *Knights*. Each comedy from the first ten years of
the war contrasts the sufferings of Athens as a result of the
war with the desirability of peace, and in 421 these culminated in a play whose title is, simply, *Peace*.[27]

By a happy congruence with Aristophanes' comedy, a
peace treaty (the Peace of Nikias) was signed that very year.
However, small hostilities soon occurred, and in 418 the war
resumed. Then Athens disastrously overreached itself when
it dispatched an expedition to Sicily to conquer Syracuse. In
413 the expedition was annihilated; not one man returned.
With the ensuing desperation came political instability. Many
blamed an excessively democratic system for Athens's wrong
decisions. This led to a right-wing coup in 411, followed by a
restoration of full democracy in 410. But the threat of defeat
loomed ever greater in the years that followed, and in 404
Athens surrendered to Sparta.

This turbulent period is the background for the three
plays in this book. They contain notably less satire of individual politicians than do the plays of the 420s, partly because
Aristophanes had already moved on, in *Birds* (414), to a new
kind of comedy, and partly because the political situation
was extremely sensitive—especially when he was creating
The Women's Festival. But it would be a mistake to regard
these plays as less politically engaged simply because the
overt vitriol of *Knights* (an atypical play) is absent. Nothing
Aristophanes wrote during the war is without a message to
the polis about how to conduct its affairs.[28]

27. *Acharnians, Knights,* and *Peace* will be collected in the sequel to this volume, *Aristophanes:* Acharnians, Knights, *and* Peace.
28. For more detail regarding the political context of these plays and Aristophanes' message in each of them, see below. I totally oppose the view, entertained briefly by McLeish in 1993*b*, xviii, and more fully expressed by Silk (2000,
318–19) and Halliwell (1998, xlff. and 81ff.) that Aristophanic comedy was not
politically engaged. I find strong support in McDowell 1995 (see below, note 44)

Women in Aristophanes

Two of these three plays—*Lysistrata* and *The Women's Festival*—place women at the center to an extent not only unprecedented in Aristophanes' earlier output, but also quite unexpected. Women were in every way second-class citizens in classical Greece. Men regarded them as less intelligent and less logical than themselves. Indeed, Aristophanes expects his audience to find it funny that in his imaginary version of the secret rites of the Thesmophoria, the women have a president, a secretary, and a meeting procedure that, in real life, only the male administration of Athens would have possessed.[29] Women had no voice in civic affairs—a feature of the polis against which Lysistrata reasonably objects.[30] Respectable free-born females were expected to confine themselves as much as possible to the *oikos*, and their duties were to remain chaste, to produce children (preferably sons), and to manage the household.[31]

Perhaps following a well-worn comic path, Aristophanes satirizes women for lust and a fondness for alcohol,[32] but in *Lysistrata* the women (especially the heroine) outwit and defeat the men, and the playwright presents very strongly the sufferings of the women as a result of war. Then, as the play reaches its climax, he affirms the value of female inclusiveness and bonding, in contrast to the men's petty warmongering and their squandering of the city's wealth.[33]

---

and Henderson 2000, 264 (on *Lysistrata*). Robson 2009, 163, tries to make a distinction between what Aristophanes himself thought on political matters and what his plays say about them. I do not believe this distinction can be made.

29. *TWF* 295ff., especially 372ff. Women and children did attend the festivals. See Henderson 1991 and Czapo and Slater 1995, 286–87.

30. *Lys* 507ff.

31. For more detail on the role of women in Athenian society, cf. Henderson 1996, 20–29.

32. See, for example, *Lys* 201–39, *TWF* 733ff. (alcohol); *Lys* 706ff., *TWF* 477ff. (lust).

33. 506ff., 588ff., 648ff., 1122ff.

Aristophanes and Euripides

In *The Women's Festival,* Aristophanes opposes the ingenuity of the women to the almost equal ingenuity of the great contemporary tragic playwright Euripides, who tries to penetrate the secret rites of the festival and then devises two successive tragic strategies to rescue his In-Law from the women. Both strategies fail, and in the end he must resort to a compromise with the women and must use a comic, rather than a tragic, stratagem to free the In-Law from the Policeman who is guarding him.

We know that Aristophanes' senior rival, Kratinos, accused a character in one of his comedies of "Euripidaristophanizing."[34] I do not interpret this brilliant coinage as referring to the fact that Aristophanes sometimes parodied Euripidean tragedy[35] (although he does this with great effect in *Acharnians, The Women's Festival,* and *Frogs*).[36] Kratinos was, in my view, suggesting that the two enfants terribles, who were creating a new kind of tragedy and a new kind of comedy at around the same time, had much in common. Both Aristophanes and Euripides were theatrical innovators who renewed tradition by rethinking the conventions of their respective genres and exploring the boundaries between tragedy and comedy. Both were alert to, and made great creative use of, the rich pool of ideas that the "new thought" of the sophists had brought to late fifth-century Athens, and both had a fascination with the Greek language and a desire to explore how it might be used innovatively in the theater—in particular by adapting the techniques of the forensic orator to the stage *agōn*.[37]

34. Kratinos, fragment 342.
35. Pace Halliwell 1998, xx–xxi.
36. On the relationship of Aristophanes and Euripides, cf. Robson 2009, 103–19.
37. See, for example, Euripides, *Andromache* 590ff.; Aristophanes, *Knights* 756ff. and *Clouds* 889ff.

In *The Women's Festival*, Aristophanes parodies *Helen* and *Andromeda*, two of the plays Euripides had presented the previous year, trusting that most of the audience would still have them fresh in its memory.[38] The parodies are sheer fun; in this play, for good political reasons,[39] the ethical dimensions strongly present in *Lysistrata* and *Frogs* are almost—but not entirely—muted.

The second half of *Frogs* constructs "Aischylos" and "Euripides" as a pair of diametrically opposed moral stereotypes: Aischylos is made to represent the courage and upright morality of the generation that defeated Persia at Marathon and Salamis (virtues viewed nostalgically and through rose-tinted spectacles), while Euripides stands for all that is trendy and immoral in contemporary Athenian society. Euripides loses the contest between them, for reasons analyzed below;[40] but it is important to note that in *Frogs* both tragedians are equally (and affectionately) lampooned and that in all three plays in which Euripides is a character, Aristophanes shows a clear fascination with his verbal style and dramatic technique. In *Frogs*, which was written shortly after Euripides' death, Aristophanes asserted, with extraordinary prescience, that with the deaths of Sophokles and Euripides (in the same year, 406), the era of the great tragic playwrights had come to its end.[41]

Comedy and Politics

At *Frogs* 1053ff., Aristophanes' Aischylos makes the claim that tragedy has a moral—which for the ancient

38. 850ff. and 1009ff. He also parodies a famous scene from *Telephos*, an obviously notorious tragedy he had milked for comic effect many years earlier in *Acharnians* (*Ach* 408ff., *TWF* 689ff.).

39. See below, Comedy and Politics: *The Women's Festival*.

40. See below, Comedy and Politics: *Frogs*.

41. So too, indeed, with *Frogs* itself (in 405), the great era of Athenian Old Comedy came to an end. Whatever their merits as prototypes of the New

Athenians inevitably implied a political—dimension:

> The playwright must hide evil, not show
> and teach it to the audience. Boys have schoolteachers
> to explain things to them; young men have the
>   playwrights.
> That's why we have to teach what's right.

And in his first surviving play, *Acharnians* (425 B.C.E.), Aristophanes, punning between *tragōidia* (tragedy), and *trugōidia* ("song of the ripe grapes," that is, comedy), makes a parallel claim for his own medium:

> DIKAIOPOLIS   Spectators, don't be angry with me, if
>   although I am a beggar,[42] I presume to speak to the
>   Athenians   500
>   about the city when composing comedy.
>   Even Comedy knows what's just, and I will say
>   some things that may be hard to take, but are still just.
>   (*Ach* 496ff.) [43]

He then mounts an argument—half comic, half serious—that the Athenians are at least as much to blame for starting the Peloponnesian War as are the Spartans. While the war continued (from *Acharnians* right through to *Frogs*), Aristophanes never ceased to use the medium of comedy both to

---

Comedy, the two surviving Aristophanic comedies from the fourth century—*Assemblywomen* and *Wealth*—completely lack the political engagement, exuberance, and variety both of tone and of comic technique that make his comedies from the Peloponnesian War period so extraordinary.

42. The hero has borrowed the ragged costume of Telephos (and several helpful props) from Euripides and makes his supplication in this outfit to increase the pathos of his speech; hence the reference to himself as "a beggar." However, neither the costume and props nor the context of tragic parody undermines the seriousness of Aristophanes' point here—pace Halliwell 1998, xliv–xlv. See my commentary on the scene in *Aristophanes:* Acharnians, Knights, *and* Peace (forthcoming).

43. See also *Ach* 630–58.

entertain the democracy and to speak out, from the privileged position of a playwright selected to compete at the festival, about serious political issues.[44] His comedy, like much of the best humor throughout history, comes from pain—his anger at the appalling toll taken by the war, which he blamed on bad policies and on leaders whom he regarded as totally misguided. I believe it is no accident that the plays collected here, three of his finest and funniest comedies, were created when he and his democratic polis were undergoing the worst disaster in their history.

Lysistrata

Lysistrata was written for a performance in January 411, when Athens's fortunes had declined to a low ebb. Renewed fighting on the mainland had followed the disastrous loss of the entire expedition to Sicily in 413, and the Athenians had embarked on an expensive rearmament program. They still retained a bridgehead in Spartan territory at Pylos, but the Spartans had countered by building and occupying a fort at Dekeleia, only eighteen miles (thirty kilometers) from Athens. Some allied states were in revolt from the Athenian empire, and morale had been affected by the religious scandal of the mutilation of the Hermai—ritual statues of the god Hermes placed in front of homes and public buildings.[45]

One important consequence of the Sicilian disaster was the beginning, in 412, of active moves by right-wing oligarchic, antidemocratic cliques. The disaffection with democracy began among troops in Samos and soon spread to Athens.[46] A central passage in *Lysistrata* (574ff.) is devoted

44. In the sheer extent to which he pursues these objectives simultaneously, offering his audiences both a wide range of kinds of humor and a high degree of political engagement, Aristophanes is perhaps unique among comic playwrights. (See Macdowell 1995, 34 and 356.)
    45. Thoukydides, *Histories* 6.27–28; cf. *Lys* 1094.
    46. Thoukydides 8.45ff.

to denouncing these cliques and proclaiming the need for the democracy to remove them:

> First you should wash it [the city] like a fleece,
> to get out all the sheep droppings. Then lay it on a bench
> and beat it with a rod to pick out all the troublemakers,
>   burs and thorns,
> and the conspirators and those who form tight cliques
> to gain high office; discard them, pluck out all the knots.

But the warning came too late; the conspirators, led by Peisandros (*Lys* 490) inaugurated a reign of terror, with political assassinations, two months after the performance of this play. Their coup, three months after the performance, installed a right-wing junta of Four Hundred.[47]

At the start of *Lysistrata* the sex strike—one of the most enduring and universal of Aristophanes' comic fantasy-ideas—creates a startling contrast between what the women are going to do and the failures of the males in politics (for the Greeks an exclusively masculine preserve). Whereas the men of the cities of Greece are hopelessly divided by the war, Lysistrata plans and executes a Panhellenic alliance of women for peace, which specifically includes three women from enemy states (Sparta, Korinth, and Boiotia), and in which her most loyal collaborator is the delegate from Sparta, Athens's principal enemy. In her *agōn* with the Bureaucrat (507ff.), it emerges powerfully that Lysistrata has taken action because of her frustration at the continuing bellicose behavior of the men, who have squandered both the financial resources of Athens (490ff.) and the young men whom the women have nurtured at great personal cost only to see them die as soldiers (523ff., 588ff.). This is why Lysistrata's plan to fulfill the meaning of her name

47. Ibid., 8.53ff. The festival at which *Lysistrata* was performed has been disputed, but Sommerstein's arguments (1977) for the Lenaian Festival of February 411 are convincing. See also Hubbard 1991, appendix 4.

("disbander of armies") evolves from a sex strike by individual women at home to an occupation by all the wives of the iconic Akropolis, which prevents the Bureaucrat from accessing the funds in Athena's treasury to build ships.[48]

Then, in the finale, Lysistrata rebukes both the Spartans and the Athenians for their mutual ingratitude and asks them (1133-34):

Why, when we have enemies abroad to fight,
do you kill fellow Greeks and wreck Greek cities?

The reference to enemies abroad is to Persia, which was starting to take an ominous interest in the outcome of the Peloponnesian War.[49] Here, following hints in some of his earlier comedies, Aristophanes openly advocates a joint Spartan-Athenian hegemony,[50] all the Greek cities being at peace with each other and having a common focus on the foreign enemy, Persia. This was a fantasy in the real world but is fulfilled in the finale of this play, together with the end of the war and its disruption of family life.

When the terms of peace have been sworn between the Athenians and Spartans, the Spartan Ambassador sings of the great battles against the Persians seventy years ago, at Thermopylai and Salamis, in which the Spartans and the Athenians distinguished themselves, united in their opposition to the invasion from Asia. As he does this and then celebrates his native city at a play performed in the heart of

48. The best analysis of the relationship between the two plans and its implications for the structure and meaning of the comedy is Vaio 1973. See also Neuburg 1992, xixff. There is a third, parallel strand in the plot of *Lysistrata*—the conflict and eventual reconciliation between the Old Men and the Old Women of the *choros*.

49. Around this time both Spartan and right-wing Athenian delegations were seeking to invite the Persian satrap Tissaphernes to join the war on their side. The Spartans succeeded (Thoukydides 8.56–58).

50. Note that Lysistrata managed to persuade the other women to undertake the sex strike in the first place only because she had the backing of the Spartan delegate, Lampito; 140ff., N.B. 167.

enemy territory, men and women from Athens, Boiotia, Korinth, and Sparta dance in harmony. It must have been difficult for the audience to reflect on the gulf between this *kōmos* of fulfillment in the comic theater and the fact that in real life the Spartans, scenting victory, would not now settle with Athens on any tolerable terms.

Aristophanes' comedies normally contain their main political commentary in the choral *parabasis*. But in *Lysistrata* there is no real *parabasis*, because the divided *choros* is still in a state of mutual gender hostility in the choros (3) at the midpoint of the comedy.[51] Instead, Aristophanes entrusts his critique of Athenian politics to Lysistrata, the most resolute and single-minded of his heroes and heroines.[52] Elsewhere she shares in the humor of the play, but in the closing section of the *agōn* with the Bureaucrat, as she makes her famous comparison between running the city and making garments from wool (574ff., quoted above), she is completely serious. If we remove the metaphor from Lysistrata's speech, she argues that the men must cleanse the city of troublemakers, conspirators, and cliques and that resident aliens, prospective resident aliens from other Greek cities, debtors to the state, and those still loyal to Athens from the colonies must be absorbed into Athens and made citizens.

It has been claimed that this program was too radical for any (male) politicians to have supported it in real life,[53] but Aristophanes was deeply concerned that the democracy suffered from unnecessary disenfranchisements (a theme he returned to in the *parabasis* of *Frogs*)—and he saw clearly that the duty of the comic poet was to teach the citizens what they ought to do, without confining himself to the political proposals being debated in the Assembly. If Aristophanes'

---

51. The women, however (surpassing the men in this as everywhere in *Lysistrata*), do present a mini-*parabasis* of their own at 638–58.

52. I cannot share Westlake's view (1980, 44) that Lysistrata's speeches in the *agōn* are not to be taken seriously because they are not part of a *parabasis*.

53. Westlake 1980, 43.

proposals had been implemented before Peisandros and his fellow oligarchs had begun their intrigues, the citizens would have made the democracy more inclusive and might perhaps have protected it against the reign of terror and coup that were, as Aristophanes had sensed (576–78), imminent.[54] And Lysistrata's proposal is given added depth when she cries out passionately against the sufferings that war inflicts upon the helpless and voteless women of the city (588ff).

At the end of the play a woman appears as a statesman (1124ff.)—and Lysistrata has, as H. Foley remarks, transcended the follies of both sexes.[55] As she herself claims, she is a special woman, with a brain, intelligent ideas, and a political education from her father and other elders. Lysistrata's reading of history is somewhat idealistic and selective: Kimon's expedition to Sparta was ignominiously dismissed in real life, and indeed the hostilities between the two states arose largely from that debacle. But in that she is no worse (if no better) than any other politician, ancient or modern, and her aim, however impractical it may have been in reality, was and remains admirable: to make both sides agree to a peace treaty.

It is true that, this being the climactic scene of an Aristophanic comedy, the negotiations are inscribed upon the body of a naked woman, personifying the goddess Reconciliation, but this must be read properly. As a personification of that which has eluded the males of both cities, Reconciliation is naturally both female and sexy; female cunning, tenacity, and sexuality have led in the play to the point at which Lysistrata needs only to exert this last influence upon the sexually desperate Ambassadors for the "impossible" peace agreement to be attained. If it is argued that reconciliation could not be

54. In late January/early February 411 Peisandros made a speech at Athens advocating change in the constitution and what he claimed might be only a temporary abandonment of democracy (Thoukydides, *History* 8.53–54). This was the beginning of the overt oligarchic campaign that culminated in the coup d'état in May.

55. Foley 1982, 5.

attained by such means in real life (where men whose wives went on a sex strike could avail themselves of slave girls and prostitutes), this misses the serious point of *Lysistrata*—the first comedy by Aristophanes in which women play principal roles and a woman is the heroine. In the dire straits to which the war has reduced the cities of Greece, and Athens in particular, the female virtues of bonding, inclusiveness, and interstate cooperation must prevail over the macho male code of exclusiveness, competitiveness, and aggression.

When we gave the first performances of this translation, Australia had, under the leadership of a male-dominated government, joined the United States and Great Britain in invading Iraq in an attempt to impose a system of government upon a country that, by tradition, history, and religious custom, is wholly opposed to that system. Public support for the invasion had been solicited by a series of mendacious statements based on trumped-up "intelligence." The occupation of Iraq was just the latest of a number of wars that have disfigured the planet since the end of World War II. But most Western democracies now have a proud tradition of peace protest that stretches back fifty years to Campaign for Nuclear Disarmament protests against the threat of nuclear holocaust during the height of the Cold War and that was at its finest during the sustained campaigns against U.S. government involvement in the Vietnam War.

It is therefore not surprising that *Lysistrata* is one of the Aristophanic comedies performed most frequently today. Modern audiences can relate closely to the situation in the play without knowing all the details of the political situation in 411 B.C.E.. Although in modern Western democracies women are not disenfranchised, as they were in classical Athens, their voice is hardly heard when the war machine goes into action. Mothers who receive the corpses of their sons in flag-draped coffins have as much reason to protest the slaughter as did Lysistrata. In the United States they did just that, forming an action group to call for the removal of their nation's troops from Iraq. And Lysistrata's attack on the dangers of oligarchic cliques, so prophetic at the time of production in February 411, still had resonance at the time of our production in April 2005, when it was becoming apparent just how few, and how fanatical, were the men who drove the policy of U.S. military intervention in Iraq. In our production we felt no need to update or modify the text. But we did help our audiences think about *Lysistrata's* relevance to them: our otherwise classic Greek temple facade was adorned with spray-painted graffiti, which included a CND logo and "NO MORE BUSH WARS." In this way we expressed the continuity of women's opposition to male-initiated wars from Lysistrata and her companions to our own immediate present.

The Women's Festival

The Women's Festival was written at a turbulent time in Athenian domestic politics: January–March 411. Peisandros and his fellow conspirators had promulgated their plan for a change to a less-democratic form of government, and Peisandros himself had set off with a delegation to the Persian satrap Tissaphernes in an attempt to bring Persia into the war on the Athenian side. Meanwhile at Athens the conspirators were recruiting their four hundred fellow oligarchs—sometimes, as Thoukydides comments,[56] in surprising places—but when the play was performed, in March, they had not yet commenced the reign of terror by political assassinations that immediately preceded their coup d'état.[57]

In this climate Aristophanes elected to create a comedy without the concrete political proposals prominent in *Lysistrata* and *Frogs*. Euripides, Agathon, and Kleisthenes, the principal victims of his satire, were of course not politicians, and the two politicians singled out for special abuse—Kleophon

56. Thoukydides 8.66.
57. Sommerstein 2001, 3.

and Hyperbolos (805, 840)—were unpopular with large sections of the community. (Indeed, the oligarchs were shortly to assassinate Hyperbolos.) The audience could relax from their political cares and enjoy one of Aristophanes' funniest comedies as a riot of cross-dressing, role play, and brilliant parody filled the *orchēstra*. Apart from the insults to these two politicians and a sardonic reference at 804 to the superiority of the infantry over the navy (which recently had suffered a minor defeat under Charminos at Syme),[58] the *parabasis* is empty of political comment.

However, the playwright makes his political position crystal clear. Aristophanes firmly declares his hostility to the conspirators and their plans. Twice the Women denounce anyone who makes treaties with the Persians against the interests of the democracy (337, 365–66). The failure of Peisandros's delegation to Tissaphernes was not yet known at Athens, but Aristophanes signals his opposition to it with these two comments. Even more significantly, the play champions the full democracy and its freedom from tyranny: "This is a free / society, and any citizen may speak" (540–41). Among those cursed in Kritylla's ritual invocation is anyone "who plans to set up a dictatorship / or bring the tyrants back" (338–39); the women respond to her by denouncing all who try "to change our laws / and make decrees instead" (361–62). And the address to Athena in choros 6 includes two lines referring specifically to the crisis: "Show yourself—we need you— / enemy of tyranny!" (1143–44).

Fortunately for the playwright, the Four Hundred did not place him on their hit list—or if they did, he somehow evaded assassination during the next five chaotic and dangerous months. But these six strong statements in *The Women's Festival* made his firm opposition to the oligarchs perfectly evident to the entire audience. Given the political situation in March 411, this was a courageous move.

---

58. Thoukydides 8.42.

Frogs

The oligarchy of the Four Hundred was overthrown in August 411, and full democracy was restored at Athens in 410. Over the next few years the fortunes of the Athenians fluctuated. They lost a sea battle at Notion in 407, but when the Persians began helping the Spartans build up their fleet, the Athenians, realizing the crucial importance of a naval victory, recruited slaves, whom they rewarded with freedom for the victory at Arginousai in the summer of 406 (the "all-or-nothing sea-battle" referred to three times in *Frogs*).[59]

Despite this important victory, Athens's position was still desperate when Aristophanes composed *Frogs* for performance at the Lenaian Festival early in 405, and he confronts the situation head-on in the play. The *parabasis* (674ff.) is exceptionally serious, and its main issue is enfranchisement. Aristophanes pleads with the Athenians to restore full citizen's rights to those caught up on the wrong side in the oligarchic coup of 411. Then the famous parable of the coinage advises the Athenians to turn back to the nobler among their citizens for leadership. (Only later does the play reveal in specific terms what this might mean.) The appeal for the reenfranchisement of right-wingers is not evidence of a conservative stance, although it may be surprising after the assertive defense of full democracy in *The Women's Festival.* Faced with a grave national crisis in 405, Aristophanes revives the idea of enlarging the franchise, an idea he had first advanced in 411 through the character of Lysistrata.[60]

The *parabasis* is followed by a contest in Haides' between Aischylos, the great tragic playwright of a former generation

---

59. 33ff., 190–92, 693–99. The aftermath of Arginousai was unpleasant: six of the victorious generals were executed for failing, in appalling weather conditions, to recover the dead and wounded. One of their junior officers, Theramenes, managed both to avoid prosecution and to accuse the generals (Xenophon, *Hellenika* 1.6–7). *Frogs* refers twice to his survival skills, which had also been in evidence in his adroit maneuvering during 411–10; 534ff., 968–70.

60. 574ff., quoted and discussed above, in the section on *Lysistrata.*

(who had fought in person against the Persians at Marathon and probably also at Salamis and had died in 456) and the recently deceased Euripides (who is made to represent the atheistic attitudes of contemporary sophistry).[61] When the Initiates establish the mood for the contest, they imply that it will revolve around a contrast in poetic style (choros 4, 814ff.), but the early phases (1006–1098) show that its serious subject is political and social morality. Aischylos stands not just for a robust and solemn poetic style, but also for a generation in which Athens was militarily successful, and Aristophanes links this with the upright morals he nostalgically ascribes to those glorious times more than fifty years earlier. By contrast, Euripides' slick contemporary style is associated with social and moral corruption—sexually immoral behavior and the weakening of the Athenian fighting spirit.

The contest subsequently turns to poetic style and technique and, as it nears its conclusion, becomes increasingly frivolous. But the sociopolitical point has been made, and it is therefore with a feeling of return and narrative satisfaction that we come back to politics at the end of the competition. Dionysos, professing himself unable to choose which of the two playwrights to take back to Athens, gives his reasons for wanting one of them, and now he goes far beyond the "desire for Euripides" on purely poetic and aesthetic grounds that he had expressed to Herakles early on in the play:

> Okay, listen to me.
> I came here for a poet. Why? So Athens
> will survive and keep my drama festival.
> I'm going to take the one of you   1420
> who's going to give the city good advice.

61. Euripides' works had already been satirized for atheism at *The Women's Festival* 14ff., 272ff., and 450–51. He is explicitly linked with the skeptical philosopher Sokrates' "pompous words and scratchings / signifying nothing" in the finale of *Frogs* (1491ff.). Aristophanes had pilloried Sokrates in *Clouds*, making him represent all the absurd aspects of the sophists and the teaching of

Nothing less than the survival of Athens is at stake, and Dionysos's first question addresses the burning issue of the moment: what should be done with Alkibiades? This brilliant aristocratic general—perhaps a good example of the "old, sterling-silver" coins recommended in the *parabasis*[62]— had deserted to the Spartans after having been indicted in 415 but subsequently found favor with the Athenians again. He returned to the city in 407 and was elected to supreme command, but his popularity vanished when he was blamed for the defeat at Notion, and he retreated into voluntary exile at his castle near the Hellespont. Should he be recalled?

AISCHYLOS   What do the people think of him?
DIONYSOS   What?
   They love him, hate him, want to have him.
   Now tell me what you think.
EURIPIDES   I hate that citizen who's slow to help
   his native land but quick to do great harm,
   most helpful to himself, but useless to his city.
DIONYSOS   Good, by Poseidon. And *your* view?   1430
AISCHYLOS   A city should not rear a lion-cub,
   but if you do, accept all its demands.

Dionysos cannot decide between Euripides' clarity and Aischylos's wisdom. He therefore requires the tragedians to tell him how the city can escape from its troubles. Euripides offers a fantastic plan for aerial warfare, 2,400 years ahead of its time, but Aischylos wins the contest:

AISCHYLOS   They must realize that enemy land is theirs
   and their own land is now the enemy's; the ships
   must be their riches—other wealth is worthless.

---

philosophy. He also attacked the philosophers for amorality, especially through the victory of Wrong over Right in the *agōn* (889ff.), which prefigures the moral dimensions of Aischylos's attack on Euripides in *Frogs*.
   62. Cf. Moorton 1988.

In other words, Athens must fully readopt Perikles' original strategy from the start of the war: let the enemy occupy all of Attika without resistance, stay within the long walls (which connected the city to its port of Peiraios), and rely on sea power—recalling Alkibiades (the "lion-cub"[63]) once more to supreme command.[64]

The Athenians took part of Aristophanes' advice in the *parabasis:* in the autumn of 405, when the Spartans were besieging their city, they enacted a law to reenfranchise those who had taken the side of the Four Hundred in 411. Aristophanes himself was rewarded with a ceremonial olive wreath and a revival of *Frogs* in 404, probably at the Dionysia in March. But demagogues such as Kleophon continued to be influential in Athenian politics.[65]

In just over a year, by the time of the succeeding revival, much had changed. Alkibiades had not been recalled, and the fall of Athens was imminent. Ignoring good advice from Alkibiades, the Athenians had suffered a comprehensive defeat at Aigispotamoi, where a Spartan fleet under Lysandros destroyed virtually the entire Athenian navy. Aristophanes was obliged to rewrite Aischylos's advice to the Athenians, and in the 404 version he reiterates his observation, already made in the *parabasis*, that Athens's current leaders are drawn from the wrong stratum of society:[66]

AISCHYLOS   When we trust those we now distrust,
    and call what we now trust untrustworthy—
DIONYSOS   What? I don't understand.
    Say something that's less learned and more clear.

63. This image is quoted from a memorable allegory in Aischylos, *Agamemnon* 717ff.

64. Cf. Moorton 1988, 355–56.

65. Cf. Sommerstein 2009, 254–71.

66. Our texts contain both versions, jumbled together. Sommerstein (1996: cf. 2009, 262–68) has unscrambled them convincingly. Aristophanes also rewrote a stanza (1256ff.) stating that Aischylos excelled all others in tragedies about Dionysos. Among Euripides' posthumous papers was a new and superb drama on that theme, *Bakchai.*

AISCHYLOS   If we no longer trust those citizens in
     whom
   we trust at present, and we use those men
   whom we don't use, perhaps we might be saved.
DIONYSOS   We are so badly off right now that we're
   bound to be saved if we reverse our course.   1450

Aristophanes' disillusionment with war-mongering demagogues such as Kleophon (who had intransigently opposed
peace negotiations since his rise to power) was total.[67] But
Aristophanes no longer calls, as he did in *Lysistrata* in 411,
for negotiations to begin. In 405 and 404 he knew that the
Spartans would settle for nothing but the total surrender of
Athens. That is exactly what they achieved, one month after
the second performance of *Frogs*. And Aristophanes' advice
to reenfranchise the supporters of the oligarchic coup of 411
backfired, with lethal effects. This move may well have
smoothed the path to the brutal regime of the Thirty Tyrants,
who seized control of Athens (with Spartan encouragement)
shortly after its capitulation.

   The text of this comedy has often been adapted and
updated; productions of *Frogs* have been mounted in rewrites
in which, for example, Shakespeare and Shaw replace Aischylos and Euripides,[68] and others in which gibes at modern
politicians replace Aristophanes' original topical jokes. Such
adaptations sometimes work[69] but more often do not; to graft
a modern theme onto the sociopolitical fabric of the last few
years of the fifth century B.C.E. is almost impossible.[70]

   67. Kleophon is reviled at *Frogs* 674ff., 1504ff., and 1532ff. Cf. *TWF* 805.
   68. See, for example, the Shevelove/Sondheim version, performed at Yale
in 1974 and revived on Broadway in 2004, with additional material by Nathan
Lane (who played Dionysos) and more songs by Sondheim. See English 2005
and Gamel 2007.
   69. For example, Mary-Kay Gamel's *The Julie Thesmo Show*, discussed by
the adaptor/director in Gamel 2002.
   70. Compare Walton 2006, chap. 9, especially 173 and 178.

I believe that *Frogs* remains one of Aristophanes' most popular comedies because (apart from the excellence of the comic writing, which makes it a joy to direct) its original concerns are still pertinent today. A short program note should outline the desperate military and political position in which Athens found itself in 404.[71] Then the modern audience can enjoy the comedy on its own terms, because it is a recurrent human habit to look back nostalgically on the "good old days" and to be aghast at the trendy novelties of "modern art."[72] We also tend to compare the politicians of our own times disparagingly with the more noble figures we imagine our past leaders to have been. Thus the core of the play—the advice in the *parabasis* and the serious sociopolitical core of the contest between the playwrights—has plenty of resonance. More than *Lysistrata* or *The Women's Festival*, *Frogs* is full of names that mean nothing to a modern audience and cannot simply be glossed or replaced. But the general thrust of the comedy is absolutely intelligible. Accordingly I oppose "modernized" scripts.

Performance

These comedies were first performed in a large open-air theater. The *theatron* (auditorium) consisted of tiers of wooden seats rising steeply on the hillside below the Akropolis. The performance space, both for solo-part actors and for the *choros*, was a flat *orchēstra* or dance floor,[73] about

71. The 404 version should be played; see recommended cuts.
72. Aristophanes was careful to make the humor of the poetic contest intelligible to members of his audience who had not seen, or did not remember, the specific tragedies that he parodies. This makes it possible for modern audiences to appreciate it as well (Dover 1993, 34).
73. There has been much controversy about the shape of the playing space in the fifth century B.C.E. The latest archaeological findings from the Theater of Dionysos point toward a *theatron* (auditorium) consisting of straight banks of

sixty-six feet (twenty meters) square, that the audience surrounded on three sides.[74] Behind this was a long, low wooden building called the *skēnē*, with a practicable roof on which actors could perform, some windows, and one set of double doors opening onto the extreme rear center of the *orchēstra*.[75] The *skēnē* building normally represented a place: in *Lysistrata*, the Propylaia (the gates at the entrance to the Akropolis); in *The Women's Festival*, first the house of Agathon and after that a temple in the background at the festival site; and in *Frogs*, first the house of Herakles and later that of Plouton, god of the underworld. But during "journey" sequences (e.g., the section of *Frogs* between Dionysos's visit to Herakles and his arrival before Plouton's palace) the *skēnē* doors are shut and its presence is ignored.

There were two entrances into the *orchēstra* called *eisodoi*, one at each side of the *skēnē* building, next to the retaining walls at the ends of the *theatron*. By a convention that reflected the real-life location of the theater, the *eisodos* at the actor's right represented entrance from out of town or from overseas, and that on the actor's left represented entrance from downtown in the city near which the action was located.[76] There were also two mechanical devices for special effects (both of which Aristophanes used in *The Women's Festival*): the

---

wooden seats raked up the hill, behind the stone seats in the front rows reserved for dignitaries, in three blocks at right angles to each other. Cf. Goette 2007.

74. There was no raised stage behind the *orchēstra*; Ewans 1995, xxff.; cf. Wiles 1997, chap. 2, especially 53, and Ley 2006, ixff. In the *orchēstra*, actors playing solo roles interacted closely with each other and with the *choros*. The hypothetical reconstructions of the action in Dearden 1967, 144ff., are completely flawed by the impractical assumption of a large raised stage behind the *orchēstra*. It is obvious that Dearden and other advocates of a raised stage (e.g., Henderson 1996, 18) have never workshopped or performed the plays.

75. Some comedies seem at first sight to require one or two extra doors toward the outside ends of the *skēnē*. Dale's argument (1969, 103–18) that one pair of central doors is all that is needed for comedy (as it certainly was for tragedy) has often been challenged but has yet to be refuted. She was firmly supported by Dearden 1976, 20ff. The three plays in this volume definitely require only the one pair of central doors (for *Lysistrata* scene 1, see Theatrical Commentary).

76. Rehm 1992, 54.

ekkuklēma, or "rolling-out machine," used to disclose scenes
from inside the *skēnē* building, and the *mēchanē,* a crane used
to swing into view gods and other characters to be imagined
as flying into the playing space.

A *choros* of twenty-four, representing a collective character, played an important part in the drama. They partici-
pated in the action both in their choral lyrics and in the
dialogue.[77] The traditional belief that there was one "chorus
leader" who spoke all their dialogue lines has no support
in ancient evidence and is almost never adopted in modern
performance, because it makes for a very static effect.[78]

The actors were all male. They wore padded costumes
and large linen *prosōpa,* which concealed the whole head and
were about two-and-one-half times life size. *Prosōpa,* literally
"faces," are normally rendered in English as "masks," but
they were not designed to conceal anything. Rather, their
function was to reveal the gender and age of the characters
to audience members up to 325 feet (100 meters) away up
the hillside. Fair skin and long hair denoted female characters. Darker skin and short hair denoted males. A beard
signified an adult male. (In *The Women's Festival,* the effemi-
nacy of Agathon and Kleisthenes was marked by the fact
that both wore beardless masks.[79]) White hair denoted old
age. Most comic masks showed mildly distorted features, and
some special masks were used. Portrait masks, for example,
caricatured real contemporary characters such as Euripides
in both *The Women's Festival* and *Frogs* and Agathon and
Kleisthenes in *The Women's Festival.*

Actors playing male characters in comedy wore large
phalluses (fake leather penises) that protruded from beneath

77. In *Lysistrata* the *choros* is divided into two groups of twelve, representing
the Old Men and the Old Women. In *Frogs* I believe that the *choros* (or perhaps a
semi-*choros* of twelve) first appeared as the Frogs and then changed costume to
play the Initiates. See below, Theatrical Commentary, *Frogs* choros 1.

78. Against the belief that the Greek technical term *koryphaios* means "chorus
leader" in the sense of spokesman, see Ewans 1995, xxii–xxiv, with footnote 22.

79. *TWF* 98, 574–75 and 583.

their short *chitons*.[80] A small number of actors played all the spoken roles, changing masks and costumes as needed.[81] There were also plenty of "silent faces"—extras. Because of the size of the theater, it is clear that gesture was an important element, but it is notable, in both tragedy and comedy, that moments in which detailed gestures are important are always narrated carefully in the spoken or sung text—presumably so that distant spectators, who would miss seeing small-scale actions, could (thanks to the excellent acoustics of the *theatron*) follow what was happening through the dialogue.[82] The chief means of visual communication was blocking—the grouping of actors and their patterns of movement.[83]

Because this theater and its performance conventions are radically different from anything we know today, the translation of the performance into modern terms involves deciding what to preserve and what to change from Aristophanes' original mode of production. In the remarks that follow I provide examples based on twenty-two years of experience in directing ancient Athenian tragedy and comedy, both in full productions and in workshops of individual scenes—in

80. For representative images of comic actors, see the plates in Revermann 2006. See also *TWF* 214ff. and 642ff., where the phallus is used to virtuoso effect. Phalluses normally were limp, but in the second half of *Lysistrata*, Aristophanes has great fun introducing a succession of male characters with ill-concealed *erect* phalluses, visible proof of their sexual deprivation as a result of the success of Lysistrata's plan.

81. Three principal actors played most of the roles. In *Frogs* one more, in *Lysistrata* and *The Women's Festival* two more actors are needed for brief appearances. A conjectural layout of Aristophanes' doublings is presented in appendix 2.

82. At *The Women's Festival* 643ff., the virtuoso manipulation of the phallus by the actor playing the In-Law would be invisible to distant spectators, especially since Kritylla and The Queen are circling around him. See also *Frogs* 640ff., where the precise moments at which the Doorkeeper's whip strikes Dionysos and Xanthias can be reconstructed from the spoken text. *Lys* 124ff. show how facial expressions—impossible in the Greek masked theater—and small movements are described in the text, so the spectators can be aware of them. For an excellent discussion of the implications of masked acting, see McCart 2007, passim; for the inscribing of emotions onto the mask by the audience, ibid., 251.

an experimental studio and a natural outdoor amphitheater in Newcastle, and in the ancient Odeion at Paphos.[84]

Because movement and blocking were the central visual dimensions of performance, the aspect of Athenian performance that must be preserved if at all possible is the actor-audience relationship. A modern production of Aristophanes cannot aspire to an audience of more than ten thousand, but a space that replicates the dynamic of the Greek performance space—with the audience in raked seating on three sides of an acting area with a facade behind it—is superior to any other venue. Fortunately, some modern theaters have been designed with the Greek performance space in mind. There are also natural and man-made outdoor amphitheaters that replicate the shape of the Greek theater, and it is possible as well to configure an experimental drama studio to this pattern. To a director who can work with a replica of the original actor-audience relationship, the "unwritten rules" of the Greek shape become evident with practice, and scenes very difficult to play in modern performance space (especially behind a proscenium arch) become quite transparent.

In the Greek space the most powerful position is C,[85] unless the *skēnē* doors are open and in use, in which case an actor can pull the focus back toward them. Positions forward of center are in general weaker than those behind it, and an

---

83. See Ewans 1995, xviii–xx.

84. I am also indebted to the results of practical research by Graham Ley and Gregory McCart, who collaborated with me on an edition of Sophokles in new, accurate, and actable translations with theatrical commentaries based on our productions in replicas of the Greek actor-audience relationship (Ewans, with Ley and McCart, 1999 and 2000). McCart's production of *The Women's Festival* and performances of Aristophanes at Epidavros have also been instructive.

85. C = Center, R = Right, L = Left, B = Back, F = Front, E = Extreme. Thus, for example, "EBC" means just in front of the doors of the *skēnē* facade, and "FC" means approximately halfway from the center of the *orchēstra* to "EFC," which is just in front of the central seat of honor accorded to the priest of Dionysos. Note that "R" and "L" are viewed from the performer's perspective, meaning to the right and left of an actor entering the *orchēstra* from the *skēnē*, *not* to the left and right of a spectator in the central segment of the *theatron*. See diagram facing the start of the Theatrical Commentary.

actor's position is weaker the farther away she or he is from
C—again, unless the actor has just entered at EBC.[86]

Here is an example from my own *Frogs* workshops, with
full stage directions to display the movements and blocking
that we developed to bring out the humor implicit in the text:

DIONYSOS *(leaving Charon's boat, which stagehands pull off by
the right* eisodos, *and tiptoeing blindly and cautiously through
the "darkness" of Haides', around EBR)*
                    Xanthias! Where's Xanthias? Oh Xanthias!
(Xanthias calls back from where he completed his circuit of the
orchēstra, *possibly ECR.)*
XANTHIAS   Cooee!
DIONYSOS   Come here!
*(Miming movement in total darkness, as if neither of them is able
to see, they grope their way toward each other's voice and bump
into each other.)*
XANTHIAS   *(recovering from the collision)*
                                                    Welcome, master.
DIONYSOS   What did you find on your way?
XANTHIAS   *(miming the difficulties of walking blindly through
mud)*   Darkness and mud.
DIONYSOS   Did you see anywhere those father-beaters
    and perjurers he told us about?
(Both characters now act as if they can see perfectly.)
XANTHIAS   *(drawing D to FC and indicating the audience with
a large gesture)*
                                                    Don't you?
DIONYSOS   *(his face surveying the central sector of the audience)*
    Yes, by Poseidon, now I can see them.
    (beat. Then turning to X)
    What will we do next?
XANTHIAS   We'd better get out of here.
    (moves a few paces back toward the R eisodos*)*

86. See Ewans and Ley 1985.

This is the place where that fellow said
we'd find wild beasts.

DIONYSOS   He'll be sorry he said that.

(He starts to move, and his movements become more expansive as he delivers this speech, striding in an arc around part of the front half of the orchēstra *to indicate his increasing overconfidence.)*

He was just telling lies to scare me   280
out of sheer jealousy because I am so brave.
There's no one as conceited as that Herakles.
Myself, I rather hoped we would encounter one
and do a deed that's worthy of our noble quest.

XANTHIAS *(who has moved from BR to C to observe D's vainglo-rious manner more closely, heartily agrees)* Absolutely! *(with a total change of tone)* But listen, I can hear a sound.

DIONYSOS   Where is it?

XANTHIAS   Behind us. *(i.e, at the rear of the* orchēstra*)*

DIONYSOS   *(races to X and makes him stand between himself and the imaginary monster)*

Go behind.

XANTHIAS   Now it's in front. *(pointing toward EFL)*[87]

DIONYSOS   *(forcing X to reverse their positions so X is nearer to EFL than D)*

You go in front.

XANTHIAS   *(retreating slightly from C toward BR)* By Zeus, I see a gigantic monster.

DIONYSOS   *(cowering behind X and retreating even more toward EBR)* What's it like?

XANTHIAS   *(peering toward EFL)* Terrible! It is all kinds of shapes;
now it's a cow, now it's a mule, and now *(moving toward FL)* . . . it's
a beautiful girl.   290

---

87. It could just as well be EFR, so this choice is arbitrary to that extent. But the Empousa cannot be imagined as being in the rear half of the *orchēstra*, or the actors will be placing their backs to too much of the audience at once in

DIONYSOS   (*pushes X aside and races to FL*) Where is she?
   Let me at her.
XANTHIAS   No! It's not a girl any more; now it's a dog.
DIONYSOS   (*stops instantly, turns, and runs back behind X
   toward BR*) It must be the Empousa.
XANTHIAS   (*perhaps stepping slightly forward toward EFL to "see
more clearly"*)

                                          Yes, her whole face
   is shining like a fire.
DIONYSOS   (*still cowering BR*) And has she got a copper
   leg?
XANTHIAS   Yes, by Poseidon; and the other one is made
   of donkey dung.
DIONYSOS   (*turns away from X, to address the R side of
   audience, and makes a gesture of despair*) Where can I go?
XANTHIAS   (*turns away from D, to address the other [L] side of
the audience, and copies D's gesture*)   And me?
(*Dionysos rushes to EFC, to the center front row of the audience,
where the VIPs sit, and begs:*)
DIONYSOS   My priest, please save me; let me drink with
   you after the show.

At 285ff. Xanthias stands at or near C, controlling Dionysos
like a puppet on an invisible string as he runs between the
rear-right and front-left sections of the *orchēstra*. The full effect
of this physically active sequence cannot really be replicated
in any other theater shape, nor should we expect it to be.
Because Aristophanes knew only the Theater of Dionysos, he
conceived his comedies with that space in mind.

   The advantages of the three-sided shape are even more
evident when the *choros* is present. The "parked" position for
the *choros*—the place where they should be when they are
not taking a major part in the action, as for example in the

the following sequence; and it cannot be EFC, or this will preempt Dionysos's
desperate run for safety to his priest at the end of the beat.

agōn between Lysistrata and the Bureaucrat (scene 3, 483ff.), in the parodies of Euripides in *The Women's Festival*, and in the contest between Aischylos and Euripides in *Frogs*—is *not* toward the rear of the *orchēstra*, where they would constantly pull focus from the action in front of them,[88] but in a semicircle[89] around the front of the playing space.[90] This allows them to easily rejoin and participate in the action whenever they are needed. The director must forget proscenium-arch habits and frequently allow one participant in a dialogue to face away from some of the audience for some of the time, such as the position of the Old Woman at FR during *Lys* 706ff., when Lysistrata occupies the focus point at C.[91]

The Greek space totally opposes the basic rules of the proscenium-arch shape, in which participants in dialogue can almost never face away from the audience. Provided that most of the audience in the *theatron* can see one of the faces engaged in a dialogue, they can empathize with the situation of both characters even if the other face is turned away from them. Because the characters face each other directly, the *orchēstra* permits a much more natural way of playing dialogue than the "cheating" required in the proscenium-arch space. It also lends itself to a fluid, effective realization of the text in performance, allowing the director to bring out the power relationships between the characters.

* * *

88. They faced the main section of the audience almost constantly in Peter Hall's very unsatisfactory British National Theatre production of the *Oresteia*.

89. In *Lysistrata*, until the *choros* is reunited in choros 5, two separate segments of a semicircle are required, one EFL and the other EFR.

90. In this position, unless they are sitting on the *orchēstra* floor (which is recommended for long scenes involving solo actors alone), the *choros* get in the way of the view from the front row of seats. Like the noble spectators in the royal boxes, which were located right beside the proscenium arches in the grandiose theaters of the nineteenth century, the VIPs in the front row in the Theater of Dionysos had to put up with some of the poorest seats in the house in terms of sightlines and appreciation of the patterns of movement, in return for being seen by the rest of the audience to be present in seats of honor.

91. See Theatrical Commentary, *Lysistrata* scene 4.

Modern performances that try to replicate the masks, padding, and all-male acting company that Aristophanes employed are doomed to be historical curiosities. In our smaller, indoor theaters, masks conceal identity and personality. Should the modern actor be deprived of one of his or her most powerful means of expression, simply because it was impossible to use facial expression in the vast space of the Theater of Dionysos?[92] *Prosōpa*, exaggerated padding, male actors in female roles, and large phalluses on the actors playing male roles were accepted without question by an audience for whom these conventions were grounded in tradition and religious custom and who knew no other way to represent comedy. However, a modern audience would read these practices, if they were employed in a production today, as indicating that the whole performance would be grotesque, farcical, and "over the top." Although there are elements of extravagance, farce, and excess in Aristophanic comedy, there is far more than this to the total theater experience that his scripts imply. In my judgment these comedies should be played today by mixed companies of actors and actresses without masks (but using the modern resource of makeup) and with unexaggerated, realistic costumes.

However, some U.S. feminists have sought to argue that the gender politics of ancient Athens are so remote from the due recognition of their equality (which women rightly demand in modern Western democracies) that women should not consent to act in classical Greek plays.[93] In a postfeminist society these objections to ancient Greek drama read rather oddly; although Aischylos, Sophokles, and Euripides were male and wrote for male actors, they created tragic roles that show a deep understanding of what it is to be female, and

92. There were also religious and ritual reasons, connected with the act of impersonation, behind the use of masks for Athenian drama. See Wiles 2007, passim, on tragedy.

93. Taaffe 1993, 146, on *Lysistrata*. Case hoped that "feminist practitioners and scholars may decide that such plays do not belong in the canon" (1988, 19).

actresses have competed fiercely to be cast as Klytaimestra, Antigone, Phaidra, Medeia, and Elektra since modern revivals began. And in *Lysistrata*, the serious core of the comedy lies in Lysistrata's diagnosis of how to cure Athenian democracy of its current problems and in her passionate sequence of speeches about what it is to be a woman in time of war (567–97). For this alone, though there is much else involved in her part, the title role holds a powerful attraction. Indeed, when I directed the first performance of this translation in 2005, not one actress found anything objectionable in the comedy—not even the beautiful young woman who played the role of Reconciliation, a sex object if ever there was one. Reconciliation is not to be played today, in a relatively small theater, by a man in a padded body suit with fake breasts and a painted-on pubic triangle, as she probably was in Kallistratos's original production in the Theater of Dionysos.[94] The modern audience requires an image that explains for them the Ambassadors' lust to make peace—and my actress, glorying in her bronzed body and resplendent in golden tiara, abbreviated golden bikini, and gold high-heeled sandals with golden straps extending up her calves, provided exactly that.[95] All those connected with the production—a highly intelligent, largely female, cast and crew—were proud to have communicated to their modern audiences Aristophanes' compelling comic fantasy of how women might use their sexual power to stop a self-destructive war. I do not believe that an all-male company could achieve this today.

94. Holzinger 1928, 37ff.; see also Vaio 1973, 379, and Ley 2007, 271. The other theory, that nude slave girls played the silent, desirable young women who often appear in the *kōmos* at the end of Aristophanes' comedies, is less likely, because in such a large theater their sexuality would make very little visual impact. But see Zweig 1992, and also Revermann 2006, 158–59, whose arguments I find attractive.

95. In modern performance both the lap dancer Fawn, at the end of *TWF*, and the Servant who, at *Frogs* 503ff., induces Xanthias (disguised as Herakles) to come into Persephone's halls must look and sound seductive. The fact that in ancient Athens they were probably played by padded male actors in body stockings is irrelevant.

Should we use ancient costumes or modern? I favor modern. Today's costume designer can use costumes of our period to make statements about the characters that simply are not possible when the actors wear classical dress. Aristophanes wrote these plays for immediate contemporary impact, and we should attempt to re-create this effect as far as possible. Simply clothing the Bureaucrat[96] in a suit and equipping him with a briefcase makes a precise statement of who he is and what he does. With this understanding, today's audience is ready for the undermining of his identity: first as an administrator, when he is made to card wool; next as a man, when Lysistrata puts her veil over his head; and finally as a living being, when Lysistrata and two other Women drape their crown and garlands on his head and around his neck, ready for his funeral (*Lys* 531ff. and 602ff.).

These comedies place considerable demands on the modern actor, who must be able to perform in a variety of styles. Among Aristophanes' requirements for playing all his lead parts are the ability to perform complex verbal comic routines and highly physical slapstick, to sing and act both straight and in parody of tragic style, and to convey both intellectual humor (demanded especially in the tragic contest in *Frogs*) and the pure crudity that often punctuates the texts.[97]

Finally, there is the choice of music. Aristophanes' scripts alternate between spoken verse and sung verse accompanied by choreography. It would be presumptuous to prescribe a choice of music or soundscape to prospective directors, but I will express my belief that ancient Greek plays are far more effective if the original distinction between spoken and sung passages is preserved—not necessarily by composing an entire new vocal score and singing the passages that were

96. In the original Greek the Bureaucrat is a *Proboulos*—one of ten senior Athenians selected as Special Commissioners after the disaster in Sicily.

97. Notes on acting style will be found below in the Theatrical Commentary on the three plays.

originally sung, but by using musical accompaniment for those passages, choreographing them, and (in an indoor production) changing the lighting. In this way an important aspect of the original script can be re-created in the modern theater.

Translation

Translation is a difficult, often undervalued, and sometimes controversial task, and the translation of Aristophanic comedy into a modern language is a complex undertaking.[98] In this book I have tried to give Aristophanes a viable voice for the contemporary English-language stage.

Aristophanes wrote his plays in verse—not rhyming verse (the Greeks used rhyme only in drinking songs), but patterns of long and short syllables, which in the lyric (sung) parts of the comedy can become quite complex. It is astonishing how many translators simply abandon verse, rendering the dialogue scenes in prose.[99]

One of my first principles is that the translation not only must be in (unrhymed) verse throughout, but also must be in a verse that reflects for actors the formidable range of Aristophanes' own verse—from the truly lyrical (e.g., *TWF* 947ff., *Frogs* 323 ff.) via both parody of the high tragic style (e.g., *Lys* 706ff., *TWF* 1015ff.) and the freely conversational (e.g., *Frogs* 738ff.) to crisp exchanges that are often the vehicle for a slapstick comic routine (e.g., *TWF* 643ff., *Frogs* 642ff.). Because this

98. See Walton 2006 passim (specifically on comedy, 145–78), Robson 2008, and Robson 2009, 193–211.

99. Sometimes, perhaps to counterbalance the prose, the choroses and monodies have been freely translated into rhymed Gilbertian verse (e.g., Sommerstein 2002, originally published in 1973, but still in print and widely distributed) that today sounds totally anachronistic. There is a world of difference between the comedic styles of Aristophanes and Gilbert. (See Halliwell 1998, lxiii, on the contrast between Gilbert's "arch tweeness" and Aristophanes' "earthy, profane brio.")

demands a degree of flexibility, the main dialogue meter of Greek drama, the iambic trimeter, is normally rendered into an English pentameter (five stresses). But because Greek and English frequently demand a very different number of words to express the same concept, when the sense requires it, I expand to six stresses or contract to four or, rarely, three. Similarly, the "recitative" sections (Greek tetrameters) are translated in verses of six to seven stresses, and the lyrics, which have a norm of three stresses, I sometimes reduce to two or expand to four. In many passages the tone is constantly shifting, and the modern verse must be alive to the rapid changes of tone and half-hidden implications, which give the actors the "hooks" they need to develop a performance.

For all the "permissiveness" we were supposed to have developed in the 1960s and 1970s, few translators to this day are prepared to render fully into English the total lack of inhibition in sexual and scatological allusion that pervades Athenian comedy. A translator of a comedy about a sex strike who is unwilling to follow Aristophanes when he calls a prick by the Greek word for a prick (*peos*) and a cunt by the Greek word for a cunt (*kusthos*) has no chance of being adequate to the original. And as far as I know, you will find nowhere but herein an accurate English translation of *Frogs* line 10:

XANTHIAS   No other clever jokes?
DIONYSOS   Except "I'm tightly squeezed."
XANTHIAS   Well, can I tell the best one of them all?
DIONYSOS   By Zeus,
     get on with it—but just don't say—
XANTHIAS   say what?
DIONYSOS   That when you shift your load you need a crap.
XANTHIAS   I can't say I am carrying so great a weight
     that if no one relieves me, I will fart out all my shit?   10

This is literally what the actor playing Xanthias said in the Theater of Dionysos in 405 (and again in 404). Why should

the pleasure of hearing Aristophanes' joke in all its scatological glory be denied to the audiences of the twenty-first
century, who can read De Sade's horrific scenes in unexpur-
gated English versions and can summon up on the Internet
pornographic images far more disgusting than anything
Aristophanes ever suggested for the delight of his Athenian
audience?[100] The "impossible" ideal toward which the translator of drama must strive is a version that is *accurate*—a
representation of as much as possible of the meaning(s) with
which the original playwright imbued his Greek text—and
also *actable*, capable of being delivered effectively by an actor
on the modern stage.[101]

As soon as we demand a high degree of accuracy or
fidelity to the source text as well as actability, practical problems arise. I have found these to be relatively containable
when translating tragedy,[102] but in comedy closely accurate
translation cannot always be maintained.[103] Sometimes using
a lateral approach is best—especially when dealing with
Aristophanes' frequent puns and double entendres. For
example in *Lysistrata*, when Kinesias (whose name means
"prick") approaches the Akropolis, he announces himself
as "Kinesias from [the deme] Paionidai." *Paiein* can be a synonym for *binein*, fucking, so he is, as J. Henderson notes, "Mr
Screw from Bangtown."[104] It was the Athenian norm to identify yourself by your name and your deme (suburb/village)
of origin, but attempts at a pun on these lines in English fall
rather flat in performance, because none of us in modern

100. On the differences between ancient Greek and modern Western attitudes regarding "obscenity" (a Roman, not a Greek, word) and on the roles of
sexual and scatological allusion in Aristophanic comedy, see Henderson 1975,
2ff. and 32–33.
101. Ewans 1995, xxxv. It is surprising (and disappointing) that actability
has not been an important criterion for many translators of Aristophanes. See,
for example, Halliwell 1998, preface, in which the only criteria are "readabil-
ity" and "historical accuracy."
102. Ewans 1995, 1996; Ewans, with Ley and McCart, 1999, 2000.
103. Cf. Walton 2006, 158–59.
104. Henderson 1987, 176.

Western society normally announces him- or herself as
Mr./Mrs./Ms. *X* from *Y*. We need to stand back a little and
bring out the *effective meaning* of Kinesias's line:

KINESIAS   Then please, by all the gods, send Myrrhine
   to me.   850
LYSISTRATA   Why? Who are you?
KINESIAS   Her husband, Kinesias; I'm a fantastic fuck.

It must, however, be acknowledged that some puns are
impossible to translate. The multiple puns in the joke about
Theogenes' wife, at *Lys* 64–65, for example, cannot be coaxed
into English. I have done my best to bring over some of the
sense of the original, but I recommend cutting these lines
from modern performance.

   Aristophanes reasonably expected from his Athenian
audiences a total familiarity with their own daily life and
with their more prominent fellow citizens. Here is a literal
translation of the opening lines of *Lysistrata*, which are fast
and furious—and highly allusive:

LYSISTRATA   But if someone had summoned them to a
      place of bakchic revelry,
   or [a grotto] of Pan or to Kolias or [a shrine of]
      Genetyllis,
   you wouldn't be able to move for all the wild drumming.
   As it is, there's not a single woman here—

Line 2 needs at least three footnotes, and in most published
translations that is exactly what you get. But no one can act
a footnote.[105] The translator must first know exactly what
kind of celebrations Aristophanes is evoking[106] and then

105. See Walton 2006, 151.
106. See Henderson 1987, 66–67, or 1996, 208–209.

bring the effective meaning of what Lysistrata is saying before a modern audience:

LYSISTRATA   But if someone had summoned them for
   an orgy,
   or a sleep-out or a celebration of the love goddess,
   you wouldn't be able to move for all the wild
      drumming.
   As it is, there's not a single woman here—

Aristophanes often uses cult titles and other allusions. The translator can help with these by inserting a gloss, either to replace the god's name or title ("the Kyprian, the Paphian" can become "the goddess of love") or to supplement it ("Apollo, god of healing"). Where Aristophanes uses a name because it evokes something specific, I replace it with the thing evoked:

[KALONIKE]   But look—here are some coming for you,   65
LYSISTRATA   —and over here some more.
KALONIKE   Phew!
   Where are they from?
LYSISTRATA   The stinky swamp.
KALONIKE   Oh yes,
   someone's just stirred it up.

Where I have written "the stinky swamp," Aristophanes named without comment the particularly malodorous swamp at Anagyrous, knowing that his audience would understand the allusion. Naming it in the English version can only cause puzzlement, and cute English puns (e.g., "Stinkton")[107] are not as effective for actors as the strategy adopted here. Similarly, when the notorious homosexual Kleisthenes is referred to in *Lysistrata* (1093), I replace his name with "a queen." (Given

107. Henderson 2000, 277.

Kleisthenes' actual appearance in *The Women's Festival* and his three mentions in *Frogs*, he is upgraded in those comedies to The Queen.) On the other hand, there are some passages in which the original Greek names must be preserved.[108]

Frogs demands a slightly different approach. *Lysistrata* can be rendered almost transparent (with a little hard work), since its subject matter, sex, is universal, and it is relatively free from personal invective when compared with most of Aristophanes' other surviving comedies. The same is more or less true of *The Women's Festival*, despite the inclusion of parodies of recent tragedies by Euripides. However, the theme of *Frogs* demands that considerably more names be retained unglossed in the English version. The second part of *Frogs* is a contest between tragic playwrights, with extensive quotations and allusions, and the only possible approach for the translator is to help with unobtrusive glosses where possible and hope that the production can adopt a "crash through or crash" approach, catching up the modern audience in the sweep of the feelings of the contestants rather than hoping they will understand every reference.

Lysistrata and *Frogs* do not raise a problem that affects the translation of many other plays by Aristophanes, including *The Women's Festival*. To caricature the barbarian god Triballos in *Birds* and the Skythian Policeman in *The Women's Festival*, for example, Aristophanes writes their parts in mangled, half-incoherent Greek. However, the Scottish, Irish, Italian, deep Southern, and Russian forms of mangled English used in many translations of these scenes strike a politically incorrect note now that the superiority of those who speak English with the accents of southeast England or WASP New England cannot (and should not) be assumed.[109]

None of the characters given dialogue in the Lakonian dialect (e.g., Lampito, the Spartan Herald, and the Ambassadors in *Lysistrata*) are being caricatured. They use it simply

---

108. See *Lysistrata* 1161ff.
109. So too Halliwell 1998, liii–liv.

because that is how they would have spoken in real life. Accordingly, I have decided to translate their words into the same modern Australian English as the rest of the play. Directors who want to mark them off decisively from the Athenian characters have plenty of options: costumes, mannerisms, or an English dialect or accent of their own choice.[110] There is an element of racist caricature in the barbarous Greek spoken by the Skythian Policeman in *The Women's Festival*, but here again, the means by which to present his stupidity and lust in performance should be left to the director and actor. (In my production, the character's absurdity was expressed in body language and behavior, without recourse to mutilating the English text.)

Aristophanes does make life difficult for his translators, but in my view some have made it worse for themselves. Many seem to feel compelled to add touches of their own humor. Why do they have so little confidence in the playwright? We may have to insert glosses in the text and to take lateral paths to bring out Aristophanes' meaning(s) to modern actors, audiences, and readers, but there is no excuse for interposing our own inventions between our contemporaries and what the playwright actually wrote.

Note on the Presentation of the Translations

For each play I have used the two most modern scholarly editions: *Lysistrata* as edited by J. Henderson 1987 and A. Sommerstein 1990, *The Women's Festival* as edited by Sommerstein 2001 and C. Austin and S. D. Olson 2004, and *Frogs* as edited by K. Dover 1993 and Sommerstein 1996. I have also consulted the close prose versions by Henderson in the Loeb series (2000, 2002). I am deeply indebted to these excellent editors, who have provided up-to-date texts and detailed commentaries, which analyze the richness of

110. Cf. Robson 2009, 200–201.

Aristophanes' Greek and elucidate as far as possible the obscure and problematic passages.

The attributions of speeches, and all stage directions in any translation from Greek drama, are modern. The directions in this edition are for the Greek theater shape, viewed from the perspective of an actor facing forward at BC, and are based on the logic of that shape and on experience gained in rehearsal and performance. Modern directors who need to modify these directions to suit a different-shaped performance space must still be aware of Aristophanes' own practice.

A sudden entry could be made only through the doors leading from the *skēnē*. All other entries were gradual, down one of the two *eisodoi*. Long before he stepped into the *orchēstra,* a character entering down an *eisodos* was visible to some actors and to those in the audience on the side opposite that from which he was making his entry. The convention must have been that the actor was in character from the moment he became visible to any of the audience but that only after he stepped into the *orchēstra* did he interact with players already there. So for side entries the direction *Enter X* is positioned at the moment X enters the *orchēstra*, not when the actor first comes into sight of some of the audience.

The text is divided into scenes (predominantly spoken dialogue) and choroses (passages sung and danced by the *choros* alone). These are numbered in two separate consecutive series. The notations A1, A2, and so on beside the lyric portions of the choral odes denote groups of "strophic" responding stanzas. Each new system inside an individual choral ode is lettered A, B, and so on. Within each system, the 1 stanza was precisely matched in meter by the 2 stanza in the original and was probably choreographed identically.

A choral ode usually marks a division between scenes; however, Aristophanes frequently inserts a choral stanza too short to interrupt the development of the scene as a whole. I have numbered these as new odes, but the number is placed in parentheses, and the scene is not ended when they begin. See, for example, *Frogs* (choros 6).

All double-indented lines were sung and choreographed in the original production.

When the *choros* was not singing, its spoken contributions to the dialogue were almost certainly divided between different members of the group. Accordingly I prefix lines spoken by "the *choros*" with, for example, 1 OLD MAN, 1 OLD WOMAN, 1 WOMAN, 1 INITIATE. Directors will choose which individual choros member is to speak each line as they develop their interpretation of each scene.

Square brackets denote recommended cuts for the modern theater. A note on these is to be found after the plays.

In this edition, following the practice of an increasing number of classical scholars, proper names are transliterated directly from the Greek original and the traditional Latinized spellings are not employed. *Chi* is transliterated by *ch*, not *kh*.

For uniformity of referencing, all modern scholars use the line numbering of one nineteenth-century edition of Aristophanes. However, there has been much research, particularly in the last fifty years, on the nature of Greek lyric verse. This has led to revisions in the line structure. I follow the layout of the Greek texts I used. Accordingly, in lyric sections there are sometimes more, sometimes fewer than ten lines of English verse between the line markers.

Lysistrata

Characters

In order of appearance

Lysistrata ("disbander of armies"): Athenian woman
Kalonike ("beautiful victory"): Lysistrata's neighbor
Myrrhine ("sexpot")*
Women from Athens (3) (Together with the Korinthian
    woman, they can play the four women in scene 4.)
Lampito: Spartan woman
Korinthian: Woman
Boiotian: Woman
[Archer Girl]
Old Men: Half *Choros*
Old Women: Half *Choros*
Bureaucrat
Policemen (3)
Kinesias ("Prick")
Slave with Baby
Spartan Herald
Spartan Ambassadors (2)
Athenian Ambassadors (2)
Reconciliation (naked girl)
[Slaves and Revelers]

The play was first performed in 411 B.C.E.

Props

Scene 1

[Shield]
Large black mixing bowl
Large bottle of red wine

*Literally "myrtle," but this was slang for the vagina.

Choros 1

Logs
Torches
Coal buckets with coals
1 Old Man, ring
Pitchers

Scene 3

Crowbars
Basket with wool, stool
Garland, crown, ribbons

Scene 4

Bronze helmet
Oracle

Scene 5

Bed
Mattress
Pillow
Blanket
Pots of ointment (2) (second one tall and thin)

Scene 1

(Enter LYSISTRATA, *left.)*

LYSISTRATA   But if someone had summoned them
    for an orgy,
  or a sleep-out, or a celebration of the love goddess,
  you wouldn't be able to move for all the wild
    drumming.
  As it is, there's not a single woman here—
(Enter KALONIKE, *left.)*
  except my neighbor who has just come out.
  Hello, Kalonike.

KALONIKE   Hello, Lysistrata.
  Why are you so upset? Don't frown, my dear;
  arching the eyebrows doesn't suit you.

LYSISTRATA   Kalonike, my heart is burning,
  and I'm very upset with us women,   10
  because all the men think
  we are very devious—

KALONIKE   —and they're right—

LYSISTRATA   but when I told them to come here
  to make plans about something really important,
  they're sleeping in; they are not coming.

KALONIKE   Darling,
  they *will* come; it's difficult for women to get out.
  We're always busy servicing our men,
  waking up servants, putting the baby off to sleep,
  or washing it or feeding it.

LYSISTRATA   But this is something even more
  important for them.   20

KALONIKE   What is it, Lysistrata?
  What is this thing? How big?

LYSISTRATA   It's large.

KALONIKE   And thick as well?

LYSISTRATA   Yes, pretty thick.

KALONIKE   Then why aren't they coming?

LYSISTRATA   I don't mean *that*! They'd have been here
   quick enough.
  This is something I've thought out for myself,
  and tossed about on many sleepless nights.
KALONIKE   It must have got exhausted with that tossing.
LYSISTRATA   So exhausted that the whole of Greece
  depends for its salvation on the women.   30
KALONIKE   On the women? There's no hope at all.
LYSISTRATA   We've got to run the city,
  or there won't be any Spartans—
KALONIKE   Wouldn't that be great?
LYSISTRATA   —and all the Boiotians would be destroyed—
KALONIKE   Oh no, not all of them. Leave me some eels!
LYSISTRATA   I'm not going to say anything ill omened
  about Athens; you can guess what I mean.
  But if the women gather here
  —the Boiotians, the Spartans   40
  and us—together we will save Greece.
KALONIKE   How on earth could we do something like
   that—sensible
  and marvelous? We sit around all tarted up
  in sexy clothes and lots of makeup,
  expensive negligees and fancy shoes.
LYSISTRATA   And that's exactly what is going to help
  —our sexy clothes, perfume, and fancy shoes
  and rouge and see-through lingerie.
KALONIKE   What do you mean?
LYSISTRATA   None of the men
  will raise his spear against another—   50
KALONIKE   Great! I'll just slip on a sexy dress—
LYSISTRATA   or take a shield—
KALONIKE   —something extravagant—
LYSISTRATA   or little sword—
KALONIKE   —and buy some fancy shoes.
LYSISTRATA   So don't you think the women should be here?
KALONIKE   Yes, they should all have flown in long ago.

LYSISTRATA   My friend, you'll always see Athenian girls
   do everything much later than they should.
   There's not a woman here from Paralia
   or Salamis.
KALONIKE   Them? First thing each day
   they're hard at it, woman on top.   60
LYSISTRATA   I expected and counted on the women
   of Acharnai to be the first ones here
—but they've not come.
KALONIKE   [Theogenes' wife
   hoisted her wine cup in the air and lost her way.]
(Enter MYRRHINE and 3 other ATHENIAN WOMEN, left and right.)
[KALONIKE]   But look—here are some coming for you,
LYSISTRATA   —and over here some more.
KALONIKE   Phew!
   Where are they from?
LYSISTRATA   The stinky swamp.
KALONIKE   Oh yes,
   someone's just stirred it up.
MYRRHINE   Are we too late, Lysistrata?
   What do you say? Why won't you speak?
LYSISTRATA   Myrrhine, I cannot praise   70
   a woman who is late for something this important.
MYRRHINE   I couldn't find my panties in the dark.
   If it is really so important, tell us now.
LYSISTRATA   No, let us wait a little longer
   for the women from Boiotia and Sparta
   to arrive.
MYRRHINE   Good idea.
(Enter LAMPITO and WOMEN from KORINTH and BOIOTIA, right.)
   But look, here comes Lampito.
LYSISTRATA   My dearest, welcome Lampito from Sparta.
   You look just great.
   Your skin is glowing, your whole body's firm.   80
   You could strangle a bull.

LAMPITO   You bet.
  I work out hard and do kickboxing.
KALONIKE   Wow! Your tits are fantastic.
LAMPITO   Hey! Don't feel me up! I'm not a sacred cow.
LYSISTRATA   And where is this young woman from?
LAMPITO   She came with me, and has authority to speak
  for the Boiotian women.
MYRRHINE   Ah, Boiotia, land
  of beautiful and fertile plains.
KALONIKE   —please note,
  the grass has just been elegantly trimmed.
LYSISTRATA   And who is this?
LAMPITO   A splendid lady,   90
  and she hails from Korinth.
KALONIKE   Splendid indeed—
  great tits and butt.
LAMPITO   Who summoned this assembly
  of the women?
LYSISTRATA   I did.
LAMPITO   Tell us what
  you want from us.
KALONIKE   Yes, darling,
  please tell us your great idea.
LYSISTRATA   I will. But first, let me
  just ask you something small.
KALONIKE   Of course.
LYSISTRATA   Don't you miss the fathers of your children
  when they're off at war? I know   100
  that all your husbands are away.
KALONIKE   Yes; mine, poor dear, has been away
  five months in Thrakia [guarding Eurykrates].
MYRRHINE   And mine has been away for seven whole
  months in Pylos.
LAMPITO   And mine; if ever he comes back home from
  his post,
  he puts a new strap on his shield and off he flies again.

LYSISTRATA   And we don't even have adulterers to fan
     our flames.
   Worse still; since the Milesians deserted us,
   I haven't even seen a compact dildo,
   not one little leather friend.   110
   So if I find a way, d'you want
   to help me end the war?
KALONIKE   Yes,
   count me in, even if I have to pawn
   my finest dress—and drink the proceeds that same day.
MYRRHINE   And me—I'd cut myself in two
   like a flatfish, and give half to the cause.
LAMPITO   And I would climb up Mount Taïgetos,
   to see if I could catch a glimpse of peace.
LYSISTRATA   All right. The truth must not be hidden any
     more.
   If we are going to force   120
   the men to sue for peace,
   we must give up—
KALONIKE   —what, tell us—
LYSISTRATA   —will you do it?
KALONIKE   We'll do it, even if we have to die.
LYSISTRATA   OK; we must give up the prick.
   Why do you turn away? Where are you going?
   You, why purse your lips and shake your heads?
   Your skin's turned pale, you're crying.
   Will you do it or won't you?
KALONIKE   I won't do it. Let the war go on.
MYRRHINE   Me neither. Let the war go on.   130
LYSISTRATA   Is that what you say, flatfish?
   You just said you'd cut yourself in half.
KALONIKE   Anything, anything you want. If I have to,
   I'll walk through fire. But not the prick.
   There's nothing like it, dearest Lysistrata.
LYSISTRATA   What about you?
1st ATHENIAN WOMAN   Me too. I'd rather walk through fire.

LYSISTRATA   Then we're all nymphomaniacs!
No wonder the tragedies are all about us;
we just fuck and get rid of the babies.   140
Lampito, my dearest, if you alone
stand by me now, we might still save the plan.
Vote with me.
LAMPITO   It's pretty hard
For us to sleep without an erect prick,
but still, I'll do it. We really need peace.
LYSISTRATA   You're marvelous—the only real woman here.
KALONIKE   But if we go without . . . the thing you said
—which I hope will never happen—just how
would this bring peace?
LYSISTRATA   Easily.
We'll sit at home, perfumed
and in our see-through nighties we'll   150
parade ourselves, neatly Brazilian waxed.
The men will get erect and want to fuck us,
but we won't go to them; we will hold off
and they'll make peace pretty damned fast, I'm sure.
LAMPITO   When Menelaos saw the breasts
of naked Helen, he threw down his sword.
KALONIKE   But what if they divorce us?
LYSISTRATA   We'll have to get out the dildos.
KALONIKE   Artificial substitutes are just no good.
MYRRHINE   What if they grab us and drag us   160
into the bedroom?
LYSISTRATA   Hold on to the door.
MYRRHINE   And if they hit us?
LYSISTRATA   Then submit—reluctantly.
They don't get as much pleasure from forced sex.
And make them suffer. Soon enough
they will give in. A man will never really enjoy sex,
unless the woman wants it too.
KALONIKE   If you both think that this will work, we'll
    go along.

LAMPITO   Just suppose *we* can persuade our men
   to make peace fairly and without deceit;   170
   how can *you* persuade the common herd
   of the Athenians to make a sensible decision?
LYSISTRATA   Don't worry, we'll persuade them.
LAMPITO   Not while they have their ships
   and boundless wealth stored in Athena's treasury.
LYSISTRATA   We've worked that out as well;
   we'll capture the Akropolis today.
   I ordered the older women to do this,
   while we agreed on our plan here.
   They will pretend to sacrifice, then seize the citadel.
LAMPITO   This is another great idea of yours.   180
LYSISTRATA   Then let us right away, Lampito, swear
   a solemn, binding oath.
LAMPITO   Disclose the oath, and we will swear to it.
LYSISTRATA [A good idea; where is that foreign girl?
(Enter a slave girl with a large shield, left.)
                                        Pay attention;
   place your shield face down in front of us,
   and someone give me sacrificial offerings.
KALONIKE   Lysistrata,
   what kind of oath will you make us swear?
LYSISTRATA   What kind?
   We'll sacrifice a lamb onto a shield, as they say Aischylos
      once did.
KALONIKE   No, Lysistrata, you must not
   make us swear something about peace upon a
      shield!   190
      (Exit Slave Girl, left.)]
LYSISTRATA   What kind of oath do you want?
KALONIKE   Suppose
   we got a white horse and made it our sacrifice?
LYSISTRATA   Ridiculous.
KALONIKE   Then just how
   shall we swear?

LYSISTRATA   I've got a good idea.
   Let's take a large black drinking bowl
   and sacrifice a great big bottle of best Thasian
   and swear not to dilute the wine with water.
LAMPITO   Wow, what a fantastic oath.
LYSISTRATA   Someone bring out the bottle and the bowl.
(One of the women does this.)
MYRRHINE   Ladies, look at the size of that bowl.   200
KALONIKE   Just let me get my hands on it!
LYSISTRATA   Let go, and place your hands upon the victim.
   Goddess Persuasion and Drinking-bowl of Fellowship,
   be favorable to us and receive our sacrifice.
(She pours the offering.)
KALONIKE   The blood is a good color, and it flows out well.
LAMPITO   It smells good too.
MYRRHINE   Ladies, let me be first to seal the oath.
KALONIKE   No, by the love goddess; we will draw lots to
      take our turn.
LYSISTRATA   All take hold of the bowl,
   and one of you repeat for all what I shall say.   210
   The rest, swear to it too and make a binding oath.
   No lover or husband—
KALONIKE   No lover or husband—
LYSISTRATA   —shall come near me with an erection. Say it!
KALONIKE   —shall come near me with an erection. Oh,
   Lysistrata, I'm going weak at the knees.
LYSISTRATA   I shall live my life at home unfucked—
KALONIKE   I shall live my life at home unfucked—
LYSISTRATA   —dressed in my sexy clothes and perfectly
      made up—
KALONIKE   —dressed in my sexy clothes and perfectly
      made up—   220
LYSISTRATA   —so that my husband will burn with desire
      for me.
KALONIKE   —so that my husband will burn with desire
      for me.

LYSISTRATA   And I will never voluntarily yield to him—
KALONIKE   And I will never voluntarily yield to him—
LYSISTRATA   —but if he takes me by force—
KALONIKE   —but if he takes me by force—
LYSISTRATA   —I won't cooperate or respond with my body.
KALONIKE   —I won't cooperate or respond with my body.
LYSISTRATA   I will not lift my silken slippers up toward
   the ceiling.
KALONIKE   I will not lift my silken slippers up toward
   the ceiling.   230
LYSISTRATA   I will not adopt the lioness on a cheese grater
   position.
KALONIKE   I will not adopt the lioness on a cheese grater
   position.
LYSISTRATA   If I confirm these oaths, may I drink from this
   sacred bowl—
KALONIKE   If I confirm these oaths, may I drink from this
   sacred bowl—
LYSISTRATA   And if I break the oath, may the wine be
   changed to water.
KALONIKE   And if I break the oath, may the wine be
   changed to water.
LYSISTRATA   Do you all swear to these conditions?
ALL   Yes.
LYSISTRATA   Then let me sanctify the bowl.
KALONIKE   Only your share!
   Let's all stay friends.
(*Shouts of joy are heard from inside the* skēnē.)
LAMPITO   Who cried out?
LYSISTRATA   That's what I told you earlier;   240
   the women have now captured the Akropolis.
   Lampito, you get going,
   and fix everything back home.
   Leave these women here as hostages.
   We'll join the others in the citadel;
   once we're inside, we'll bolt the doors.

KALONIKE   Don't you think the men will come and try
    to take it back it from us at once?
LYSISTRATA   I don't care.
    If they bring threats or fire against us,   250
    they will not make us open up the doors
    unless they agree to do what we say.
KALONIKE   No, never! If they did, in vain
    are women called unbeatable and devilish.
(Exit Lampito, right.)
(All others exeunt into the skēnē.*)*

Choros 1

*(Enter OLD MEN, left, carrying logs on their shoulders, torches,
and a bucket of coals.)*
1 OLD MAN   Lead on, my friend, go step by step, although
    your shoulder hurts from carrying these heavy logs.
                        * * *
1 OLD MAN (A1)   When you live long, things happen
            that you never would believe.
            Who would have ever thought the women,   260
            wicked cows we feed at home,
            would seize the sacred image,
            occupy *my* citadel,
            and bar the gates against us?
                        * * *
1 OLD MAN   Let's rush to the Akropolis,
    and drop these logs around them!
    The women who thought up this idea and executed it—
    we'll heap a pyre with our own hands
    and burn them all[, starting with Lykon's wife].   270
1 OLD MAN (A2)   By the gods, they will not laugh at us
            while I am still alive.
            Kleomenes, who first captured the citadel,
            did not get off scot-free;

he breathed the true Spartan spirit,
but still gave all his weapons up to me.
He left here in a tiny cloak—
hungry, filthy, hairy,
six years without a bath.   280
                    * * *

1 OLD MAN   That's how I conquered him—with valor!
  We camped out here in seventeen rows of shields.
  I was brave then, and I'll defeat these women,
  hated by Euripides and all the gods.
  If not, take down my victory monument at Marathon.
                    * * *

1 OLD MAN (B1)   Only the little steep bit
    of my path is left.
    But how will we climb up
    without a donkey?   290
    The logs are crushing my shoulders.
    Still, we must press on
    and blow on the fire
    so it does not go out
    when we are nearly there.
    Puff! Puff!
    Look, look at the smoke!
                    * * *

1 OLD MAN (B2)   Ow! It's leapt up
    and attacks me;
    it bites my eyes like a mad dog.
    It's a volcanic fire
    the way it spurts;   300
    it's chewing up the gunk in my eyes.
    Go on ahead to the Akropolis,
    rescue the goddess.
    Is there a better time than this?
    Puff! Puff!
    Look, look at the smoke!
                    * * *

1 OLD MAN   The fire's alive and blazing, with divine
        support.
1 OLD MAN   Let's put the logs down here,
     light the vine-torch in the coal bucket,
     then attack the door like rams.   310
     If the women don't undo the locks when we tell them,
     we'll have to burn the doors and make them suffocate.
1 OLD MAN   OK, let's drop our burden; watch out for the
        smoke!
     [Would any of the generals at Samos like to help?]
1 OLD MAN   At least this bloody log has stopped wrecking
        my back.
1 OLD MAN   Now it is your duty, bucket, to make the
        coal-fire burn,
     so I can have a blazing torch.
1 OLD MAN   Gracious Victory, be with us; we will reward
        you with a trophy
     when we have overcome these women
     who have dared to take the Akropolis.
(Enter OLD WOMEN, left, with pitchers of water.)
1 OLD WOMAN   I think I see thick smoke and haze,
     as if there's burning fire; let's hurry up.   320
                        * * *
1 OLD WOMAN (A1)   Fly, fly,
        before our friends are burnt
        to death, blown from all sides
        by bitter winds
        and horrible old men.
        I am afraid; are we too late?
                        * * *
1 OLD WOMAN   This morning I filled up my water-vessel
        from the well
     with difficulty. There was a crowd, commotion,
                                pitchers clashing;
     slave girls jostled me, covered with whip-marks   330

and tattoos. But I filled up my pitcher eagerly
and I am bringing water; I will help my sisters
who are under siege from fire.

* * *

1 OLD WOMAN (A2)   I've heard there are some burnt-out
men
who've carried up their weighty sticks, like slaves
heating the public baths, right to the citadel,
making most terrible threats
that they would kill those hated women with
a fire.   340

* * *

1 OLD WOMAN   Athena, I don't want to see them burnt!
They must free Greece and Athens from the madness
of this war;
that's why, O goddess of the golden crown,
I call on you to be our ally;
if a man sets them on fire,
join us in bringing water.

Scene 2

1 OLD WOMAN   Stop! What's this? Those miserable
men!   350
How can they be good or reverent, if they do this?
1 OLD MAN   This is unbelievable!
A swarm of women coming to defend the gates.
1 OLD WOMAN   Why be afraid of us? We aren't many.
You haven't seen a fraction of our forces yet.
1 OLD MAN   My friend, shall we just let them babble on?
Shouldn't we hit them with our sticks?
1 OLD WOMAN   Put your pitchers down, so they're not
in the way, if someone tries to hit us.
1 OLD MAN   If someone punched them in the jaw   360
two or three times, we wouldn't have to listen to them
now.

1 OLD WOMAN   OK, here is my jaw. Take your best shot.
    I'm ready—
  and I will be the last bitch ever who will grab your balls!
1 OLD MAN   Shut up, or I'll beat your old arse to pulp.
1 OLD WOMAN   Just touch her with your little finger.
1 OLD MAN   What if I hit you with my fists? How would
    you get back at me?
1 OLD WOMAN   I will devour your lungs and cut out all
    your guts.
1 OLD MAN   Euripides is wisest of all poets;
  'there is no beast as shameless as a woman.'
1 OLD WOMAN   Let's pick up our pitchers.   370
1 OLD MAN   You horrible creatures, what did you bring
    the water for?
1 OLD WOMAN   Why did you bring the fire, old corpse?
        To light your funeral pyre?
1 OLD MAN   No—to kindle a blaze under your friends.
1 OLD WOMAN   I'll use my water to put out your fire.
1 OLD MAN   You're going to put out my fire?
1 OLD WOMAN   Yes, right now.
1 OLD MAN   I think I'd better roast you with this torch.
1 OLD WOMAN   If you've got some soap, I'll give you a bath.
1 OLD MAN   *You*'ll bath *me*, you smelly bitch?
1 OLD WOMAN   Yes—your bridal bath.
1 OLD MAN   You wouldn't dare!
1 OLD WOMAN   I'm a free woman.
1 OLD MAN   I'll stop you shouting.
1 OLD WOMAN   You're not in court now.   380
1 OLD MAN   Set fire to their hair!
1 OLD WOMAN   Time for the water.
1 OLD MAN   Ow!
1 OLD WOMAN   Was it too hot?
1 OLD MAN   What d'you mean, hot? Stop! What are you
    doing?
1 OLD WOMAN   I'm watering you well so you will grow
  again.

1 OLD MAN   But I am dead from shivering.

1 OLD WOMAN   I thought you had an inner fire to warm
     yourself.

Scene 3

(Enter the BUREAUCRAT, left, with 3 POLICEMEN.)

BUREAUCRAT   It seems there's been a flare-up of unbridled
     female misbehavior—loud music, orgies,
     and the rooftop worship of a dead heartthrob.
     I once witnessed an incident in parliament;   390
     that wretch Demostratos was speaking in favor
     of the expedition to Sicily, but his wife was dancing
     in the gallery and shouting "poor Adonis." Next
          Demostratos
     said we should recruit troops from Zakynthos, and then
     his drunken wife screamed "suffer for Adonis!" He just
          carried on—
     the wretched man who's hated by the gods.
     But that's the way women behave.

1 OLD MAN   What would you say if you knew what they're
     doing now!
     They have insulted us, and thrown the water   400
     from their pitchers on us; when we shake
     our cloaks, it looks as if we've peed ourselves.

BUREAUCRAT   By the sea-god, yes—but that's what we
     deserve!
     We go along with all our women's wicked ways,
     and teach them how to live in luxury—so they
     come up with clever schemes like this.
     We go to a tradesman and we say,
     "Goldsmith, you made a necklace for my wife;
     last night when she was dancing,
     the pin fell out of her hole.   410
     I've got to go away on business;

if you have time, you must go over to my place tonight
and fit it in again for her."
Another man says to a shoemaker—
a young one, with a hefty prick—
"Shoemaker, the sandal strap is hurting
my wife's little toe because
it is so soft and tender; in the middle of the day,
please go and enlarge her opening a little."
Here are the consequences.   420
I am a senior public servant, and I've ordered
wood to make new oars—so I need money,
and these women are preventing me from getting in.
But don't just stand about. Bring crowbars,
so I can stop this outrage.
What are you gawping for, you wretch; where are you
looking? Dreaming about the nearest pub?
Get the crowbars under the doors
and force them open; I'll help
over here.
(Enter LYSISTRATA, wearing a garland, from the skēnē.*)*
LYSISTRATA   Do not force the doors;   430
  I'm coming of my own free will. Why use crowbars?
  Instead of crowbars you need brains and common sense.
BUREAUCRAT   Is that right, bitch?
  Grab her and tie her hands behind her back.
LYSISTRATA   If that little bastard lays a fingertip
  on me, he'll suffer for it.
(The POLICEMAN hesitates.)
BUREAUCRAT   Are you afraid? Grab her by the waist,
  And you, too; hurry, tie her up.
*(Enter a formidable WOMAN, wearing ribbons in her hair, from
the* skēnē.*)*
1st WOMAN   If you just lay a hand on her
  we'll beat you till you shit yourself.   440
BUREAUCRAT   Shit yourself?! Where's another policeman?
  Grab this one first, because she talks too much.

(Enter a second formidable WOMAN, *wearing a tiara, from the* skēnē.*)*

2nd WOMAN   If you touch her with the tip of your finger,
   I'll give you a black eye.

BUREAUCRAT   What? Where's a policeman? Seize her.
   I'll stop at least one of you.

(Enter a third formidable WOMAN, *from the* skēnē.*)*

3rd WOMAN   If you go near her, I will pull out all your hair
   and make you scream.

(The POLICEMEN *hesitate.)*

BUREAUCRAT   This is seriously bad. I've no more
      policemen.
   But there's no way I'll let the women   450
   beat us. Troops, fall in;
   get ready to attack.

LYSISTRATA   You'd better know
   I have four companies of fighting women
   in the citadel, all fully armed.

BUREAUCRAT   Troops, tie them up.

LYSISTRATA   Women, get ready;
   market-pease-pudding-gardenveg-stallholdergirls,
   garlic-barmaid-breadbakergirls,
   come on, hit them, strike them,
   abuse them, humiliate them.   460

(The three WOMEN *take on the* POLICEMEN, *who lose and exeunt rapidly, left.)*

   Stop, fall back, do not take spoils of victory.

BUREAUCRAT   Looks like my lot have lost.

LYSISTRATA   What did you expect? Did you think
   you were attacking slave-girls; don't you realize
   women can be courageous?

BUREAUCRAT   Sure they can—
   very courageous, if they've had enough to drink.

1 OLD MAN   Dear bureaucrat, you've wasted many
      words.
   Why are you trying to talk to these wild beasts?

Don't you remember the bath they gave us recently
still in our clothes, and with no soap?   470
1 OLD WOMAN   My dear man, you shouldn't raise your
      hand
   in reckless violence against your neighbors;
   if you do, you'll get black eyes.
   I want to sit down quietly like a little girl,
   no trouble to anybody, not moving a muscle—
   unless my honey's stolen and I'm stirred up like an
      angry bee.

(Choros 2—A1)

1 OLD MAN   What can we do
      with these animals?
      It's intolerable! You must
      examine this disaster carefully.
      What did they think they were doing when   480
      they seized our citadel,
      the sacred place, the holy shrine
      on the great rock?
                                          * * *

1 OLD MAN   Interrogate, do not give in, ask probing
      questions.
   It would be disgraceful if we let this go without a
      searching test.
BUREAUCRAT   I agree, and first I want to find out
   the reason why you locked us out of the Akropolis.
LYSISTRATA   To keep the treasury intact and stop you
      waging war.
BUREAUCRAT   We use the money to wage war?
LYSISTRATA   And stir up everything.
   It's there for Peisandros and all the other politicians
      to steal—   490
   they always used to stir up trouble. Well,

    they can do what they want,
    but they won't get the money any more.
BUREAUCRAT   What will you do?
LYSISTRATA   What do you think? We'll run the economy.
BUREAUCRAT   *You* will?
LYSISTRATA   Is that so strange?
    Don't we run your household finances for you?
BUREAUCRAT   That is not the same.
LYSISTRATA   Why not?
BUREAUCRAT   We need the money for the war.
LYSISTRATA   You shouldn't be fighting at all.
BUREAUCRAT   How else can we save the city?
LYSISTRATA   We will save you.
BUREAUCRAT   You?
LYSISTRATA   Yes, us—
BUREAUCRAT   That's outrageous—
LYSISTRATA   —whether you like it or not.
BUREAUCRAT   —just terrible.
LYSISTRATA   Get angry,
    but you'll have to do it anyway.
BUREAUCRAT   Unfair!   500
LYSISTRATA   You must be saved, old friend.
BUREAUCRAT   If I don't need it?
LYSISTRATA   All the more reason.
BUREAUCRAT   And why are war and peace *your* business?
LYSISTRATA   I'll tell you.
BUREAUCRAT   Quickly, or I'll hurt you.
LYSISTRATA   Listen,
    and try to control yourself.
BUREAUCRAT   I can't;
    I'm too angry.
1 OLD WOMAN   You'll regret it!
BUREAUCRAT   Oh, stop screeching. Now, speak to me.
LYSISTRATA   I will.
    For a long time we suffered in silence; because we knew
    our place, we let you do just anything you wanted.

You didn't even let us grumble—and we didn't like it!
We saw right through you, and often we found out   510
that you had made a bad decision about something
     important.
Although we were hurting inside, we asked you with
     a smile;
"In the assembly today, what did you do about
the peace treaty?" "Mind your own business!" said my
     husband;
"Keep quiet." So I did.
1 OLD WOMAN   *I* wouldn't have!
BUREAUCRAT   You'd have been sorry if you hadn't.
LYSISTRATA   *That's* why I kept quiet.
So then we heard you'd passed an even worse decree,
And I would ask; "Dear husband, why do you persist
in such a stupid policy?"
He'd give me a nasty look, and say if I did not get on
     with spinning
he'd give me a headache; "War is men's business!"   520
BUREAUCRAT   Absolutely right!
LYSISTRATA   How can it be right, you idiot,
if nobody can give you good advice when you go
     wrong?
But when we finally heard you saying in the streets;
"There's not a single soldier left in the country," "Yes,
     you're right,"
then we decided to save Greece
by getting together with the other women.
How long do you think we should have waited?
If you would listen to our good advice
and be quiet like we did, we could set you straight.
BUREAUCRAT   *You* will set *us* straight? Outrageous and
     intolerable!
LYSISTRATA   Be quiet!
BUREAUCRAT   *I've* got to be quiet for *you*, a woman
     with a veil   530

upon her head? I'd rather die.

LYSISTRATA   If that's a problem,
   take my veil, and then be quiet.

1 OLD WOMAN   Here's your little basket.

LYSISTRATA   Do some knitting,
   chew on some gum,
   and leave the war to women.

1 OLD WOMAN   Leap up, leave your pitchers,
   let us take our turn to help our friends.   540

(Choros 2—A2)

1 OLD WOMAN   I'll never stop dancing—
   old age won't wear out my knees.
   I'll go to any lengths
   to help these wonderful women, who
   are noble, charming, courageous,
   and wise; they love their city
   and can think.

* * *

1 OLD WOMAN   Now, granddaughter of heroines, daughter
   of stinging nettles,
   let rip; do not go soft; you're sailing well.   550

LYSISTRATA   If Eros and his mother, the goddess of love,
   breathe hot desire into our breasts and thighs
   and this gives men sweet tension and stiff pricks,
   I think we will be called the women who have stopped
   the war.

BUREAUCRAT   How?

LYSISTRATA   First we must stop men charging crazily
   across the marketplace in full armor.

1 OLD WOMAN   Good idea!

LYSISTRATA   They go past pottery and vegetable stalls
   clashing their arms like manic dancers.

BUREAUCRAT   Of course; that is a mark of courage.

LYSISTRATA   No, it's just ridiculous
  to go round with a Gorgon shield to buy your fish.   560
1 OLD WOMAN   Yes, I once saw a cavalry commander on
      his horse
    buy porridge from an old woman and put it in his
      helmet.
    Then there was a foreign soldier menacing with shield
      and javelin;
    he terrified the fig-seller, and gulped down all her fruit.
BUREAUCRAT   But how can you solve the knotty problems
  in the cities?
LYSISTRATA   Very easily.
BUREAUCRAT   Then show me how.
LYSISTRATA   Given a knotted skein of wool, we take it and
      we draw
    it with the spindle, first from one side and then from the
      other.
    That is how we will resolve this war, if we just get the
      chance,
    untangling it with embassies, to one side then the
      other.   570
BUREAUCRAT   You think that you can stop this terrible
      affair with wool and skeins
    and spindles? You're out of your mind.
LYSISTRATA   If you had any brains,
  you'd run the city like we treat this wool of ours.
BUREAUCRAT   This I have to hear.
LYSISTRATA   First you should wash it like a fleece,
    to get out all the sheep droppings. Then lie it on a bench
    and beat it with a rod to pick out all the troublemakers,
                    burrs and thorns,
    and the conspirators and those who form tight cliques
    to gain high office; discard them, cut off all the knots.
    Then card the wool into a basket filled with general
      goodwill.

Mix everybody in—the immigrants, and friendly
    foreigners,   580
or men who owe the state a debt—mix them in as well.
Next, all the cities that are colonies of ours,
you have to realize these are many separate piles
of unspun wool; we need to take the wool from all of
    them,
and bring it home and mix it into one, and make
a giant ball of wool—then weave a new cloak for the
    people.
BUREAUCRAT   Isn't it terrible for women to speak of
    beating fleece and spinning wool?
You do nothing to help with the war.
LYSISTRATA   You bastard, we do
more than double what you do. First we give birth
and send our sons as soldiers off—
BUREAUCRAT   Don't say it; no past sufferings.   590
LYSISTRATA   Then, when we should be having pleasure
                  and enjoying being young,
we sleep alone because of war. Never mind us wives,
think of unmarried girls who're growing old in bed
    alone.
BUREAUCRAT   Don't men get old as well?
LYSISTRATA   Yes, but it's not the same.
When one gets back from service, even with grey hair,
he'll soon get a young girl to marry him;
a woman's time is short, and if she's lost her chance,
nobody wants to marry her; she just sits at home and
    hopes.
BUREAUCRAT   Right! If a man can still get an erection—
LYSISTRATA   Why don't you just die?
There's plenty of space; buy a coffin;   600
I'll even knead your honey cake myself.
Take this garland for your funeral.
1st WOMAN   Here are some ribbons from me—

2nd WOMAN   And a crown from me.
LYSISTRATA   What do you need? What do you want?
    Just go!
    The ferryman of the dead is calling you,
    but you're preventing him from setting sail.
BUREAUCRAT   Oh, how terrible are my sufferings!
    I'm going straight to my colleagues
    to show them what these women did to me.   610
LYSISTRATA   Are you complaining about our funeral
        service?
    Don't worry; very first thing, two days from now,
    we'll come—and dance upon your grave!
*(Exit BUREAUCRAT, left; exeunt LYSISTRATA and THREE WOMEN
into the skēnē.)*

Choros 3

1 OLD MAN   Now is the time for all free men to rise.
    Take off your cloaks, gentlemen; get ready for action.
                              * * *

1 OLD MAN (A1)   This business has the stench
        of something sinister; I smell a whiff
        of tyranny. And I'm afraid some Spartans   620
        may have met here in secret to incite
        these women, hated by the gods,
        to seize the treasure; that's the jury pay
        on which I live!
                              * * *

1 OLD MAN   It's terrible that *they* are telling *us*, the citizens,
    what we must do—women just babbling on about the
        war—
    and making peace with Spartans,
    whom I trust less than hungry wolves.
    They're weaving a web of tyranny.   630
    I will not endure it; I will stand on guard

and sing heroic songs of victory.
I will parade in arms like the great tyrant-killer
and strike the same pose as his statue—nicely placed
to hit this horrible old woman on the jaw.

* * *

1 OLD WOMAN   Your own mother won't recognize you if
     you do.
Take off your cloaks, dear ladies.

* * *

1 OLD WOMAN (A2)   Citizens, we will begin
     with words of value to the city.
     This is just, because the city nourished us   640
     in luxury and comfort.
     When I was seven I served the goddess for eight
          months,
     I ground corn for the sacred cakes at ten, and then
          stripped off
     my saffron robe, and went through rites of passage
          before puberty.
     And when I was a beautiful young woman, I carried
     the sacred basket, wearing a necklace made of figs.

* * *

1 OLD WOMAN   So don't I have a duty to give the city
     good advice?
Do not begrudge me, just because I am a woman,
if I bring changes for the better.   650
I have contributed my share; I've borne you sons.
You miserable old men have not contributed;
you squandered all the wealth your ancestors had won
from war with Persia, and you've not made up the
     deficit.
Indeed, we're going bankrupt thanks to you.
D'you dare to grumble? Don't annoy us,
or I will use my boot to kick you on the jaw.

* * *

1 OLD MAN (B1)   This is a total outrage!

—and it's getting worse.   660
Now is the time for every man with balls to fight.
Off with your shirts; a man should smell
just like a man, and not be wrapped away.
Come on, foot soldiers,
just as we went to battle when
we were still young.
We must rise up again, take wing   670
and slough off this old skin.
                    * * *

1 OLD MAN   If we give them even a tiny chance,
   there's nothing slippery that they won't do;
   they will build ships, and try to fight
   at sea against us, like the Karian queen.
   And if they turn to horses, we won't have a chance;
   women just love horses and mounting up,
   and they don't fall off. Think of the Amazons,
   whom Mikon painted fighting men on horseback.
   We've got to get them all and put them   680
   in the stocks—so grab their necks!
                    * * *

1 OLD WOMAN (B2)   If you inflame me, I'll let loose
      my inner sow on you, and shear your fleece.
      You'll beg your friends to rescue your shorn-off
         carcasses.
      We'll strip for action too,
      so we will smell like women mad enough to bite. 690
      Come on, attack me, if you never want
      to eat garlic again
      or chew black beans.
      Just one bad word—I'm so enraged—
      and I will crush your nuts.
                    * * *

1 OLD WOMAN   I don't give a shit for you, as long as
      Lampito still lives
   and that dear noble girl from Thebes, Ismenia.

No matter if you voted seven times, you are quite
    powerless—
you wretched man whom all your neighbors hate.
Only yesterday I tried to have a party   700
for the local wives and kids. I sent an invite to
a dear and special friend from Boiotia—an eel;
but they said they could not send her, because of your
    decrees.
You won't stop voting stupidly, until one of us grabs
    your leg,
gives a good heave, and breaks your neck.

Scene 4

(Enter Lysistrata from the skēnē.*)*
(mock tragic)

1 OLD WOMAN   Queen of our mighty enterprise,
   why have you come forth frowning from the temple?

LYSISTRATA   The deeds of wicked women and the female
    mind
   have made me lose my courage, and I wander restlessly.

1 OLD WOMAN   What are you saying? What are you
    saying?   710

LYSISTRATA   It's true. It's all too true.

1 OLD WOMAN   What is so terrible? Please share it with
    your friends.

LYSISTRATA   It is shameful to speak, and difficult to be
    silent.

1 OLD WOMAN   Please do not hide from me this evil we
    have suffered.

LYSISTRATA   We need a fuck. That's it in short.

1 OLD WOMAN   O Zeus!

LYSISTRATA   Why call on Zeus? Here's how it is.
   I just can't keep them away from their men
   any longer. They're deserting.

First I caught one digging a hole in the wall   720
near the grotto of Pan,
then another letting herself down the wall
with a rope and running off. Then I caught by the hair
another one who tried to fly
on a sparrow down to her lover.
They're trotting out any excuse to go
back home.

(Enter 1st WOMAN from the skēnē.*)*

Here's one right now.

Hey, you; where are you off to?

1st WOMAN   I want to go home.
I've got a special fleece,
and moths are wrecking it.

LYSISTRATA   What do you mean, moths?   730
Get back in.

1st WOMAN   But I'll be very quick—
just long enough to spread it on the bed.

LYSISTRATA   No spreading on the bed; you're not going
        anywhere.

1st WOMAN   Should I just let my fleece be destroyed?

LYSISTRATA   If necessary.

(Enter 2nd WOMAN from the skēnē.*)*

2nd WOMAN   Unhappy me, alas for the beautiful flax
which I left untreated at home.

LYSISTRATA   Here's another one
who wants to have her flax worked on.
Get back inside.

2nd WOMAN   But I promise;
I'll just strip it off and come straight back.

LYSISTRATA   No stripping off; if I let you,   740
another woman will want to do the same.

(Enter 3rd WOMAN from the skēnē, *apparently heavily pregnant.)*

3rd WOMAN   Goddess of childbirth, may I not bear my
        child
until I leave this sacred place.

LYSISTRATA   What is this nonsense?

3rd WOMAN   I'm going to have a baby.

LYSISTRATA   You weren't pregnant yesterday.

3rd WOMAN   But I am now.
    Dear Lysistrata, please send me home at once,
    so I can find a midwife.

LYSISTRATA   What's the story?
    What is this hard thing?

3rd WOMAN   A baby boy.

LYSISTRATA   No, it's something hollow,
    made of bronze. I'll find out for myself.   750
    This is absurd! You've taken the sacred helmet
    and pretended you were pregnant?

3rd WOMAN   Yes I did, and I *am* pregnant.

LYSISTRATA   Then why did you take it?

3rd WOMAN   So if the child came out
    still in the citadel, I could give birth into the helmet,
    like the pigeons do.

LYSISTRATA   What's this excuse? Your plan's exposed.
    Wait for the ceremony five days after birth.

3rd WOMAN   But I can't even sleep up there,
    ever since I saw the sacred snake.

(Enter 4th WOMAN from the skēnē.*)*

4th WOMAN   I'm being destroyed by those owls—   760
    their awful racket! I can't get a wink of sleep.

LYSISTRATA   You miserable creatures, stop these
        preposterous excuses.
    Sure, you want your men; do you not think
    they want us too? I'm certain they are having
    troubled nights. Stand firm, good ladies,
    hold out for a little longer.
    There is an oracle which says that we shall win,
    if we don't fall into internal strife. And here it is.

3rd WOMAN   Tell us what it says.

LYSISTRATA   Maintain a reverent silence.
    "When the swallows fly to a single place,   770

in flight from the hoopoes, and abstain from the phallus,
that will be the end of our troubles. Zeus the thunderer
    on high
will turn everything upside down—"
2nd WOMAN   —does that mean we get to go on top?
LYSISTRATA   "but if the swallows separate and fly out from
    the sacred temple, then it will be shown
    they are the horniest of all birds."
1st WOMAN   The oracle is clear. Praise to the gods.
LYSISTRATA   Let's not give up the hard work we have done.
    Come on inside. My friends, it would be shameful if
    we failed to do our duty by the oracle.   780
(*Exeunt LYSISTRATA and FOUR WOMEN into the* skēnē.)

Choros 4

1 OLD MAN (A1)   I want to tell you a story
        I heard when I was a boy.
        There once was a young man called Melanion,
        who was afraid of marriage; he went off into the wild
        and lived in the mountains.
        There he made traps
        and hunted hares   790
        and kept a dog
        and never came back home.
        He found women disgusting; so do all
        men of good sense like us.
1 OLD MAN   I'd like to kiss you—
1 OLD WOMAN   Eat less onions!
1 OLD MAN   Stretch my legs and kick—
1 OLD WOMAN   You've got a lot of pubic hair!   800
1 OLD MAN   Myronides was fierce
        to all his enemies
        because his pubic hair was thick
        and black, and so was Phormio.

* * *

1 OLD WOMAN (A2) I'd like to tell a little story
        in reply to yours about Melanion.
        Timon the vagabond
        used to hide away in thick bushland   810
        like an offshoot of the Furies.
        He left the city
        and lived in the mountains
        with curses upon human wickedness.
        He hated, as we do, all wicked men—
        but he loved women!   820
(Enter LYSISTRATA on the roof of the skēnē.*)*
1 OLD WOMAN Shall I punch your jaw?
1 OLD MAN Please don't; I'm terrified.
1 OLD WOMAN Then I'll kick you.
1 OLD MAN You'll show your hair.
1 OLD WOMAN Then you would see
        I may be old,
        but I don't let it grow;
        it's neatly trimmed.

Scene 5

LYSISTRATA Come here, ladies, come to me quickly.
(Enter MYRRHINE and two other WOMEN on the roof.)
1st WOMAN What is it? Tell me why you're shouting. 830
LYSISTRATA I see a man, maddened and smitten
    by the holy mysteries of sex.
    Goddess of love, ruler of Kypros, Kythera,
    and Paphos, may he make his way straight here.
2nd WOMAN Where is he, whoever he is?
LYSISTRATA   By the shrine of Chloe.
1st WOMAN Yes, there he is. And who is he?
LYSISTRATA Look. Does any of you recognize him?
MYRRHINE   Yes,
    I do. It's my husband, Kinesias.

LYSISTRATA   It's your job now to make him burn,
     torment him,
     cheat him, make love but not make love,   840
     and give him everything except what we swore we
          wouldn't.
MYRRHINE   Easy. I'll do it.
LYSISTRATA   I'll stay here;
     I'll help to work him up
     and get him on heat. Off you go.
(Exeunt MYRRHINE and other WOMEN down into the skēnē.*)*
*(Enter KINESIAS, left, hugely erect. A SLAVE follows with his
baby son.)*
KINESIAS   Poor me, I'm in convulsions, and my prick
     is straight as if it had been stretched upon the rack.
LYSISTRATA   Who's penetrated our defenses?
KINESIAS   Me.
LYSISTRATA   A man?
KINESIAS   Can't you see that?
LYSISTRATA   Then go!
KINESIAS   What right have you to throw me out?
LYSISTRATA   I'm the guard of the day.
KINESIAS   Then please, by all the gods, send Myrrhine
     to me.   850
LYSISTRATA   Why? Who are you?
KINESIAS   Her husband, Kinesias; I'm a fantastic fuck.
LYSISTRATA   Welcome, dear man. Your name
     is famous and is celebrated here.
     Your wife is always mentioning you,
     and if she eats an egg or an apple,
     'This is for Kinesias,' she says.
KINESIAS   Then please—
LYSISTRATA   Just a moment. If we're talking
     about our men, she says at once all of the rest
     are nobodies compared to her Kinesias.   860
KINESIAS   Please call her out.
LYSISTRATA   Will you give me a fee?

KINESIAS   Well, yes, if you want.

　　I've got this; and what I've got, I'll give to you.

LYSISTRATA   I'll just go down and call her out.

KINESIAS　　　　　　　　　　　　Please hurry up.

(LYSISTRATA descends into the skēnē.*)*

　　I have no pleasure in my life

　　since she left home.

　　I ache when I come home, and everything

　　seems empty; I cannot enjoy

　　my food or drink. I'm permanently stiff.

MYRRHINE   *(offstage, to LYSISTRATA, as she climbs to the*
　　skēnē *roof)*

　　I love him, yes, I love him. But he doesn't want　　870

　　me to. Don't make me go to him.

KINESIAS   Dearest, darling Myrrhie, why are you doing
　　this?

　　Come down here.

MYRRHINE *(on the roof)* No, I won't.

KINESIAS   Won't you come down? I'm begging you,
　　Myrrhine.

MYRRHINE   No, you don't need anything from me.

KINESIAS   I don't? I'm suffering.

MYRRHINE   I'm off.

KINESIAS　　　　　　Please don't go. Listen to

　　your baby son. You, call out to Mummy.

BABY   Mummy, Mummy, Mummy.

KINESIAS   What's the matter with you? Six days　　880

　　he's gone without a bath or a breast-feed.

MYRRHINE   I do pity him; but his father

　　neglects him.

KINESIAS   Do the right thing—come down to your baby.

MYRRHINE   Motherhood has awesome power. I must go
　　down.

　　　　　　　　　　　　　　　I have no choice.

(MYRRHINE goes down inside the skēnē.*)*

KINESIAS   She looks much younger and much sexier;
   OK, she's angry and treats me like dirt,
   but that's exactly why I long for her so much.
(Enter MYRRHINE from the skēnē.*)*
MYRRHINE   My dearest, darling child of a wicked father,
   let me give you a kiss, you sweet little thing.   890
KINESIAS   Myrrhie, I'm sick of this. Why have you been
   persuaded by those other women? You're making
      me sore,
   and doing yourself no good.
MYRRHINE   Don't touch me!
KINESIAS Our household management
   has gone to pieces.
MYRRHINE   I don't care.
KINESIAS   You don't care if the cockerels are ruining
   your finest dress?
MYRRHINE   I don't.
KINESIAS   And you haven't celebrated the sacred rites of
      Love
   for all this time. Please come back home.
MYRRHINE   No, I won't, unless you come to terms with
      the enemy   900
   and stop the war.
KINESIAS   If the people vote for it,
   we will do that.
MYRRHINE   If they vote for it,
   I will come home; but right now, I am bound by my
      oath.
KINESIAS   Then at least lie down with me—it's been so
      long.
MYRRHINE   No way. But I'm not saying I don't love you.
KINESIAS   You do? Then please lie down with me,
   Myrrhine.
MYRRHINE   What? You idiot! In front of the baby?
KINESIAS   Manes, take the baby home.
(Exit SLAVE with baby.)

Look—no more baby.

Let's lie down.

MYRRHINE But where could we possibly 910
do it, darling?

KINESIAS Where? Pan's grotto looks good.

MYRRHINE But how could I go back into the sanctuary?
I'd be impure.

KINESIAS Wash in the nearby spring and you'll be pure
and beautiful.

MYRRHINE But darling, I'd be breaking an oath.

KINESIAS Let that be on my head. Don't worry about it.

MYRRHINE OK; I'll just get us a little bed.

KINESIAS No!
The ground will do.

MYRRHINE No! Even though
you have your faults, I won't lie with you on the
ground.

(Exit MYRRHINE into the skēnē.*)*

KINESIAS You can all see how much my wife loves me.

(Enter MYRRHINE with bed.)

MYRRHINE There, lie down quickly, and I'll get
undressed. 920
But wait—we need a mattress.

KINESIAS What? I don't!

MYRRHINE No, we can't do it
just on the springs.

KINESIAS Give us a kiss.

MYRRHINE Of course.

(And after a really sexy kiss, she goes back into the skēnē.*)*

KINESIAS Wow! Come back quickly.

(Reenter MYRRHINE with mattress.)

MYRRHINE Here's the mattress. Lie down, and I'll undress.
But this is awful; you don't have a pillow.

KINESIAS I don't need one.

MYRRHINE Well, I do.

(Exit MYRRHINE into the skēnē.*)*

KINESIAS   How long will this poor prick be forced to wait?
(Reenter MYRRHINE with pillow.)
MYRRHINE   Lift up now, lift. There, I've got
    everything.   930
KINESIAS   Yes, everything. Come here, my darling.
MYRRHINE   I'm taking off my bra. But just remember;
   don't cheat me about the peace treaty.
KINESIAS   I swear I won't.
MYRRHINE   You don't have a blanket.
KINESIAS   I don't need one; I just want a fuck.
MYRRHINE   Don't worry; you'll get one. I'll be right back.
(Exit MYRRHINE into the skēnē.*)*
KINESIAS   She's ruining me with all these bedclothes.
(Reenter MYRRHINE with blanket and ointment.)
MYRRHINE   Raise yourself up.
KINESIAS   This bit's already up.
MYRRHINE   Would you like me to rub ointment on you?
KINESIAS   Absolutely not.
MYRRHINE   Oh yes I will, whether you want it or not.
KINESIAS   I wish she'd spill the lot.   940
MYRRHINE   Hold out your hand and you can rub it on.
KINESIAS   Look here, I don't like this stuff;
   it's just making us wait and it doesn't smell sexy.
MYRRHINE   Oh stupid me, I brought the wrong one.
KINESIAS   It's fine. Leave it, please.
MYRRHINE   Don't talk nonsense.
(Exit MYRRHINE into the skēnē, *with ointment jar.)*
KINESIAS   I'd like to kill the man who invented perfume.
(Reenter MYRRHINE with a tall, phallic-shaped bottle.)
MYRRHINE   Try this.
KINESIAS   I've got one of those already.
   You irritating girl, just lie down and don't bring me
   anything more.
MYRRHINE   OK. I'm taking off
   my shoes.

(She tiptoes towards the skēnē *without his noticing.)*
      But just remember, darling,   950
 you must vote for peace.
KINESIAS   I'll think about it.
(Exit MYRRHINE *into the* skēnē.*)*
 Aah!
 She's destroyed me and ruined me
 and stripped me and left me.
  What shall I do? Whom shall I fuck,
  betrayed by the fairest of all creatures?
  How shall I nurture this poor little orphan?
  Where's a pimp?
  I need to hire a nurse.
1 OLD MAN You poor man, you are suffering.
  Your soul is worn down by this awful trick. 960
  I pity you. Alas!
  What kidneys could stand this,
  what soul, what testicles,
  what groin, what prick
  stretched out like this
  without a fuck?
KINESIAS Oh God, more pain!
1 OLD MAN She's a disgusting bitch
 for doing this to you.
KINESIAS No, she's loving and sweet.   970
1 OLD MAN What d'you mean, sweet? She's a bitch.
KINESIAS OK, she's a bitch. O Zeus, Zeus,
  if only you could carry her off
  like a pile of leaves in a gigantic hurricane,
  spin her around and shake her up
  and then let go,
  so she was carried back to earth
  and suddenly
  landed on my prick.

Scene 6

(Enter a SPARTAN HERALD, massively erect, right.)

HERALD   Where are the Elders of Athens   980
   or the Executive? I need to let them know some news.

KINESIAS   Who are you? A man, or a walking phallic
      symbol?

HERALD   Young man, I am a Herald, and I've come
   from Sparta to negotiate for peace.

KINESIAS   Is that why you're hiding a weapon under
      your clothes?

HERALD   No, I'm not.

KINESIAS   Why turn away?
   Don't try to hide it. Did your groin swell up
   on the long journey?

HERALD   He's crazy.

KINESIAS   Liar! You've got a hard-on.

HERALD   No I haven't. Don't talk nonsense.   990

KINESIAS   Then what's this?

HERALD   A Spartan message-stick.

KINESIAS   If that's one, here's another.
   Trust me, I know—so tell the truth.
   How are things down in Sparta?

HERALD   Everyone's erect and all the allies
   have been aroused; we're desperate for a good firm
      thrust.

KINESIAS   What god inflicted this suffering on you?
   Was it Pan?

HERALD   No. It all began, I believe, with Lampito,
   and then all the other Spartan women
   decided suddenly to deprive   1000
   their menfolk of their pussies.

KINESIAS   How are you going?

HERALD   Very badly. We all walk around
   bent over like lamp-carriers on a windy day.
   The women will not let us touch their cunts

unless we all agree to make
peace with the other Greeks.
KINESIAS   Now I get it! This is a conspiracy between
the women everywhere. You must advise
your government to send as fast as possible
ambassadors with full power to negotiate.   1010
I'll just show the Athenian Council this prick,
and they'll appoint negotiators as well.
HERALD   I'll fly; yours is the best advice.
(Exeunt HERALD, right, and KINESIAS, left.)
1 OLD MAN   No wild beast is harder to fight than women;
not fire or panthers are so dangerous.
1 OLD WOMAN   If you know that, do you intend to go on
fighting us,
you silly man, when you and I could be true friends?
1 OLD MAN   I'll never stop hating women.
1 OLD WOMAN   OK, stop when you want to. But I can't
ignore
the fact that you're half naked. It's ridiculous.   1020
Let me help you put your shirt back on.
(She does so.)
1 OLD MAN   That was very nice of you;
I was bad-tempered when I took it off.
1 OLD WOMAN   Now you look like a man, and not
ridiculous at all.
If you'd behaved, I would have got that bug
out of your eye.
1 OLD MAN   Yes, it's been troubling me. Here is a ring;
scrape it out, then show me.
My eye's been hurting for ages.
1 OLD WOMAN   I'll do it, even though you've been
so grumpy.   1030
My god, look at the size of this insect;
it has to be a Hexham grey.*

*Aristophanes here named the notorious mosquitoes of the Trikorythos
marshes in the Tetrapolis, NW of Athens. We substituted the large and fierce

1 OLD MAN   Thanks for the help; it was digging boreholes
      into me.
   That's why, now it's come out, I'm crying.
1 OLD WOMAN   I'll wipe these tears off, even though you
      are a pest,
   and give you a kiss.
1 OLD MAN   Oh, don't.
1 OLD WOMAN   Whether you want it or not!
1 OLD MAN   Oh, shit! You're so persuasive,
   and the old proverb is right; we can't
   live with you or without you.
   I will make peace with you, and for the rest of time   1040
   I won't abuse you and you will not do the same to me.
   So let us stand together and join in this song.

Choros 5

1 OLD MAN (A1)   From now on we will not say cruel words
      about any of our fellow-citizens;
      no, quite the opposite! We'll say and do
      good things; there's been enough suffering already.
      All of you—men and women—if you need   1050
      a little bit of money—just a few thousand bucks—
      come to us; we've got the cash.
      When peace and prosperity come,
      if you've borrowed from us you need never repay
      'cos we may not have lent you a cent!
                              * * *
1 OLD WOMAN (A2)   We're going to have a feast for some
      most loyal allies, noble gentlemen.   1060
      There'll be a hearty pea soup, and I've got a suckling pig

---

mosquitoes of the mangrove swamps at Hexham, west of Newcastle, Australia,
where this translation was first performed. Insert your own audience's least
favorite insect here!

ready to eat—the finest, tenderest bits of pork.
Come to my place today—come early!
You must all have baths (the kids as well)
then come on over, walk straight in
as if you were at home. One problem, though;   1070
we will have locked and barred the door!

Scene 7

(Enter TWO SPARTAN AMBASSADORS, right, with large erections.)
1 OLD WOMAN   Here are the ambassadors from Sparta,
    looking like they're wearing panty pads.
  Spartans, greetings to you; tell us
  in what state you are.
1st SPARTAN   What need of words?
  Just look and see.
1 OLD MAN   Oh dear. The disease has got really intense;
  it looks inflamed and far worse than before.
2nd SPARTAN   Unspeakable! What can we say?
    Whatever way you want,   1080
  get someone to come here and let's make peace.
(Enter ATHENIAN AMBASSADORS, left, also erect [attended by slaves].)
1 OLD WOMAN   Here are our local ambassadors
  bent over like wrestlers, and with their clothes
  pushed out from their bellies. It's clear
  this is a swelling disease.
1st ATHENIAN   Who can tell us where Lysistrata is?
  Look at the state we're in.
1 OLD MAN   Looks like they've got the same illness.
  D'you get a special seizure around dawn?
1st ATHENIAN   It's driving us mad all the time.   1090
  If someone doesn't reconcile us very soon,
  we'll have to fuck a queen.

1 OLD WOMAN   If you have any sense, you'll cover up; or
     else the men
  who knocked the pricks off all those statues might see
     you.
2nd ATHENIAN   Good advice.
2nd SPARTAN   Agreed.
  Let's fold our cloaks around us.
1st ATHENIAN   Greetings, Spartans. We have suffered
     terribly.
1st SPARTAN   Dear friend, we might have suffered even
     worse
  if those statue-mutilators had found us in this state.
1st ATHENIAN   All right, Spartans, let's get down to
     business.   1100
  Why are you here?
1st SPARTAN   We are ambassadors
  for peace.
1st ATHENIAN   Great. So are we.
  Let us call out Lysistrata,
  the only person who can bring us reconciliation.
[1st SPARTAN   Bring Lysistratos as well, if he can help.]
(Enter LYSISTRATA from the skēnē*.)*
2nd ATHENIAN   I don't think we have to call her;
  she heard us, and here she is.
1 OLD WOMAN   Greetings, bravest of all! Now you must be
  fierce but soft, honest but tricky, stern but gentle—
  brilliantly multiskilled. Your charm has conquered
                              two great cities;   1110
  they both defer to you and trust you to resolve their
     grievances.
LYSISTRATA   It will not be too difficult, provided the
     ambassadors are all
  eager for peace and not just scoring points.
  I will soon see. Where's Reconciliation?
(Enter RECONCILIATION, a beautiful, naked girl, from the skēnē*.)*

First bring me the Spartans,
with a gentle, not an angry hand,
not in the stupid way our men have treated us,
but as a woman should—affectionately.
If he doesn't give you his hand, pull him by the prick.
Now bring the Athenians;   1120
whatever they give you, grab it and bring them here.
Now, men of Sparta, stand near me,
Athenians over here, and listen to what I say.
I am a woman, but I have a brain,
I'm old enough to have intelligent ideas,
and I've learnt much about our great traditions
listening to my father and to other elders.
First I'm going to rebuke both of you
with justice on my side;
at the Olympic games and other festivals   1130
(I could name many, but I won't) you share one bowl
to sprinkle altars just like kinsmen;
why, when we have enemies abroad to fight,
do you kill fellow-Greeks and wreck Greek cities?
That's my first point.

1st ATHENIAN   I'm dying from this hard-on.

LYSISTRATA   Now, Spartans, I'm turning to you.
  Don't you remember how a mighty Spartan general
     once
  came here to Athens as a suppliant, and sat down at
     an altar
  in his scarlet cloak—his face was white with fear—   1140
  begging us for an army? You could hardly cope
  with both an earthquake and a slave revolt.
  The great Kimon marched down there with 4,000 men
  and saved the whole of Sparta.
  So we Athenians did that for you, and yet
  you're ravaging this land that helped you out?

2nd ATHENIAN   Yes, they are doing wrong.

1st SPARTAN   We are—but that girl's bum is beautiful.

LYSISTRATA   D'you think I'm going to let off you
    Athenians?
  Don't you remember how the Spartans, when the
    tyrants   1150
    had reduced us all to poverty, came fully armed?
    They killed a host of foreign occupying troops,
    and many of the tyrant's friends and allies.
    They also helped you, by themselves, to throw him out
    and gave us freedom, so instead of slavish rags,
    we once more wore the cloak of freedom and
    democracy!
2nd SPARTAN   I've never seen a girl with such great tits
    and buns.
1st ATHENIAN   I've never seen a cunt more beautiful.
LYSISTRATA   You've done so many good things for each
    other;
  why are you still fighting? Why won't you stop this
    wickedness?   1160
  Why not be reconciled? What's standing in the way?
1st SPARTAN   We're willing, if we can have
  this nice round bit.
LYSISTRATA   Which one?
1st SPARTAN   Pylos, the secret entrance.
  We've always wanted it, and now I'm going to grope it.
1st ATHENIAN   No way, they can't have that.
LYSISTRATA   Let them have it.
1st ATHENIAN   Where can we attack them from?
LYSISTRATA   Ask for another place instead.
1st ATHENIAN   This is terrible; give us instead of that
  the Hedgehog, and the Malian Gulf
  just behind it, and the Legs of Megara.   1170
1st SPARTAN   No way, not all of those, good sir.
LYSISTRATA   Back off; don't argue about a pair of legs.
1st ATHENIAN   I want to get my clothes off and farm my
    patch.
1st SPARTAN   I want to get in first with the manure.

(Exit RECONCILIATION, discomfited and in haste, into the skēnē.)

LYSISTRATA   When you are reconciled, this shall be done.
  If you've agreed, then go,
  and tell your allies the good news.
1st ATHENIAN   What allies? We are stiff.
  The allies will all say the same as us;
  "We need a fuck."
1st SPARTAN   That's pretty much what ours   1180
  will say as well.
1st ATHENIAN   Even the warmongers.
LYSISTRATA   Well spoken. Now let's go and solemnize
      the treaty,
  so the women can entertain you in the citadel
                      with what we've got inside our boxes,
  and you can swear your oaths and give each other
    pledges.
  Then each of you can take
  his wife and go back home.
1st ATHENIAN   Let's do it now—
1st SPARTAN   I'll follow you.
1st ATHENIAN   —as fast as possible.
(Exeunt AMBASSADORS and LYSISTRATA into the skēnē.*)*

Choros 6

1 OLD WOMAN (A1)   This ceremony will need sons to
      carry things, and basket-girls;
  I won't begrudge them spreads and fancy
    clothes   1190
  and cloaks and stately robes, and gold.
  I tell you all—take everything that's in
  my house; nothing is so well sealed
  that you can't break the seal and take
                        what's there.   1200

Unfortunately—you won't find a thing,
unless your eyesight is better far than mine!

* * *

1 OLD MAN (A2)   If you've no grain, and you have got
     to feed
your slaves and lots of little kids,
you can come and get flour from my store—
little grains, but they will make a good-sized loaf.
If you are poor, come to my house   1210
with sacks and baskets for the flour;
my slave will fill them up.
I should just mention—you cannot come in!
I have a savage dog.

Scene 8 (Finale)

[1st ATHENIAN *(inside the* skēnē*)*
  Open the door!
(enters; to slaves)
                 You should have got out of my way!
  Why are you lying around?
  I'll burn you with my torch!
             (to the audience)
                      No; that's an old
  comic routine, and I won't do it. *(pause)* Well, OK,
  if I must—anything to please you.   1220
(Enter 2nd ATHENIAN from the skēnē*.)*
2nd ATHENIAN   And I'll help you.
  Go away, or I'll pull your hair.
1st ATHENIAN   Go away, so the Spartans inside
  can leave in peace when the banquet is over.
(The slaves retreat toward an eisodos*.)*]
2nd ATHENIAN   I've never seen such a good feast.
  What great company the Spartans were,
  and we are very witty when we're pissed.

1st ATHENIAN   That's fair enough; we're pretty stupid
      when we're not.
   If I can persuade the Athenians,
   we'll always be drunk when we negotiate.   1230
   When we go to Sparta sober,
   we're always looking for something suspicious.
   We don't listen to what they're really saying,
   and we suspect they're saying things they're not,
   and we come back with differing accounts.
   Today has been fantastic; if someone sang
   the wrong song, we'd just praise him
   and congratulate him.
             [(The slaves come back toward the door.)
   Oh, here come the slaves again.
   Get out of here, you wretches!   1240
2nd ATHENIAN   Yes, here come the Spartans now.]
(Enter SPARTAN AMBASSADORS from the skēnē.*)*
1st SPARTAN   Good friend, play the bagpipes,
   so I can dance and sing
   to honor the Athenians and ourselves.
1st ATHENIAN   Please do; we love your Spartan dances.
(Enter LAMPITO, 3 WOMEN, KORINTHIAN and BOIOTIAN women,
Athenians (three policemen and KINESIAS) from the skēnē.*)*
1st SPARTAN   Goddess of Memory,
      inspire me through the Muse
      who knows how we and the Athenians
      made war like gods at sea   1250
      and beat the Persians.
   Our own Leonidas
   led men who fought like boars
   sharpening their teeth.
   Sweat flowered on their cheeks,
   and dripped down to their knees.
   There were as many Persians as   1260
   the grains of sand.
                    * * *

Wild virgin goddess of the hunt,
come here to seal our treaty,
so we may be united forever.
Be kind to us, and help us to be rich
because we have made peace,
and we'll be rid of men who act
like wily foxes.   1270
Come here, come here,
goddess of the hunt.

(Enter LYSISTRATA, KALONIKE, and MYRRHINE from the skēnē.)

LYSISTRATA   Now everything has been done well,
    so Spartans and Athenians, each take your wives;
    let man stand next to woman, woman
    next to man, and we will celebrate our fortunes
    dancing for the gods. Let us make sure
    we never make the same mistakes again.

(as the couples begin to dance)

1 OLD MAN   Bring on the dance,
    call the goddess of the hunt to us,   1280
    and her twin brother, god of healing,
    leader of the dance;

1 OLD WOMAN   call the god of ecstasy,
    who dances with his maenads, eyes ablaze,
    and Zeus, lit by his thunderbolt—also
    his noble, happy wife.

1 OLD MAN   We call the gods, who don't forget,
    as witnesses
    of this serene Tranquillity
    which the goddess of love has given us.   1290

CHOROS   Hooray!
    Dance off to victory!
    Hooray!

(They are about to exit, when they are detained by this drunken request from the 1st Athenian:)

1st ATHENIAN   Let's have an encore!

1st SPARTAN   Muse of Sparta, come—
    leave beautiful Taïgetos once more, and praise
    Apollo, and Athena,
    and the noble Twins   1300
    who race beside the river.
    Dance on, dance on;
    step nimbly. We'll praise Sparta,
    where we dance for the gods
    and stamp our feet
    and where like colts the girls
    leap by the river.
    Their feet raise dust,   1310
    their long hair streams,
    their bodies twirl like maenads;
    Helen leads the sacred dance.

            * * *

    Come, bind up your hair, and leap
    like deer, and clap your hands;
    let's praise the conquering goddess; praise
        Athena!   1320
(Exeunt ALL.)

The Women's Festival
(Thesmophoriazousai)

Characters

In order of appearance

Euripides: famous tragic playwright
In-Law: of Euripides; an elderly man
Servant: of Agathon
Agathon: young tragic playwright
Women: played by the *Choros*
Mika: young mother
Garland-Seller
Kritylla: priestess, leader of the women
The Queen: Kleisthenes, Athens's most notorious passive
    homosexual
Council Executive: senior government official
Policeman
Echo: mysterious figure

Silent Roles

Mania: nursemaid for Mika's "baby"
Fawn: dancing girl
Woodworm: boy flute player

Props

Preset

Altar with sacrificial knife; wooden votive tablets
    concealed behind it.

Scene 1

Torch and myrtle twigs (Servant)
Lyre (Agathon)

Couch; small table with razor (in case) and mirror; wig,
     hairnet, and headband; woman's shawl; yellow dress
     and belt (on *ekkuklēma* with Agathon)
Torch (for Euripides)
Torches (Women of the *Choros*)
Wine bladder wrapped as baby (Mania)
Speaker's garland (Kritylla)

Scene 2

Brushwood, sacrificial bowl (Mania)

Scene 5

Plank with clamps
Mat
Whip, knife, holster (Policeman)
Sack, winged sandals and helmet (Euripides as Perseus)

Scene 6

Small harp (Euripides)
Old Woman's wig and cloak (Euripides)
Pipe (Woodworm)

Scene 1

(Enter EURIPIDES, followed by his elderly IN-LAW, left.)

IN-LAW   O Zeus, bring me a sign of spring!
   This man will be the death of me; we've been
      wandering since dawn.
   Euripides, before I vomit up my guts,
   please tell me where you're taking me.

EURIPIDES   You must not hear things, all of which
   you will see straightaway.
                              IN-LAW   What? Say that again.
   I must not hear?

                  EURIPIDES   Not things you're going to see.

IN-LAW   I must not see?

                  EURIPIDES   Not things you must soon hear.

IN-LAW   What are you telling me? It certainly sounds
      clever!
   You're saying I must not see or hear?   10

EURIPIDES   The concepts are entirely different.

IN-LAW   You mean not seeing and not hearing?
                              EURIPIDES   That's right.

IN-LAW   How are they different?
            EURIPIDES   This is how they came to be distinct.
   When Ether first became a separate entity,
   and gave birth in himself to living creatures that could
      move,
   first he contrived an instrument of sight
   —the eye, shaped as a ball just like the sun;
   for hearing he then bored a funnel—that's the ear.

IN-LAW   Because of the funnel I can't see or hear?
   I'm *so* grateful for the explanation.   20
   This is what happens when you hang around with
      clever men.

EURIPIDES   You can learn lots of things like this from me.
                              IN-LAW   It's marvelous

to gain such wisdom, but I only want to learn
how to be lame in *both* my legs.
EURIPIDES   Come here and pay attention.
                                                      IN-LAW   Right.
EURIPIDES   D'you see this door?
                                          IN-LAW   Yes, I
most certainly do.
                        EURIPIDES   Be quiet now.
                              IN-LAW   Quiet about the door?
EURIPIDES   Listen.
                    IN-LAW   Listen, and be quiet about the door?
EURIPIDES   This is the place where Agathon, the famous
     tragic playwright, lives.
IN-LAW   Which Agathon is that?   30
EURIPIDES   He is—
IN-LAW   Dark skinned and strong?
EURIPIDES   No, another one. Haven't you ever seen him?
IN-LAW   The one with a thick beard.
                        EURIPIDES   Haven't you *ever* seen him?
IN-LAW   Not so I'd recognize him.
EURIPIDES   I bet you've fucked him, but you probably
     don't know it.
(Enter SERVANT from the skēnē.*)*
     Let's crouch out of the way. Here comes a servant
     carrying out fire and myrtle twigs;
     he's going to sacrifice so Agathon may gain poetic
     inspiration.
(They retreat to the mouth of the left eisodos.*)*
SERVANT   Abstain from inauspicious words,
     let everyone be silent, for the holy band   40
     of Muses now resides within these halls—
     and they're creating poetry.
     The air must hold its breath, windless;
     the gleaming sea must not be heard
     to splash—

IN-LAW Rubbish!
>EURIPIDES   Shush!
>>IN-LAW   What's he saying?

SERVANT   Let every wingèd creature lay itself to rest,
and let no wild beast of the forest
move its feet.
>IN-LAW   Total rubbish!

SERVANT   For Agathon our lord, creator of fine words,
is going to—
>IN-LAW   Get fucked?   50

SERVANT   Who spoke?
>IN-LAW   The windless air.

SERVANT   —lay down the keel, on which to build a
brand-new play.
He's bending new planks made of words,
planing some and gluing others,
forging ideas, inventing metaphors, and melting
wax; he rounds the words to shape,
then casts them in the mold—
>IN-LAW   And sucks some cocks.

SERVANT   What vulgar peasant has approached these
halls?

IN-LAW   A man who's ready to take you and Agathon,
creator
of fine words, turn you around, bend you,   60
and bugger you with this prick!

SERVANT   When you were young, were you this coarse,
old man?

EURIPIDES   My good friend, just ignore him, and please ask
if Agathon could come out here.

SERVANT   You do not need to ask; he'll soon be out.
He's just about to start creating poetry; and when
it's winter it is hard to bend the verse,
unless he comes outdoors to catch the sun.

EURIPIDES   What shall I do, then?
>SERVANT Wait here till he comes.   70

(Exit SERVANT.*)*

EURIPIDES *(mock-tragic)* O Zeus, what fate have you in store
    for me today?

IN-LAW   I would just like to know
    what's going on. Why the despair? Why be so stressed?
    You are my in-law; you should not keep secrets from me.

EURIPIDES   A dread misfortune's been cooked up for me.

IN-LAW   What is it?

                EURIPIDES   On this day it will be judged
    whether Euripides will live or be destroyed.

IN-LAW   But how? The courts are idle, so they can't
    cast verdicts, and the Council's not in session,
    since the Women's Festival is in its middle day.   80

EURIPIDES   And that's exactly how I'm going to be
    destroyed.
    The women have conspired against me, and
    in their shrine, this very day,
    they'll vote for my destruction.

                      IN-LAW   Why?

EURIPIDES   Because I slander women in my tragedies.

IN-LAW   Well then, you'll only get what you deserve.
    So what is your escape plan?

EURIPIDES   I'm going to persuade the tragic playwright
    Agathon
    to penetrate the festival.

                IN-LAW   What will he do?

EURIPIDES   Join the assembly of the women, and then
    if need be   90
    speak up for me.

              IN-LAW   Will he go openly or in disguise?

EURIPIDES   In a disguise, dressed as a woman.

IN-LAW   Splendid idea, well worthy of your style;
    in scheming we just take the cake.

(Enter AGATHON *on the* ekkuklēma, *clean shaven and dressed
as a woman in a yellow dress. He is lying on a couch beside a
small table, which has on it a razor [in its case], a mirror, and a*

wig with hairnet and band. On the couch are another yellow
woman's dress, belt, and scarf, and somewhere on the ekkuklēma
are some sandals. He is accompanied by the SERVANT.)
EURIPIDES   Quiet!

          IN-LAW   What's happening?

              EURIPIDES   Agathon is coming out.

IN-LAW   Where is he?

      EURIPIDES   There—the man they're wheeling out.

IN-LAW   I must be blind! I cannot see
   a man at all—just Kyrene the whore.

EURIPIDES   Be quiet! He's going to sing.

IN-LAW   Melisma like a swarm of ants, or just a plaintive
     ode?   100

AGATHON   (*as solo*) Maidens, take up the torch
     sacred to the two goddesses below the earth;
     dance, raise your voices; we are free,
     and the whole city sings with us.
                 * * *

     (**as choros**) Which gods are we to celebrate?
     Tell us. We're happy if we worship
     anyone.
                 * * *

     (**as solo**) Come, make Apollo happy with your song,
     the god who shoots the golden arrows,
     and who built our city in the vales of Simois.   110
                 * * *

     (**as choros**) Enjoy these songs of fairest beauty,
     Phoibos; be the first to receive
     our beautiful tribute of song.
                 * * *

     (**as solo**) Now sing the praises of the
         goddess Artemis,
     virgin who hunts up in the wooded hills.
                 * * *

     (**as choros**) I follow you; I call upon the blessed,
     holy child of Leto,

Artemis, pure maid.

                          * * *

(*as solo*) And Leto and the dance-notes of   120
the Asian lute, keeping the cross-beat time,
directed by the Graces.

                          * * *

(*as* **choros**) Yes; I worship Leto, who is queen and
     mother
of our songs, and the lyre,
the manly instrument,

                          * * *

(*as solo*) that makes light sparkle in the god's eyes,
like your unexpected song. For this joy
honor lord Apollo.

                          * * *

(*as* **choros**) Hail, O happy son of Leto.
Hail!

                          * * *

IN-LAW   What a sweet song,   130
     and so effeminate, and fully tongued,
     just like a French kiss; when I heard it,
     I felt a thrill come right up to my arse.
     And as for you, young man, I'd like to ask,
     using the words of Aischylos [in his Lykourgos plays],
     "Where are you from, womanish creature?
     What's your fatherland, and what's the reason for
          this dress?"
     What is this freak of nature? Why d'you strum
     dressed up in yellow? With a lyre and hairnet?
     Male deodorant and bra? It does not add up.
     How can you have a mirror and a sword?   140
     What are you, boy? Were you brought up to be a man?
     And if so, where's your prick? Your cloak? Your proper
          shoes?
     If you're a woman, then where are your tits?
     No comment? Well, if you won't tell the truth,

I'll have to make my judgment from your singing!
AGATHON   My dear old man, I hear the envy in
   all this abuse, and you will not upset me.
   I wear the clothes that suit my creativity.
   A tragic dramatist must first immerse himself
   completely in the character that he's creating.   150
   So if he is creating plays with female parts,
   his body must participate in everything they do.
IN-LAW   You must ride men on top, when you write
      about Phaidra.
AGATHON   If what you write concerns the deeds of men,
      your body has
   already got all that you need; but what we do not have,
   poetic imitation helps to find.
IN-LAW   When you're writing a satyr-play, give me a call,
   so I can help by fucking you from behind.
AGATHON   Anyway, it's inappropriate for a poet to look
   all wild and hairy; look at Ibykos,   160
   Anakreon from Teos and Alkaios;
   all their harmonies were delicate,
   they wore the proper headband, lived the soft
   Ionian lifestyle—and Phrynichos (you must have
   heard of *him*!) was beautiful and beautifully dressed.
   That's why his plays were beautiful as well.
   It is a law of nature; we write just the way we are.
IN-LAW   That's why the ugly Philokles writes ugly verse,
   and Xenokles is horrible and so's his poetry,
   Theognis is a cold man, and he writes so frigidly.   170
AGATHON   You're absolutely right. That's why
   I gave myself this treatment.
                         IN-LAW   *What* did you do?*
EURIPIDES   Stop hassling him. I myself was just the same
   when I was his age, and beginning my career.
IN-LAW   I do not envy you your upbringing.

---

* In-Law suspects that Agathon has had himself castrated!

EURIPIDES   Please let me say why we came here.

AGATHON   Go on.

EURIPIDES   Agathon, a wise man should be able to
   say much in a few words.
   I have been struck by a disaster, and
   I come to you as suppliant.

AGATHON   What do you need?   180

EURIPIDES   The women will destroy me at their festival
   this very day, because I slander them.

AGATHON   But how can *I* help you?

EURIPIDES   You're everything I need. If you took up a
      place
   among the women, looking just like one,
   and spoke up for me, I am sure you'd save my life.
   You are the only one whose words would do me justice.

AGATHON   Why don't you go yourself?

EURIPIDES   I'll tell you. First, I would be recognized.
   Then, I am grey haired and I have a beard,   190
   while you're good looking, pale skinned, clean shaven,
   gentle mannered, and you have a woman's voice;
      you look just great.

AGATHON   Euripides!

EURIPIDES   What?

AGATHON   Remember you once wrote:
   "You love your life; do you not think your father loves
      his too?"

EURIPIDES   I did.

AGATHON   Then don't expect that I
   will bear your burden. I'd be mad to do it.
   Cope with your problems by yourself.
   We aren't supposed to scheme our way
   out of misfortunes; we just have to endure them.

IN-LAW   You filthy queen, your arsehole is so wide   200
   because you open up to anyone who wants it.

EURIPIDES   Why are you afraid to go?

AGATHON   I'd suffer a worse fate than you.

EURIPIDES   Why?

           AGATHON   Because
the women think I copy all the things they do
at night, and steal their natural rights as females.

IN-LAW   Steal their rights? You just get fucked like them.
But it's a fair enough excuse.

EURIPIDES   So will you do it?

                      AGATHON   No, no way.

EURIPIDES   Oh thrice accursed! Euripides is lost!   210

IN-LAW   My dear, good relative, do not be so dismayed.

EURIPIDES   What shall I do?

              IN-LAW   Forget that bastard;
I'll do what you want.

EURIPIDES   If you are going to help me, then
take off your clothes.

(IN-LAW strips naked.)

          IN-LAW   It's done.
What are you going to do to me?

              EURIPIDES   Shave off your beard,
and singe your private parts.

                IN-LAW   OK, do it—
but I wish I'd never volunteered.

EURIPIDES   Agathon, you carry a razor everywhere;
please lend it to me.

        AGATHON   Get it yourself;
it's here.

      EURIPIDES   You are a gentleman.   220
(to IN-LAW) Sit down. Puff out your cheek.

IN-LAW   Ow!

      EURIPIDES   Be quiet! I will gag you,
if you don't shut up.

        IN-LAW   Ah! AAAH!

(IN-LAW runs toward the left eisodos.)

EURIPIDES   Where are you going?

          IN-LAW   To the nearest shrine;
I won't stay here

and get cut into pieces.

EURIPIDES   You'll look ridiculous
with half your face shaved clean.

IN-LAW   I don't care!

EURIPIDES   By all the gods, please don't
desert me; come back here.

IN-LAW *(sitting down again)*
I was born to suffer.

EURIPIDES   Keep still and lift your head up. Do not
twist.   230

IN-LAW   Oh!

EURIPIDES   Keep quiet; it has all gone well.

IN-LAW   I was born to suffer; now I'll have to fight
without a beard.

EURIPIDES   Don't worry; you'll look great.
D'you want to see yourself?

IN-LAW *(he looks in the mirror)*
No!! I see The Queen!

EURIPIDES   Stand up so I can singe you, and bend over.

IN-LAW   I was born to suffer; I'll become a suckling pig.

EURIPIDES   Someone bring a torch out from the house.
(The SERVANT does this.)
Bend over; watch out for the tip of your prick.

IN-LAW   I will—but I am burning up.   240
Ah!! Water, water, quick
before the fire spreads to another arse.

EURIPIDES   Be brave!

IN-LAW   *Be brave*, when I'm consumed by fire?

EURIPIDES   No need to worry now; you're past
the worst already.

IN-LAW   Look at the soot!
I'm burnt right from my balls through to my arsehole.

EURIPIDES   Don't worry; somebody will sponge them down.

IN-LAW   No one had better try to wash my bum.

EURIPIDES   Agathon, since you would not volunteer
yourself,

at least lend me a dress and belt   250
 for my friend; you cannot deny you have such things.
AGATHON   Take them and use them; I don't mind.
             IN-LAW   What should I get?
EURIPIDES   First take this dress and put it on.
IN-LAW   By the love-goddess, it has a pleasant smell of
     prick.
 Put it on, and do it up. And now fasten the belt.
                       EURIPIDES   All done.
IN-LAW   Now, arrange the dress around my legs.
EURIPIDES   We need a hairnet and a band.
                 AGATHON   Here is a prestyled wig—
 I wear this gear myself when I go out at night.
EURIPIDES   Great! You have everything we need.
IN-LAW   Does it fit me?
                         EURIPIDES   Absolutely!   260
 Bring a scarf.
                 AGATHON   Take this one from the couch.
EURIPIDES   And we need shoes.
                       AGATHON   OK then, borrow mine.
IN-LAW   Will they fit me? Wow, you like to wear things
     loose.
AGATHON   Whatever you say. And now that you've got
                                       all you need,
 let someone wheel me back into the house.
(*AGATHON is wheeled back inside on the* ekkuklêma.)
EURIPIDES   Great. Now our man looks absolutely
 like a woman. If you gossip, make your voice
 all feminine; do it properly, and be convincing.
                 IN-LAW   (*falsetto*) I will do my best.
EURIPIDES   Get going now.
                       IN-LAW   No way, unless
 you swear to me—
             EURIPIDES   What?
                       IN-LAW   That you will come   270
 and rescue me with all your skill, if anything goes wrong.

EURIPIDES   I swear then by the Ether, residence of Zeus.
IN-LAW   You might as well swear by a block of shonky
      flats.
EURIPIDES   OK, I swear by all the gods on high.
IN-LAW   And just remember that it is your heart that
      swore;
   your tongue did not, nor did I ask it to.
EURIPIDES   *(who has looked down the left* eisodos)
   Go on, and hurry. I can see the signal for
   the Women's Festival Assembly.
   I am off.
(Exit EURIPIDES, right.)
                              IN-LAW *(to an imaginary female slave)*
                              Thratta, follow me.
   Oh, Thratta, look at all the burning torches, and the
      crowd   280
   making its way here through the smoke.
   O beautiful goddesses of the Festival, I beg you,
      welcome me;
   grant me good fortune coming here and going home.
(During the rest of this speech, the CHOROS *of* WOMEN, MIKA
[with MANIA *nursing her "baby"], and* GARLAND-SELLER *enter
in small groups, left.)*
   Thratta, bring the casket, and take out
   the sacrificial cake, so I can make my offering.
   O glorious mistress, dear Demeter,
   and Persephone, may I be rich and make you many
   offerings—or at least not be caught out today.
   And may my little daughter Pussy find a husband
   who is rich, but also stupid and a good-for-nothing,   290
   and give my little Prickie brains and common sense.
   Where's a good place for me to sit, to hear
   the speeches properly? Thratta, go away;
   slaves aren't allowed to hear these words.
*(Enter KRITYLLA, left, with garland. Very businesslike and con-
scious of her importance as the Priestess.)*

KRITYLLA   Let there be no ill-omened speech. Pray to the
goddesses of this festival, Demeter and her daughter,
and to Wealth and to the Bearer of Fair Offspring, and
Earth the Nurturer, and Hermes and the Graces   300
for this assembly to be the best ever, and for it to help
the city of Athens, and bring good fortune to us all. And
she who gives the best advice for the people of Athens
and the women of Athens shall be victorious. Pray for
all this, and good things for yourselves.   310
Hurrah! Hurrah! Hurrah! Let us rejoice!

Choros 1, part one

WOMEN   We receive your prayer, and we beseech
the gods; be present here, and rejoice
in our prayers.
Come here, great Zeus, and lord Apollo
of the golden lyre, whose sacred place is Delos,
and Athena, virgin, all conquering,
the grey-eyed lady of the golden spear—
you fought for Athens and you now live here—
and famous Artemis, the hunting goddess,   320
daughter of Leto of the golden eyes.
Most solemn Lord Poseidon, sea-god,
leave the swirling depths of ocean, rich in fish;
come, O sea-nymphs, come
you nymphs who wander on the mountains.
Let the golden lyre sing out
to echo all our prayers;
let us, the noble women of this city,
have a perfect gathering today.   330

* * *

KRYTILLA   Pray to the Olympian gods and goddesses,
the gods and goddesses of Delphi
and of Delos and all other gods;

if anybody plots against the women
of this city, or negotiates in secret
with Euripides or with the Persians
to harm us, or plans to set up a dictatorship
or bring the tyrants back, or tells a husband that his
    wife
has passed a baby off as hers, or if a slave has been   340
the go-between in an affair, then whispers in the
    master's ear,
or someone goes on errands and brings back false news,
or if a lover lies to get a woman to put out,
and does not give her what he's promised,
or if an older woman steals a lover by giving him gifts,
or a call-girl takes presents and cheats on her boyfriend,
or if a tavern-keeper (male or female)
waters down the drinks (kegs or glasses),
now pronounce this curse; let them and their whole
    household
perish wretchedly! Then pray the gods bestow on all   350
the rest of us blessings of every kind.

Choros 1, part two

WOMEN   We pray with you that all
            we wish for will come true
            for both the city and its people,
            and all women who deserve it
            will win victory for what they say; but if
            anyone deceives us, and they disobey
            the oaths that custom's sanctioned
            to harm us for their own reward,   360
            or try to change our laws
            and make decrees instead, or tell
            our secrets to our enemies,
            or bring the Persians here

to harm us for their own reward,
we hope they'll die, because
they disrespect the gods and do injustice to the city.
All-conquering Zeus, may what we pray come true,
and may the gods stand at our side,   370
even though we are women.

* * *

Scene 2

KRITYLLA   Pay attention, everyone. The Council of the
     Women
passed this resolution. Arikleia was President,
Lysilla was Secretary, and Sostrate proposed the motion:
to hold an assembly at dawn on the middle day
of the Festival, when we have the most free time,
and first discuss what we should do
to make Euripides suffer, since we all think
he's done wrong. Who wants to speak?
MIKA   I do.
                KRITYLLA Put on this garland first.   380
(MIKA puts the speaker's garland on her head.)
1 WOMAN   Quiet, quiet, pay attention; she's clearing her
     throat
like all the public speakers do. I think we're in for a
     long speech.
MIKA   I swear to you, good ladies, I do not stand here
     to speak
for personal advantage; I've just found it very difficult
for a long time to see Euripides,
the son of a greengroceress, throw mud at you,
and have to hear all kinds of filth.
What dirt has he not smeared on us?
He slanders us wherever there   390
are live performances of tragedy;

he calls us man-mad whores,
pisspots, betrayers, gossips,
and "disgusting creatures," "the worst evil man can
    bear."
So when they come back from the show, at once
men look at us suspiciously, and check up straightaway
to see if we've a lover hidden somewhere in the house.
We can't do anything we want; he's taught our men
such awful things. If a woman plaits a garland,   400
they think she's in love; or if she drops a bowl
as she is going to and fro around the house,
her husband asks: "for whom did you wish good luck,
    when you broke that pot?
I bet it was our guest from Korinth!"
A girl is sick; her brother says:
"I think she's pregnant."
If a woman can't have children, and she needs
to smuggle in a baby, we can't get away with it—
for now the men stay right beside her bedroom door.
He's slandered us to the old men, who used   410
to fancy bright young things; they will
not marry any more, because he said
"the woman rules in an old bridegroom's house."
And then it's all because of him that they
put seals and locks on women's living areas
to keep a watch on us, and breed
gigantic hunting dogs to scare away our lovers.
                        * * *
We could forgive all that; but once we could
look after the provisions by ourselves, and take
out grain and oil and wine—   420
and now we can't. Men carry keys around
themselves—secret, awful things
made down in Sparta, with three teeth.
Before that we could open up the storage room

by buying a cheap copy of their signet ring,
but now this household spy, Euripides,
has taught them to get signets made out of
worm-eaten wood
and wear them all the time. So I propose
that we cook up some kind of death for him,
by poison or some clever trick,   430
so he may perish. That is what I tell you openly—
I'll get the secretary to help me draft the rest.

(Choros 2)

WOMEN (A1)   I've never heard
       a subtler woman or
       a more compelling speaker.
       Everything she says is just,
       she's marshalled all her arguments,
       weighed them all up, and cleverly
       expressed her views
       in cunning words.
       If Xenokles the tragic poet stood   440
       and spoke beside her,
       I think you'd all agree that he
       talks utter rubbish!
                          * * *

GARLAND-SELLER   *(placing the speaker's garland on her head)*
    I haven't much to say;
    this lady has denounced Euripides so well,
    I only want to add what I myself have suffered.
    My husband passed away in Kypros,
    leaving me with five small children, whom I just manage
            to support
    by weaving garlands in the myrtle market.
    And for a while our life was not too bad,
    but now this man who churns out tragedies   450

has made the men believe there are no gods;
it's cut our sales by more than half.
So I advise you well, and tell you this;
that man deserves a punishment for many things.
My fellow-women, he has wronged us grievously,
as you'd expect from one brought up among
            wild herbs and veg.
I'm off to the marketplace; I've got to plait
preordered garlands for a party group of twenty men.
(Exit GARLAND-SELLER, left.)

(Choros 2, continued)

WOMEN   Here's another gutsy speech,
            even more accomplished   460
            than the one before.
            What she said was timely,
            her ideas were wise and subtle,
            far from stupid—all believable.
            For what he's done to us,
            that man must suffer
            public punishment.
                              * * *

IN-LAW   *(taking the speaker's garland)*
            Ladies, it's no surprise that you are furious
            against Euripides, and your anger's boiling over,
            hearing all the wrongs he's done.
            And I too—may I lose all happiness with my children if
                I lie—
            I hate that man; I would be mad if I did not.   470
            But still, there should be room for argument;
            we're on our own, no one will publicize the things
                we say.
            So why are we accusing him
            and taking it so badly, if he knows a couple

of our tricks—when we have thousands?!
Let me not speak for others; I myself
know I've done many awful things. The worst of all
was when I'd been a bride three days,
lying beside my husband; I had a boyfriend,
who'd taken my virginity when I was seven.   480
Wanting to have me, he came scratching at the door.
I recognized the sound at once, and went down secretly.
But then my husband asked; "Where are you going?"
   "Where?
I've got a dreadful tummy-ache—I'm going
to the loo!" "OK." Then he began
to pound up juniper and dill and sage,
while I poured water on the door-sockets
and went out to my lover; I got fucked head down
beside the altar of Apollo, clutching at the laurel bush.
Well, Euripides never mentioned that, did he?   490
And he never said how we get laid by slaves
and muleteers, if we can't find a better man.
Nor how, when we've been screwed the whole night
   long,
we chew garlic first thing, so when
our husband gets back home from guard duty,
he smells us and does not suspect at all. Look here,
he never mentioned *that*. OK, he hurls abuse at
   Phaidra—
what's that got to do with us? He never told about
the woman who, while showing off a new top
to her husband, smuggled out a lover   500
wrapped up in a cloak—he never mentioned that!
I know another woman who pretended for ten days
she was in labor, until she could buy a baby;
her husband ran round everywhere to buy
     a medicine for induction.
An old woman brought in the baby hidden in a pot;
its mouth was stuffed with honeycomb to keep it quiet.

The old girl gave a nod, and the wife shouted out:
"husband, husband, go away—I'm going to
give birth." (The baby'd kicked the inside of the pot.)
He went away all joyful, then she pulled the honey
    comb   510
out of the baby's mouth, and it cried out.
The horrible old woman who'd brought in the baby boy
smiles at the husband, puts it in his arms, and says:
"You've got a lion there, a lion; he's the image of his
    father
every which way, right down to his little prick;
it's just like yours—a twisted acorn-cup."
Don't we do wicked things like that? By Artemis,
we do. So why are we still angry with Euripides,
when he gives us back nothing worse than what we've
    done?

(Choros 2, conclusion)

WOMEN (A2)   This is astonishing!   520
    Where is this creature from,
    what country bred
    such an outrageous woman?
    I never would have thought
    this bitch would dare to say
    such awful things so shamelessly
    and openly.
    These days anything can happen,
    but I applaud the ancient proverb: Be careful!
    For under every stone, ready to bite,
    there lies a public speaker!   530
               * * *

1 WOMAN Women have no shame; there's nothing worse
    than women—except other women!
MIKA My friends, you must be crazy,

drugged or seriously ill,
to let this wretched woman insult all of us
like this. Any volunteers? If not,
my slave and I will get some red-hot ash
and singe her pussy, so she'll learn
never again to insult other women.
IN-LAW   No, not my pussy, please! This is a free   540
society, and any citizen may speak,
so just because I said what I think's right about
Euripides,
must I be singed as punishment?
MIKA   Why shouldn't you be punished? You're the only
one who dared
to speak up for that man who has done awful things
to us,
deliberately finding stories in which women are
portrayed
as sluts, like Melanippe and Phaidra. He never wrote
about
Penelope, because she was a decent woman.
IN-LAW   And I know why. There's not a single woman
now
who's like Penelope; they're Phaidras one and all.   550
MIKA   Listen to that! This bitch is still insulting every one
of us!
        IN-LAW   I haven't finished telling
what I know. D'you want me to say more?
MIKA   You haven't any more; you've spewed out all
you know.
IN-LAW   Not a ten-thousandth part of what we do.
Listen, I didn't mention how we take curved reeds
and siphon off the wine.
                    MIKA   Watch out!
IN-LAW   And we steal meat from the Men's Banquet,
which we give

to our procurers, and then say the cat's—
   MIKA I've had enough of this rubbish!
IN-LAW Or how a woman chopped her husband into
  pieces with an axe,   560
  I didn't mention that; and what about the one who
   sent her husband mad by drugging him,
  and the woman from Acharnai who buried her father—
   MIKA Go to hell!
IN-LAW —under the bathtub.
      MIKA Do we have to listen to this?
IN-LAW And when your slave-girl had a baby boy, you
  pretended
  it was yours, and gave your baby girl to her.
MIKA You won't get away with saying that; I'm going
  to pull out all your pubic hair.
      IN-LAW Don't you dare!
MIKA Oh, yeah?
    IN-LAW Oh, yeah!
      MIKA Philiste, take my cloak.
IN-LAW Just touch me, and by Artemis I'll . . .
      MIKA Yes, what will you do?
IN-LAW That seed cake that you ate—I'll make you shit
  it out.   570
1 WOMAN Ladies, please stop; I see a woman rushing
  here
  to speak to us. Don't fight; please settle down,
  so we can hear her news respectably.
(*Enter* THE QUEEN, *left.*)
THE QUEEN Dear ladies, you are just like me. My cheeks
  make plain how similar I am to you; I'm mad
  on all things feminine, and I am always there for you.
  Now, I have just heard gossip in the marketplace
  that something big is going down which will harm you;
  I've come to tell you all about it, so
  you can look out, be on your guard, and not   580
  let a disaster catch you unprepared.

KRITYLLA   What is it, boy? I think we have to call you boy,
   since you have such clean-shaven cheeks.
THE QUEEN   They say Euripides has sent an old man here,
   a relative of his, today.
KRITYLLA   To do what? What's their plan?
THE QUEEN   So he can spy on everything you say,
   know both what you decide and what you're going
      to do.
KRITYLLA   How come we haven't found him, seeing he's
   a man?
THE QUEEN   Euripides has singed and plucked him,   590
   and disguised him as a woman.
IN-LAW   Do you believe that? What man would be so
   crazy as
   to let himself be plucked?
   By the Two Goddesses, I don't think so.
THE QUEEN   You're talking nonsense; I would not have
   come to say this,
   if I hadn't heard it from people who know.
KRITYLLA   This is shocking news.
   Ladies, we must do something;
   Let's look for this man and find out how he
   managed to sit here undetected.   600
   Dear friend, please help to find him; add
   another favor to the one you've just done us.
THE QUEEN   OK, I will examine all of you.

                                   IN-LAW   Help!
THE QUEEN   First, who are you?
                          IN-LAW   Where am I to turn?
MIKA   You ask who I am? I'm Kleonymos' wife.
THE QUEEN   Do you all know this woman?
KRITYLLA   Yes. Now try the others.
THE QUEEN   Who's this one with a baby?
            MIKA   My nurse.
                    IN-LAW   I'm done for.

THE QUEEN   Hey you, where are you going? Stay right
    here. What's wrong?
IN-LAW   I need a pee—in private!   611
THE QUEEN   OK, go right ahead, and I'll stay here.
(IN-LAW retreats to the mouth of the right eisodos.*)*
KRITYLLA   Yes, stay—and keep a beady eye on her;
   she is the only woman we don't recognize.
THE QUEEN   You're taking a long time to pee.
                    IN-LAW   I'm afraid
I'm only dribbling; I ate too much mustard yesterday.
THE QUEEN   What is this nonsense? Come back here!
(THE QUEEN drags IN-LAW back into the orchēstra.*)*
IN-LAW   I'm sick; why are you dragging me around?
          THE QUEEN   You just tell me,
who's your husband?
          IN-LAW   You want to know about my husband?
you know the guy, he's from Kothokidai.   620
THE QUEEN   *Which* guy?
          IN-LAW   The guy who once
did something to another guy—
          THE QUEEN   You're talking nonsense!
Have you been to this festival before?
          IN-LAW   Oh yes,
for years.
          THE QUEEN   Who shares a tent with you?
IN-LAW   I can't remember.
          THE QUEEN   You can't answer anything!
KRITYLLA   Hold it! I'm going to really put her to the test;
   I'll ask about the festival last year. You must stand aside;
   being a man, you must not hear. Now tell me,
   which of the sacred rites came first?
IN-LAW   Let me see, what first? We drank.   630
KRITYLLA   And after that?
          IN-LAW   We drank some toasts.
KRITYLLA   Someone must have told you! What was third?

IN-LAW   Xenylla asked for a bowl; we hadn't got a
   chamber pot.
KRITYLLA   Rubbish. Come here, Kleisthenes;
  this is the man you're after.
                    THE QUEEN   What should I do?
KRITYLLA   Strip him off; he's an impostor.
IN-LAW   Would you strip a mother of nine?
THE QUEEN   Undo your belt quickly, you bastard.
(IN-LAW'S top half is now revealed.)
MIKA   This is a pretty sturdy specimen;
  and look—there are no tits like ours at all.   640
IN-LAW   Yes, I'm barren and have never had a child.
KRITYLLA   Two minutes ago you were a mother of nine!
(IN-LAW is now naked.)
THE QUEEN   Stand up straight! *(pause)* Where have you
   hidden your prick?
KRIYLLA   *(behind IN-LAW)* It's peeking out here, and it's
   really nice!
THE QUEEN   *(coming round the back)* Now where is it?
         KRITYLLA *(changing position)*
            It's gone back to the front.
THE QUEEN *(joining her)* It is not here.
         KRITYLLA *(changing position again)*
            No, now it's come back here.
THE QUEEN   What's this? A game of high-speed *shuttlecock*?
KRITYLLA   You wretch! No wonder he said all those
   awful things
  about us—it was for Euripides!
        IN-LAW   I've had it now—   650
  look at the mess I'm in.
KRITYLLA   What shall we do?
          THE QUEEN   Guard him well,
  so he does not escape.
  I'm off to tell the Council's chief executives.
(Exit THE QUEEN, left. IN-LAW gets dressed again.)

1 WOMAN   Now we must light our torches, hitch
    our skirts for action and take off our cloaks,
      to see if any other men have got into our festival;
    search right around the meeting-place,
            the tents and passageways.
    First we must set out with a gentle tread;
    look everywhere—and stealthily. We must not   660
    be slow; this is a time for no delay,
    so let me lead you running in a circle, now.
                    * * *

WOMEN   Go on! Hunt and search,
        to see if any other man
        is sitting here among us secretly.
        Cast your eyes everywhere,
        look carefully
        in all directions!

Choros 3, part one

(A1)   If I catch anyone committing this
        impiety, he will be punished and
        be an example to all other men
        of outrage and injustice   670
        and irreverence.
        He'll then acknowledge that the gods
        clearly exist, and he will teach
        all mankind to show reverence
        and practise holy rituals that custom's sanctified,
        and think and do what's right.
        If they don't, this will happen;
        when one of them is caught acting impiously,
        he will go blazing mad, frenzied, deranged,   680
        and be a sign for women and all mortals to observe
        that the god punishes unlawful and unholy acts
        immediately.

* * *

1 WOMAN   I think we've searched the whole place
       thoroughly.
   We haven't found another man in hiding.
(IN-LAW seizes MIKA'S "baby" from MANIA and rushes to the
central altar, where he threatens it with the sacrificial knife.)
MIKA   Hey, you, where are you going? Here, stop, stop!
   Oh no, I'm desperate, he's snatched   690
   my baby from her nurse's breast.
IN-LAW   Shout all you like! It won't ever get another titbit,
   if you don't let me go. (mock tragic)
                                   Here, on the sacred thighbones,
   the sacrificial knife will strike it down, and its veins'
       blood
   will stain the altar red.
                               MIKA   I'm desperate!
   Women, please help! Attack him and
   defeat him; would you let me lose
   my only child?
WOMEN   Hey, hey!
   What is this new, appalling thing   700
   I see?
1 WOMAN   The whole world's full of violence and
       shamelessness
   Look what he's done now! Just look!
IN-LAW   I'll knock your arrogance right out of you.
1 WOMAN   Isn't this just terrible, and more than terrible?
MIKA   Yes, terrible! He's stolen my baby!

Choros 3, part two

WOMEN (A2)   What can you say about a man
   who does such things and has no shame?
IN-LAW   I haven't finished yet!
MIKA   But where you are you cannot   710

easily escape, and boast
    you did this, and then slipped away;
    no, you will suffer.
IN-LAW   I just pray that will never happen.
1 WOMAN   Which one of the immortal gods
    would help a wicked man like you?
IN-LAW   You're wasting words; I will not let her go.
WOMEN   No! By the Two Goddesses, you'll soon
    be sorry for your arrogance and your   720
    unholy deeds, offensive to the gods;
    we'll pay you back what you deserve for this.
    Fortune has suddenly changed course,
    and stands against you.

Scene 3

1 WOMAN You should have used these torches and have
    got some wood,
    to burn the scumbag up as quickly as we can.
MIKA   Mania, let us go and get some sticks;
    I'll turn *you* into ashes on this very day!
(*Exeunt MIKA and MANIA, into the* skēnē.)
IN-LAW   Light the fire and burn me; as for you,   730
    take off your dress, and little girl, blame for your death
    one single woman—your mother.
(*He strips the "baby."*)
    What's this?! The little girl has turned
    into a bladder full of wine[, with tiny Persian boots]!
    You sex-mad women, greatest pisspots of all times,
    who will do anything to get a drink,
    good news for tavern-keepers, bad news for all other men,
    and bad news for our crockery and woolen clothes!
(*Reenter MIKA and MANIA from the* skene, *with brushwood and
sacrificial bowl.*)
MIKA   Pile on plenty of sticks, Mania.

IN-LAW   Yes, pile them on; but just tell me one thing: 740
  is this your baby?

                    MIKA   Yes, I carried her
  a full nine months.

                         IN-LAW   You did?

                                    MIKA   Yes, by Artemis.

IN-LAW   *(suddenly showing her the naked wine bladder)*
  Pretty expensive wine?

                    MIKA   What have you done to me?
  You shameless bastard, you have stripped my tiny
  baby girl!

                    IN-LAW   Tiny?

                              MIKA   Yes, she's very small.

IN-LAW   How old is she? Three vintages or four?

MIKA   About that, plus the time since Dionysos's festival.
  Give her back.

                    IN-LAW   No way!

MIKA   Then we'll burn you.

                         IN-LAW   Just go ahead;
  but when you try, I'll cut her throat.   750

MIKA   No, no, I beg you, please; do anything you want
      with me,
  but spare my child.

                    IN-LAW   You are a natural, loving mother;
  I'm still going to cut her throat.

MIKA   Alas, poor child! Mania, give me the ritual bowl,
  so I may catch my daughter's blood as it pours out.

IN-LAW   I will grant you that favor; hold the bowl below
      the victim.

(He slashes the bladder and sprays MIKA with wine.)

MIKA   *(spluttering)* Damn you, you filth, you vermin!

IN-LAW   The skin shall be donated to the priestess.

KRITYLLA   What's going to the priestess?

                              IN-LAW   This. Here, catch.

KRITYLLA   My poor dear Mika, who has ruined you?   760
  Who's robbed you of your darling daughter?

The In-Law confronts Mika, holding her wine-bladder "baby" hostage (*The Women's Festival* 753–54). Apulian krater, fourth century B.C.E. Reproduced by permission of Maria von Wagner Museum der Universität Würzburg. Photograph by Karl Oehriein.

MIKA   This scumbag. Now, since you are here,
    guard him; I will catch up with Kleisthenes
    and tell the Council's chief executives what this man's
    done.
(*Exeunt MIKA and MANIA, left.*)
IN-LAW   How can I save myself?
    What can I try? I've no idea. The man who caused
    all this and got me in this mess
    is nowhere to be seen. How could I send
    a message to Euripides? I know; there is a way
    in his play *Palamedes*; I will write on oar-blades,   770
    and then throw them in the sea. (*pause*) I haven't any oars.

Where could I get some? Where?
What if I write, instead, upon these votive tablets
and throw them? Much better.
They are made of wood, like oars.
(He takes some votive tablets from behind the altar.)
    My hands, you must
    be clever and attempt this task.
    Come, smooth tablets,
    let me inscribe the words
    to tell about my troubles (Oh,   780
    this *r* is hard to carve!).
    (to the knife) Go on, go on! What kind of mark is *that*?
(He throws tablets in all directions.)
    Go, hurry fast, this way,
    that way! Be quick!

Choros 4 (Parabasis)

1 WOMAN   Let us women now come forward, and acclaim
    ourselves.
    Men say such awful things about our sex,
    that we are altogether bad, and every bad thing comes
        from us
    —fights, strife, disputes, trouble, vexation, war. . . . But
        think,
    if we are bad, why do you marry us? And if we really
        are so bad,
    why d'you forbid us to go out, or even peep outside?   790
    If we're so bad, why do you want to guard us very
        carefully?
    If you discover that the little woman has gone out,
    you rage and scream, when really you should be
        ecstatic, if
    you truly find that awful female's left your house.
    And if after a party we crash out at someone else's pad,

you all search everywhere for us. If a girl looks out
from her front door, you perve on her;
if she's ashamed and goes back in, you all want even
　　more
to see that "awful female" peep out once again!
1 WOMAN　[There is a test, which shows
that we are far superior to you; and here it is.　　　800
Let's see who's inferior. We say it's you,
you say it's us. Let's have a look, and do
a close comparison between some names.
Charminos is inferior to Nausimache—"sea warrior"—
　　　　　　　　　　　　　　　　　their deeds prove that.
And Kleophon is clearly worse in every way than our
　　best prostitute.
For many years you haven't even tried to rival
　　Aristomache ("best in battle"—that's
the one at Marathon) or Stratonike ("victorious army").
Tell me if a Councillor, who only held his office for last
　　year,
is better than Euboule ("excellent adviser"). None of you
　　could claim that's true.
So, we boast we're far superior to men.　　　810
No woman would steal heaps of public funds, and drive
　　up to
the citadel in chariots; if one is caught committing *her*
　　great crime
—stealing a basketful of grain—she'll pay it back that
　　very day!]
　　　　　　　　　　　　* * *
1 WOMAN　We could show many men here present
do bad things, *and*—
men are far worse
at overeating; they are thieves,
foul deceivers, kidnappers.
Indeed, men don't preserve their property

as well as women.   820
We've kept safe till this very day
the loom, the shuttle-rod, the wool-basket,
our sunshades; but
our husbands often lose
the family spear-rod, together with its metal tip,
and plenty of them on campaign find that
the shield's been ripped
from off their shoulders.

* * *

1 WOMAN   We have a multitude of just complaints   830
    against you men, but one stands out. We think
    that if a woman is the mother of a man who serves the
        city well
    —an infantry commander or a general—she should have
    her just reward—a seat of honor at the [Stenia,
    the Skira, and the other] women's festivals;
    but if a woman's mother of a coward or a worthless man—
    a useless ship's commander or a hopeless helmsman—
    she should have her hair cropped in a pudding-basin cut,
    and should sit well behind the mother of the brave man.
        City,
    how's it fair for Hyperbolos's mother to sit clothed in
        white,   840
    with flowing hair, next to Lamachos's mum,
    and lend out money? She should be forbidden
    to get interest on a loan from anyone, and you
    should take away her capital, saying: "the mother of a son
    like that does not deserve to earn a cent."

Scene 4

IN-LAW   I'm getting eyestrain looking for him; he is still
    not here.

What could be stopping him? It must be that
his *Palamedes* was a lousy play and he's ashamed of it.
So which drama would tempt him to come here?
I know; I'll be his Helen from last year.   850
I've got the female costume for it, anyway.

KRITYLLA   What are you cooking up? Why are you
     looking round?
I'll give you a Helen you'll be sorry for, if you don't
wait in peace, till an Executive shows up.

(IN-LAW veils his head.)

IN-LAW   This is the beautiful and virgin stream of Nile,
     that waters, in the place of heaven's rain,
     Egypt's white plains—for all the swarthy
          laxative-addicted people there.

KRITYLLA   You're just a scumbag.

IN-LAW   My native land is famous Sparta, and
     my father is Tyndareus.

                    KRITYLLA   Bastard, he is not   860
     your father[; I would say it's Phrynondas].

IN-LAW   My name is Helen;

               KRITYLLA   Are you pretending once again to be
     a woman, when you haven't yet been punished
                         for your first attempt?

IN-LAW   —many brave souls perished for my sake beside
     the streams of Skamander.

                    KRITYLLA   I wish you'd died as well.

IN-LAW   And here I am. But Menelaos, my poor
     suffering husband, has not yet come here.
     Why then do I still live?

               KRITYLLA   The lazy ravens haven't eaten you.

IN-LAW   But something seems to cheer my heart.
     O Zeus, do not deceive me with this rising hope!   870

*(Enter EURIPIDES, right, disguised as Menelaos in rags, and covered
with seaweed.)*

EURIPIDES   Who is the master of this splendid house?

Who could receive some foreigners who've suffered much
at sea, in storm and shipwreck?

IN-LAW   These are the halls of Proteus.

EURIPIDES   Which Proteus?

KRITYLLA   You lying scumbag! He is talking nonsense;
Proteas has now been dead ten years.

EURIPIDES   And on which kingdom have I landed with
my boat?

IN-LAW   Egypt.

EURIPIDES   Oh, alas, how far we've gone astray.

KRITYLLA   Do not believe this bastard; he is lying through
his teeth. We are in Athens, at the Women's Festival.   880

EURIPIDES   Proteus himself; is he within, or out of sight?

KRITYLLA   Good sir, you must be suffering from seasickness;
I told you just now Proteas is dead, but you
still asked "is he within, or out of sight?"

EURIPIDES   Alas, he's passed away. Where was he laid to
rest?

IN-LAW   This is his monument, on which I've taken refuge.

KRITYLLA   May you perish unpleasantly—and I am sure
you will!—
that's not a monument, it's just an altar.

EURIPIDES   Good lady, why d'you sit
upon his tomb, all veiled?

IN-LAW   I'm being forced   890
to marry, and to share the bed of Proteus's son.

KRITYLLA   You rotten bastard, why are you lying to the
stranger?
Good gentleman, he came here bent on crime,
to steal the women's gold.

IN-LAW   Snarl out your slanders, hurl abuse at me!

EURIPIDES   Fair lady, who is this old woman who's
abusing you?

IN-LAW   Theonoe, daughter of Proteus.

KRITYLLA   No I'm not;
I am Kritylla, daughter of Antitheos from Gargettos—

and you're a scumbag.
        IN-LAW Say what you will!
Your brother will not ever marry me;   900
I won't betray my husband, Menelaos, who's
  besieging Troy.
EURIPIDES Lady, what did you say? Turn your sparkling
  gaze on me.
IN-LAW I blush to show you my humiliated face.
EURIPIDES What is this? Silence holds me fast.
 O gods, what do I see? Oh lady, who are you?
IN-LAW And who are you? The same word holds both
  you and I.
EURIPIDES Are you a native woman or a Greek?
IN-LAW A Greek. I yearn to know your native land.
EURIPIDES I've never seen a woman more like Helen.
IN-LAW I know that you are Menelaos—from the
  seaweed!   910
EURIPIDES You've truly recognized this most unfortunate
  of men.
IN-LAW At last you're here; come, come into your wife's
  warm pussy!
 Take me, husband, take me, hold me tight.
 Let me kiss you. *(drops the tragic pose and female voice)*
      Get me out of here, get me out of here,
 as quick as you can!
      KRITYLLA You won't like it if you try—
 I'll hit you with this torch!
EURIPIDES Would you stop me from going home to
  Sparta with
 my own true wife, the daughter of Tyndareus?
KRITYLLA *I* think that you're a scumbag just like him, 920
 and both up to no good. No wonder you were playing
 sneaky Egyptians. He is going to be punished.
 Here come the Executive and his policeman.
EURIPIDES This is serious. I'll have to sneak away.
IN-LAW Alas, what shall I do?

EURIPIDES   Do not despair.
I never will betray you, while I still draw breath,
unless my myriad clever schemes should fail.
(Exit EURIPIDES, right.)
KRITYLLA   Well, *that* line caught no fish!
(Enter EXECUTIVE, followed by POLICEMAN, left.)
EXECUTIVE   Is this the scumbag that The Queen told us
    about?
Hey, you, get up! Policeman, take him in   930
and fix him to the plank, then stand him up
right here and guard him; no one must
come near to him. And use your whip
if anyone should try.
             KRITYLLA   That's great! Just now, a man
in sailor's rags nearly escaped with him.
IN-LAW   Dear Executive, I beg you by your right hand—
which you prefer to hold out cupped, so you can get
a bribe—grant one last favor to a man condemned to die.
EXECUTIVE   What might that be?
                          IN-LAW   Tell the policeman
he must strip me off before he ties me to the plank.   940
I'm an old man; don't leave me in these female clothes.
The carrion crows will laugh, while they are eating me.
EXECUTIVE   The Council has resolved you must be bound
    like this,
so everyone will see what a scumbag you are.
IN-LAW   Alas!! Oh yellow dress, look what you've done
    to me;
and now there's no more hope that I'll be saved.
(Exeunt POLICEMAN and IN-LAW into the skēnē; *exeunt EXEC-
UTIVE and KRITYLLA, left.)*

Choros 5

1 WOMAN   Let's let our hair down—that's our custom here,
    when at the sacred season we worship Demeter and

Persephone with secret rites.
[Poor Pauson celebrates by fasting too,
and prays to them all year   950
for that day to come round
when others fast at the same time as him!]
                              * * *

1 WOMAN   Begin, get moving,
        tread light footed in a circle,
        join your hands together,
        everyone begin the rhythm of the dance,
        and spring with nimble feet.
        Our eyes must look all round to check
        the dance is truly circular!
                              * * *

WOMEN (A1)   As you dance in ecstasy
        sing out, and honor with your voices all   960
        of the Olympian gods.
                              * * *

        (A2)   If anyone expects that I,
        a woman in this sacred place,
        will bad-mouth men, he's wrong.
                              * * *

        (A3)   We should do something new;
        first halt the graceful steps
        of this round dance.
                              * * *

        (B1)   Step forward, honor with your song   970
        Apollo of the graceful lyre, and the pure queen,
        Artemis the archer goddess.
        Hail, god whose power stretches far,
        and grant us victory!
        Now let us sing to Hera the Fulfiller,
        as is right—she joins our sportive dances and
        she keeps the holy keys of marriage.
                              * * *

        (B2)   And I entreat the shepherds' god, Hermes,

and Pan, and all the lovely nymphs—
enjoy our dances,
smile upon them;   980
let us eagerly create
the double pleasure given by a dance
to gods and dancers.
Follow the custom, let our hair down—after all,
we're fasting for these sacred rites!

        * * *

(B3)   Leap up and whirl around—keeping
your steps in time; sing out with piercing voice!
And you yourself, Dionysos, must be our leader,
ivy-crowned lord; I will adore you
with the revelry you love.

        * * *

(C1)   Euios! O son of Zeus and Semele,   990
god of loud clamor,
in the mountains you enjoy
the nymphs who sing delightful hymns;
Euios! Euios! Euoi!
You love to dance a bakchic dance.

        * * *

(C2)   Echoes sound out around you from
the slopes of Mount Kithairon;
dark-leaved shady mountains and
their rocky valleys roar with sound;
ivy-tendrils coil in circles round you,
with their lovely leaves.   1000

Scene 5

(*Enter* POLICEMAN *from the* skēnē *on the* ekkuklēma *with* IN-
LAW, *fastened to a large plank by iron collar and chains.*)
POLICEMAN   There, howl all you like; you're outdoors now.
IN-LAW   Please, I beg you—

POLICEMAN   Don't bother.

IN-LAW   Loosen the nail!

POLICEMAN   My pleasure!

IN-LAW   Aaah! You're tightening it!

POLICEMAN   How about a little more?

IN-LAW   Aaah! Oooh!
You bastard!

POLICEMAN   Shut up, you old fart.
I'll get a mat to sit on while I'm guarding you.

(Exit POLICEMAN into the skēnē. *He reenters around 1016 and goes to sleep.)*

IN-LAW   *This* is my reward because I helped Euripides!

(EURIPIDES enters on the mēchanē *disguised as Perseus, with winged cap and sandals. He flies overhead and then exits again.)*

Aha! Zeus the savior, and all other gods—there is hope
　　yet!

He will not let me down; he's just   1010
appeared as Perseus, giving me a sign
that I must play Andromeda; at least I've got
the chains the part requires. It's clear he's going to come
and rescue me; why else would he fly past?

(as Andromeda, though frequently lapsing back into his own character)

A Dear, sweet girls, how can
I get away without
I the policeman seeing me?
A D'you hear, Echo who sings
back to me from the cave?
I Grant my prayer—just let me go   1020
home to my wife!
A Pitiless was he who bound me,
I'm the most long-suffering of all.
I I only just escaped that horrible
old woman, and now look at me!
The policeman sent to guard me
bound me to this plank, doomed

and deserted, food for crows. D'you see?
A Not in the dance with girls   1030
of my own age, **I** nor with
a voting urn do I stand here,
A but enmeshed in these many chains I lie
as food for the most gluttonous of sea-monsters.
Young women, sing no bridal hymn for me,
but the lament for one in bondage;
I am wretched and have suffered wretchedly.
I'm in despair! Despair!
And I am suffering these cruel and unjust torments
for a kinsman's sake, although I pleaded with
    him,   1040
causing a tearful death-lament to blaze—
Aiai! Aiai! Ah! Ah!
I —the man who shaved me,
put me in a yellow dress,
and sent me to this holy place
where all the women are.
A I hate the unrelenting god who causes my ill fate!
I am accursed!
Who will not look upon my miserable
and awful sufferings?
I I wish a fiery bolt from heaven   1050
would utterly destroy that policeman.
A No longer is it dear to me to look
on the immortal sun, since I've been chained up
suffering appallingly, my throat half-slit—
a speedy journey to the land of shades.
(Enter ECHO, right.)
ECHO   Hello, dear girl; and may the gods destroy
  your father, Kepheus, for exposing you out here.
IN-LAW   Who are you? Why do you take pity on my
      sufferings?
ECHO   Echo; I mock and mimic words,
  and last year, in this very place,   1060

I helped Euripides compete.
But child, do what you have to do;
wail pitiably.
                    IN-LAW   You must echo me.
ECHO   No problem. You begin.
IN-LAW   O sacred Night,
        how long and far you ride,
        steering your chariot across
        the starry back of sacred Ether
        and past the holy mount, Olympos—
                                ECHO   —Olympos.
IN-LAW   Why have I, Andromeda, been fated to
        endure   1070
        a fate far worse than anyone—
                                ECHO   —than anyone—
IN-LAW   —death? Truly I'm unfortunate—
                                ECHO   —unfortunate.
IN-LAW   Shut up, you're ruining my scene!
                                ECHO   —my scene!
IN-LAW   You're just a bloody nuisance, and you talk
    too much!
                ECHO   Too much!
IN-LAW   Please let me sing my solo;
    do me a favor; stop.
                    ECHO   Stop.
IN-LAW   Go to hell!
                    ECHO   To hell.
IN-LAW   What is your problem?
        ECHO   Problem?
                    IN-LAW   You are talking nonsense!
                    ECHO   Nonsense?   1080
IN-LAW   I hate you!
                    ECHO   Hate you!
                    IN-LAW   Hope you suffer!
                                ECHO   Suffer!
POLICEMAN   Here, what's going on?
                        ECHO   What's going on?

POLICEMAN   Shall I call the Executive?

                          ECHO   Executive?

POLICEMAN   I'll get you!

                ECHO   Get you!

POLICEMAN   Where's that voice from?

                        ECHO   Voice from?

POLICEMAN Are you talking?

               ECHO   Talking?

                  POLICEMAN   You'll be sorry!

                  ECHO   Sorry!

POLICEMAN   Making fun of me?

               ECHO   Of me?

IN-LAW   No, it's this woman over here.   1090

ECHO   Over here.

           POLICEMAN   Where is the bitch?

ECHO   Where is the bitch?

              IN-LAW   She's running off.

POLICEMAN   Where are you going?

              ECHO   Where are you going?

POLICEMAN   You will not get free!

              ECHO   You will not catch me!

POLICEMAN   Still gabbling on?

              ECHO   Still gabbling on?

POLICEMAN   Get the bitch!

            ECHO   Get the bitch!

(Exit ECHO, right.)

POLICEMAN   I hate that woman—and she talks too much!

(EURIPIDES enters on the mēchanē *again, disguised as Perseus. This time he makes a perfect landing.)*

EURPIDES   O gods, what barbarous land is this where I
    have flown
  with my swift sandals? Through the middle of the air
  I cleave my path with wingèd feet—   1100
  Perseus; I'm bound for Argos carrying
  the Gorgon's head.

           POLICEMAN   What? You've got the head

of Gorgos the secretary?

EURIPIDES   I say the Gorgon's
head.

POLICEMAN   And I say Gorgos's.

EURIPIDES   Wait! What rock is this I see, and maiden fair
as any goddess, tied up to it like a ship?

IN-LAW   Stranger, take pity on me in my utter misery;
free me from these chains!

POLICEMAN   Shut up!
You bastard, you're condemned to death, and you
still dare to talk?

EURIPIDES   Dear maid, I see you hanging there and
pity you.   1110

POLICEMAN   That's not a maiden, it's a wicked old man,
a thief and a scumbag.

EURIPIDES   My good man, you are wrong.
This is Andromeda, daughter of Kepheus.

POLICEMAN *(lifts IN-LAW'S dress)* Look down here; pretty
big, isn't it?

EURIPIDES   Give me her hand, so I can touch the girl.
Good policeman, every man on earth
has some disease. Mine is this; desire for her
has overwhelmed me.

POLICEMAN   I don't envy you.
If we had tied him with his arsehole facing out,
I would have let you bugger him.   1120

EURIPIDES   Dear policeman, won't you let me free her
from her bonds,
to lie upon the sacred marriage-bed?

POLICEMAN   If you want to fuck the old man all that
much,
bore a hole in the plank and bugger him from behind!

EURIPIDES   No! I shall free her from her chains!

POLICEMAN   I'll hit you with my whip!

EURIPIDES   I'm going to do it!

POLICEMAN   I'll chop

your head off with my knife.

EURIPIDES   Alas! What shall I do? To what words shall
    I turn?
    This dumb copper wouldn't understand me anyway.
    "To bring new wisdom to men of dull wits   1130
    is waste of effort." I have got to find
    another scheme, more suited to this man.

(Exit EURIPIDES on the mēchanē.*)*

POLICEMAN   Foxy bastard! What a monkey-trick he tried
    on me!

IN-LAW   Perseus, remember how you've left me in this
    wretched plight!

POLICEMAN   D'you still fancy a crack of the whip?

(He settles down on his mat to sleep.)

Choros 6

WOMEN   It is the custom that we summon here
    Pallas Athena, virgin goddess,
    lover of the dance,   1140
    who guards our city
    —everyone bears witness to her power—
    and is the Keeper of the Keys.
    Show yourself—we need you—
    enemy of tyranny!
    The women call you;
    come, and bring us peace,
    friend of our festival.
    Sovereign goddesses, be gracious
    to us; come here to your sacred grove   1150
    where men are not allowed to see
    the holy, secret rites which you light up
    with torches—an immortal sight!
    Come, come, we pray,
    Demeter and Persephone,

if ever you have come in answer
to our call, come now, as we
implore you, come to us!

Scene 6

(Enter EURIPIDES, left, carrying a wig and cloak and a small harp,
with FAWN and WOODWORM.)
EURIPIDES   Ladies, if you would like to make a treaty
    with me for   1160
  the rest of time, now is your chance;
  I'll never say bad things about you
  any more. This is a formal offer.
1 WOMAN   Why are you saying this?
EURIPIDES   The man on the plank is a relative of mine,
  and if I can take him home, I'll never ever
  slander you. But if you won't let me,
  I'll tell your husbands, when they get back
  from the war, everything that you've been doing.
1 WOMAN   As far as we're concerned, you've got a
    deal;   1170
  as for the policeman, you must cope with him yourself.
EURIPIDES   No problem.
(He puts on the wig and cloak.)
                           Fawn, remember what
  I told you on the way;
  go over there and do a sexy dance.
  Woodworm, give her a tune—something exotic.
(WOODWORM plays and FAWN dances.)
POLICEMAN What's that noise? Some party animals have
  woken me.
EURIPIDES   Dear policeman, the girl was going to
    rehearse.
  She's got to dance tonight at a stag party.
POLICEMAN She can sing and dance, I don't mind.

Very graceful! Like a flea on a blanket! 1180

EURIPIDES   Take off your dress, dear child.

(FAWN does this.)

Sit on the policeman's knees, and stretch
your feet out; I'll undo your sandals.

POLICEMAN   Yes, please!

Sit down, sit down little girl, yes, yes.

Nice firm titties, like a turnip.

(FAWN rises and resumes her dance.)

EURIPIDES   *(to WOODWORM)* Play faster.

(to FAWN) Are you still afraid of the policeman?

(FAWN'S dance becomes more erotic.)

POLICEMAN   What a great bum!

(to his prick) You're for it if you do not stay inside!

(He gives up trying to conceal his erection.)

OK. That's the best I can do with the prick.

EURIPIDES *(to FAWN)* That'll do. Get your dress; it's time
for us
to go.

POLICEMAN   Won't she kiss me first? 1190

EURIPIDES   Of course. Give him a kiss.

POLICEMAN   Oooh!

What a sweet tongue, like our local honey.

Can she sleep with me?

EURIPIDES   Good-bye, policeman,
that just can't be done.

POLICEMAN   Please, old lady,
just this once.

EURIPIDES   Will you pay a hundred bucks?

POLICEMAN   Yes, yes, I will.

EURIPIDES   Then give me the money.

POLICEMAN   I'm broke. Take my holster instead—
but bring it back again. Girlie, follow me—
and you, old woman, keep an eye on this old man.
What is your name?

EURIPIDES   Artemisia. 1200

POLICEMAN   I won't forget the name. Artamouxia.
(He escorts FAWN into the skēnē.*)*
EURIPIDES   Hermes, god of deception, well done!
  Woodworm, take these, and run away.
(Exit WOODWORM, left, with the cloak and wig.)
  I'll set him free. And when you're free,
  run like a man, and get back home
  as fast as you can to your wife and kids.
IN-LAW   Just set me free and I'll do that.
EURIPIDES   You're free. Now you must get away
  before the policeman comes and catches you.
                                           IN-LAW   I will.
(Exeunt EURIPIDES and IN-LAW, left.)
(Enter POLICEMAN from the skene *with FAWN.)*
POLICEMAN   Old woman, your daughter was very
      nice—   1210
  sweet and cooperative. *(pause)* Where's the old woman?
  This is a disaster! Where's the old man?
  Old woman! Old woman! I'm not happy with you!
  Artamouxia!
  That old hag has cheated me. Run after her, quick as
      you can!
(Exit FAWN, left, in haste.)
  No wonder it's called a holster; I lost it by taking out
      my weapon!
  Oh!
  What shall I do? Where's the old woman? Artamouxia!
1 WOMAN   Are you after the old woman with the harp?
POLICEMAN   Yes, yes. Did you see her?
                                  1 WOMAN *(pointing right)*
                                       She went this way,
  and an old man was with her.
POLICEMAN   Was he wearing a yellow dress?
                                       1 WOMAN Yes.   1220
  You'll still catch them, if you go this way.

POLICEMAN   Bitch! Where did you go?
   Artamouxia!
1 WOMAN   Go straight up there! Where are you going?
      You must come
   this way! You're running in the wrong direction!
POLICEMAN   The gods are against me, but I've still got to
      run! Artamouxia!
(Exit POLICEMAN, right.)
1 WOMAN   Run! And may a fair wind blow you all the
      way to hell!

                         * * *

   We've had enough fun.
   It's time for each of us to go
   back home. And may the goddesses
   reward us well   1230
   for what we've done today.
(Exeunt WOMEN, left.)

Frogs

Characters

In order of appearance

Dionysos: god of ecstasy, wine, and drama; a cowardly
  buffoon
Xanthias: his slave
Herakles: hero, demigod, and glutton
Corpse
Charon: ferryman of the dead
Frogs: *Choros* or half *choros*
Choros: Initiates in the mystery cult of Demeter at Eleusis
Doorkeeper
Servant of Persephone (female)
Innkeeper
Plathane: another innkeeper
Slave (male)
Euripides: recently deceased tragic playwright
Aischylos: grand old man of tragedy, now dead for fifty
  years
Plouton (Haides): lord of the underworld (Haides')
Old Woman
Slaves, Policemen

Frogs was first produced in 405 B.C.E. and was revised for
a revival by popular demand in 404. Aristophanes was
awarded the honor of a civic crown for the advice contained
in the *parabasis*.

Props

Scene 1

Lionskin and club (Dionysos)
Donkey, baggage on stick (Xanthias)

Litter (Corpse)
Boat with oars (on wheels) (Charon)

Scene 3

Sponge (Xanthias)
Whip (Doorkeeper)

Scene 5

Altar, three thrones
Fire, incense, voting pebbles

Scene 6

Lyre (Euripides)
Castanets (Old Woman)
Giant scales

Finale

Sword, several nooses, bottle of hemlock (Plouton)

Scene 1

(*Enter* DIONYSOS, *left, in lounging slippers and a long saffron robe, over which he wears a lionskin; he is carrying a sizable club. He leads a donkey on which* XANTHIAS *rides, carrying a large amount of baggage on the end of a stick resting on his shoulder.*

They circle the orchēstra, *surveying the audience with a marked lack of enthusiasm. Eventually* XANTHIAS *begins the comedy.*)

XANTHIAS   Hey, boss, shall I tell one of the old jokes—
   the sort that always gets a laugh?
DIONYSOS   Yes, by Zeus, whatever you like—except "I'm
      in great pain":
   don't use that one; it always makes me sick.
XANTHIAS   No other clever jokes?
DIONYSOS   Except "I'm tightly squeezed."
XANTHIAS   Well, can I tell the best one of them all?
DIONYSOS   By Zeus,
   get on with it—but just don't say—
XANTHIAS   say what?
DIONYSOS   —that when you shift your load you need a
   crap.
XANTHIAS   I can't say I am carrying so great a weight
   that if no one relieves me, I will fart out all my shit?   10
DIONYSOS   No, please, I beg you, not unless I need to puke.
XANTHIAS   Then why did I have to bear all this stuff,
   if I can't do anything like Phrynichos
   and Lykis and Ameipsias?
   They carry luggage on in all their comedies.
DIONYSOS   Don't do it! I am always in the audience,
   and when I see one of their clever tricks,
   it takes more than a year out of my life.
XANTHIAS   Then thrice cursed is this neck of mine,
   it's *in great pain*, but cannot get a laugh.   20
DIONYSOS   Hang on! Is this not outrage and sheer insolence?
   I'm Dionysos, son of the great Jar of Wine,
   but I'm worn out by walking, while I let *him* ride

so he is free of pain and does not bear a burden.

XANTHIAS   I'm not bearing anything?

DIONYSOS   No, how can you? You are riding.

XANTHIAS   I *am* bearing something—look.

DIONYSOS   How?

XANTHIAS   Pretty unhappily.

DIONYSOS   Isn't the donkey bearing the weight you're
    bearing?

XANTHIAS   Not this load that I am bearing; no, by Zeus.

DIONYSOS   How can you be bearing it, when someone else
    is bearing you?

XANTHIAS   I don't know; but my shoulder is still *in*
    great pain.   30

DIONYSOS   Well, since you say the donkey is no help to you,
    take your turn; pick him up and carry him.

XANTHIAS   Oh, my cursèd fate! If only I had fought at sea,
    and won my freedom, I could tell you to go to hell!

DIONYSOS   Get down, you rogue; for I have now
    approached
near to this door, to which it was
my destiny to turn.

(He knocks on the door with his club.)

                     Slave, hey, slave, I say!

(He knocks again.)

(Enter HERAKLES from the skēnē, *followed by a slave who leads*
the donkey off.)

HERAKLES   Who struck my door? He leapt at it
    just like a centaur, whoever . . . Tell me, what's this?!

(He turns away, choking with laughter.)

DIONYSOS   Slave!

XANTHIAS   What is it?

DIONYSOS   Didn't you notice?

XANTHIAS   What?   40

DIONYSOS   How he was scared of me.

XANTHIAS   Yes, by Zeus—scared you're insane.

HERAKLES   By Demeter, I just can't stop laughing.

I'm biting my lip, but I'm still laughing.

DIONYSOS   My good friend, please come here; I need
    something from you.

HERAKLES   Sorry, I just can't keep myself from laughing
    at the lionskin over the saffron robe.
    What's the idea? A hunting club and slippers?
    Where on earth have you been?

DIONYSOS   I was on a warship—with The Queen.

HERAKLES   And did you use your ram?

DIONYSOS   Yes, indeed; we sank
    enemy ships; twelve, thirteen, or so.   50

HERAKLES   You two together?

DIONYSOS   Yes, by Apollo.

XANTHIAS   (*aside*) And then I woke up.

DIONYSOS   And . . . ! While I was on the ship,
    reading *Andromeda*, suddenly a great desire
    smote at my heart—you've no idea how big.

HERAKLES   Desire? How strong?

DIONYSOS   As small . . . as a giant.

HERAKLES   For a woman?

DIONYSOS   Well, no.

HERAKLES   A boy?

DIONYSOS   Certainly not.

HERAKLES   You don't mean . . . for a man?

DIONYSOS   Aaaah!

HERAKLES   You slept with The Queen?!

DIONYSOS   Brother, do not poke fun at me. I'm really in
    bad shape.
    So great is this desire which is destroying me.

HERAKLES   What kind of passion is it, little brother?

DIONYSOS   I can hardly say.   60
    I'll try to tell you by comparison.
    Have you ever felt a sudden desire for soup?

HERAKLES   Soup? Oh yes, a thousand times.

DIONYSOS   Shall I just tell you the plain truth, or try
    another way?

HERAKLES   Not another word about soup; I know all
     about that.

DIONYSOS   Well, a desire that great is gnawing at me for
   Euripides.

HERAKLES   Even though he's dead?

DIONYSOS   And there's no man alive who could stop me
   from going to get him.

HERAKLES   To the depths of Haides'?

DIONYSOS   Yes, and even further down, by Zeus, if there
     be such a place.   70

HERAKLES   Why?

DIONYSOS   I need a clever and creative dramatist;
   "for those that were are dead, and those who live are
        bad."

HERAKLES   But Iophon's alive?

DIONYSOS   Yes, he's the only one
   still left who's any good—that's if he is;
   I do not even know if that is true.

HERAKLES   But Sophokles is better than Euripides
   —should you not bring *him* back?

DIONYSOS   Not till I've had a look at Iophon all by himself
   and sounded out what he can do without his dad.
   Anyway, Euripides is quite a piece of work, and he   80
   would even try to run with me away from Haides' halls;
   but Sophokles was easygoing here, and he still is down
        there.

HERAKLES   So where is Agathon?

DIONYSOS   He has deserted me and gone;
   a fine playwright, and much loved by his friends.

HERAKLES   Where in the world is he, poor man?

DIONYSOS   He's "feasting with the blessed," up north.

HERAKLES   And Xenokles?

DIONYSOS   Oh, let him rot.

HERAKLES   Pythangelos?

XANTHIAS   Still not a word about me,
   although my shoulder is now worn away.

HERAKLES   But surely there's a thousand wonder-boys
    turning out tragedies in Athens, all   90
    of them kilometers more fluent than Euripides?
DIONYSOS   They're a pathetic bunch, all small talk;
    twittering swallows, who are ruining the art.
    If they are granted a performance, they just disappear
    after one piss against the Muse of Tragedy.
    You couldn't find a fruitful writer even if
    you looked, who can declaim a truly memorable phrase.
HERAKLES   What do you mean by fruitful?
DIONYSOS   A man who can
    produce a daring trope like "Ether,
    Bedroom of Zeus," or "Foot of Time,"   100
    or "my mind did not want to swear over sacred
        offerings,
    but my tongue perjured itself separately from my mind."
HERAKLES   You like that sort of stuff?
DIONYSOS   I'm mad about it.
HERAKLES   Utter rubbish—and you must know that.
DIONYSOS   Don't try to rule my mind; you've got your own.
HERAKLES   Everybody knows that's worthless drivel.
DIONYSOS   Stick to food.
XANTHIAS   Not a word about me.
DIONYSOS   The reason why I'm bringing all this luggage
    and have come disguised as you is so
    you can inform me, please, about the people whom   110
    you used as hosts when you went down for Kerberos.
    Tell me all this; the harbors, bread shops,
    brothels, resting places, roads and junctions, waterholes,
    towns, pubs and hostesses who have
    the fewest bedbugs.
XANTHIAS   Not a word about me.
HERAKLES   Rash fool, will you too dare to go?
DIONYSOS   Don't try to stop me; just tell me the route
    by which I can most quickly go to Haides'—
    but not one that's too hot or cold.

HERAKLES   Well now, what shall I tell you first?   120
   Here's one—for this you need a rope and bench;
   just hang yourself.
DIONYSOS   No, that's a bit too stifling.
HERAKLES   Then there's a short road—you just *pound*
      along—
   using a mortar.
DIONYSOS   D'you mean hemlock?
HERAKLES   Yes, I do.
DIONYSOS   It's cold and wintry;
   all at once your shins freeze up.
HERAKLES   Would you like a quick and downhill route?
DIONYSOS   Yes, by Zeus; I'm not much of a walker.
HERAKLES   Well, take a gentle stroll to Kerameikos.
DIONYSOS   Then what?
HERAKLES   Go up onto the high tower—
DIONYSOS   And then?   130
HERAKLES   Watch the start of the torch-race,
   and when the spectators say "Go!"
   off you go too.
DIONYSOS   Where?
HERAKLES   Right down.
DIONYSOS   I'd make a pâté of my brains.
   I will not go that way.
HERAKLES   Which, then?
DIONYSOS   The one you used.
HERAKLES   It's a long voyage;
   first you come to a vast,
   bottomless lake.
DIONYSOS   How shall I cross it?
HERAKLES   In a tiny little boat an old man
   will carry you across for a fare of two dollars.   140
DIONYSOS   Wow!
   Two dollars takes you everywhere these days.
   How did they get there?
HERAKLES   Theseus took them.

After that you'll see thousands of fearful beasts
and snakes.

DIONYSOS   Do not try to scare me any more;
you will not stop me going.

HERAKLES   Then there's lots of mud
and ever-flowing shit, in which lie all
who ever did injustice to a guest,
or fucked a boy and stole the money back,
or beat their mother, socked their father
on the jaw, swore perjured oaths,   150
or copied out a speech from Morsimos.

DIONYSOS   By the gods, they ought to throw in everyone
who learned that stupid war dance by Kinesias.

HERAKLES   Next you will be surrounded with the gentle
sound of flutes,
and you will see a light—most beautiful, as bright as
here—
and myrtle-groves and blessed groups of revelers,
both men and women, clapping with their hands.

DIONYSOS   Who are they?

HERAKLES   Initiates.

XANTHIAS   I'm the pack-donkey, missing out on
everything.
I won't carry this stuff any longer.   160

HERAKLES   They'll tell you all you need to know.
For they live very near the road that leads
right to the door of Plouton's house.
Good-bye, dear brother.

(*Exit HERAKLES into the* skēnē.)

DIONYSOS   And good-bye
to you as well. *(to Xanthias)* Pick up the baggage once
again.

XANTHIAS   Before I've even put it down?

DIONYSOS   Do hurry up.

XANTHIAS   No, please, I beg you, hire someone who
is being carried to his grave, if there's a porter-corpse.

DIONYSOS   And if I don't find one?
XANTHIAS   Then I will take it.
DIONYSOS   Fair enough.
(Enter CORPSE, left, carried by bearers.)
     Look—there's one right now.   170
     Hey you, I mean you, you! Corpse!
     My good man, would you carry our luggage to
          Haides'?
CORPSE   How much is there?
DIONYSOS   This lot.
CORPSE   Will you pay twenty bucks?
DIONYSOS   No, much less.
CORPSE   Bearers, get on with it.
DIONYSOS   Wait, my friend, let's bargain.
CORPSE   If you won't give me twenty bucks, forget it.
DIONYSOS   Fifteen?
CORPSE   I would rather live!
(He signs to the bearers, who take him out, right.)
XANTHIAS   Arrogant bastard! Let him rot!
     I will carry on.
DIONYSOS   You are a good and noble man.
     Let's go and find the boat.
(Enter CHARON in a boat, right. He rows it across the rear of the orchēstra to BL.)
CHARON *(talking to himself)* Pull . . . Out! Heave to!   180
DIONYSOS   What's this?
XANTHIAS   This? By Zeus, this is the lake—
     the very one he mentioned; and I see a boat.
DIONYSOS   Yes, by Poseidon, and this man is Charon.
     Hello Charon, hello Charon, HELLO CHARON!
CHARON   Who's for eternal rest from toil and trouble?
     Who's for the plain of Oblivion, endless rope-plaiting,
     the Kerberians, Raven-Hell, or Tainaros?
DIONYSOS   I am.
CHARON   Get in quick.
DIONYSOS   Where d'you think we'll land?

CHARON   Raven-Hell.

DIONYSOS   Really?

CHARON   Yes, by Zeus—for you, my pleasure.
   Get onboard.

DIONYSOS   Slave, come here.

CHARON   I won't take a slave,   190
   unless he fought the all-or-nothing sea-battle.

XANTHIAS   No, I didn't. I . . . I had eye trouble.

CHARON   Then I'm afraid you'll have to run right round
      the lake.

XANTHIAS   Where shall I wait for you?

CHARON   At the resting-place
   by the Withering Stone.

DIONYSOS   You understand?

XANTHIAS   Yes, all too well!
   I am accursed; what crossed my path when I got up?
(XANTHIAS begins to trudge wearily around the perimeter of the
orchēstra.)

CHARON   Sit to your oar. If anybody else is coming,
      hurry up.
   (to DIONYSOS) What *are* you doing?

DIONYSOS   Me? Exactly what
   you told me to; I'm sitting on my oar.

CHARON   Sit right here, Fatso.

DIONYSOS   OK.   200

CHARON   Now put your hands in front of you and
      stretch them out.

DIONYSOS   OK!

CHARON   Stop fooling around; brace your feet
   and row hard.

DIONYSOS   How can I?
   I've no experience, and I'm a landlubber.
   I'm not from Salamis.

CHARON   It is easy; you will hear
   most beautiful music, as soon as you strike water.

DIONYSOS   Whose music?

CHARON   The wonderful songs of the frog-swans.
DIONYSOS   *(dipping his oar)* Set me the time.
CHARON   Pull . . . ! Out; in. Pull . . . ! Out; in.

Choros 1

(Enter FROGS, right.)
FROGS   Brekekekex koax koax!
    Brekekekex koax koax!   210
    We are the children of the water marsh
    So let us sing in unison our festive call,
    our sweet-voiced song,
    koax, koax—
    the song we used to sing
    for Zeus's son, the god of Nysa,
    Dionysos in the Marsh,
    when every year a crowd
    of drunken revelers at the festival
    came to our sanctuary.
    Brekekekex koax koax!   220
DIONYSOS   I'm starting to feel a pain
    in my bum, koax koax.
FROGS   Brekekekex koax koax!
DIONYSOS   I don't suppose you care.
FROGS   Brekekekex koax koax!
DIONYSOS   Perish you all, with your koax;
    you're nothing but koax.
FROGS   So we should be, busybody!
    The Muses, experts on the lyre, love me,
    and goat-hoofed Pan, who plays the tuneful reed;   230
    Apollo, lyre-god, takes great pleasure from me too
    because his lyre uses the reed-stalks that
    I grow in my marsh-water.
    Brekekekex koax koax!
DIONYSOS   I'm getting blisters, and

my arsehole has been oozing for some time;
    soon it is going to come right out and say—
FROGS   Brekekekex koax koax!!
DIONYSOS   My musical friends,   240
    please stop.
FROGS   Oh no! We will
    sing all the more, if ever we have hopped
    on sunny days through galingale
    and flowering reeds, taking pleasure in
    our diving songs,
    or, fleeing from the rain,
    have sung our underwater
    dance-song shimmering
    with splutter-bubbles!
DIONYSOS   Brekekekex koax koax!   250
    I'm taking over from you.
FROGS   That's intolerable!
DIONYSOS   It'll be far worse
    if I row till I burst.
FROGS   Brekekekex koax koax!!
DIONYSOS   Croak all you like; I do not care.
FROGS   We'll yell as loudly as
    our throats can stretch all day.
DIONYSOS   Brekekekex koax koax!   260
    You won't beat me like that.
FROGS   And *you* will not beat us.
DIONYSOS   No! *You* will not beat me—
    —not ever; I will shout
    all day, so I can beat you at "koax."
    BREKEKEKEX KOAX KOAX!!!
(Silence. The FROGS exeunt, left, vanquished.)
    I *knew* I'd make you stop koax.
CHARON   Stop, stop, ship your oar.
  Disembark; pay the fare.
DIONYSOS   Here's the two dollars.   270
(Exit CHARON, right.)

Scene 2

Xanthias! Where's Xanthias? Oh Xanthias!
(XANTHIAS calls back from near the right eisodos.)

XANTHIAS   Cooee!

DIONYSOS   Come here!

XANTHIAS   Welcome, master.

DIONYSOS   What did you find on your way?

XANTHIAS   Darkness and mud.

DIONYSOS   Did you see anywhere those father-beaters
  and perjurers he told us about?

XANTHIAS   Didn't you?

DIONYSOS Yes, by Poseidon, and *(indicating the audience)*—I
  can still see them.
  What will we do next?

XANTHIAS   We'd better get out of here.
  This is the place where that fellow said
  we'd find wild beasts.

DIONYSOS   He'll be sorry he said that.
  He was just telling lies to scare me   280
  out of sheer jealousy because I am so brave.
  There's no one as conceited as that Herakles.
  Myself, I rather hoped we would encounter one
  and do a deed that's worthy of our noble quest.

XANTHIAS   Absolutely! But listen, I can hear a sound.

DIONYSOS   Where is it?

XANTHIAS   Behind us.

DIONYSOS   Go behind.

XANTHIAS   Now it's in front.

DIONYSOS   You go in front.

XANTHIAS   By Zeus, I see a gigantic monster.

DIONYSOS   What's it like?

XANTHIAS   Terrible! It is all kinds of shapes;
  now it's a cow, now it's a mule, and now . . . it's a   290
  beautiful girl.

DIONYSOS   Where is she? Let me at her.

XANTHIAS   No! It's not a girl any more; now it's a dog.
DIONYSOS   It must be the Empousa.
XANTHIAS   Yes, her whole face
    is shining like a fire.
DIONYSOS   And has she got a copper leg?
XANTHIAS   Yes, by Poseidon; and the other one is made
    of donkey-dung.
DIONYSOS   Where can I go?
XANTHIAS   And me?
*(DIONYSOS rushes to the center front row of the audience, where
the VIPS sit, and begs:)*
DIONYSOS   My priest, please save me; let me drink with
        you after the show.
XANTHIAS   Oh lord Herakles, we're done for.
DIONYSOS   Don't ever
    call me that, I beg you; do not speak the name.
XANTHIAS   Dionysos, then.
DIONYSOS   That is even worse.   300
XANTHIAS   *(to the ghost)* Pass; on your way. *(to Dionysos)*
    Master, come here.
DIONYSOS   What's up?
XANTHIAS   Take courage; we've survived,
    and like Hegelochos we can now say
    "after the storm the seal is calm once more."
    Empousa's gone.
DIONYSOS   Swear.
XANTHIAS   Gone, by Zeus.
DIONYSOS   Swear once again.
XANTHIAS   By Zeus.
DIONYSOS   Swear.
XANTHIAS   Yes, by Zeus.
DIONYSOS   Poor me, when I saw her I went quite pale.
XANTHIAS   Yes, and your arse went brown in sympathy.
DIONYSOS   Poor me, whence have these evils fallen on me?
    Which god shall I entreat to let me live?   310
XANTHIAS   The Foot of Time, or Ether, Residence of Zeus?

(music)
  Hey.
DIONYSOS   What?
XANTHIAS   Can't you hear?
DIONYSOS   What?
XANTHIAS   The sound of flutes.
DIONYSOS   Yes, and I can smell
  a whiff of torch-smoke; very mystical.
  Let's crouch down quietly and listen.
(They hide in the mouth of the left eisodos.)
(Enter INITIATES, right.)
INITIATES   Iakchos, oh Iakchos!
    Iakchos, oh Iakchos!
XANTHIAS   That's it, master; I think initiates are celebrating
  here, just as he said. This is the song
  to Iakchos that Diagoras composed.   320
DIONYSOS   I think so too. It's best for us
  to stay in silence till we're sure.

Choros 2

INITIATES (A1)   Iakchos, most honored of our gods,
    Iakchos, oh Iakchos,
    come, and dance across this meadow,
    join your holy band of revelers:
    shake your head, toss the
    fruitful wreath of myrtle   330
    on your brow, and boldly stamp your feet
    to celebrate the playful, joyous ritual
    which all the Graces bless; a dance that's sacred
    to your worshipful initiates.
             * * *
XANTHIAS   O greatly honored, holy lady Persephone,
  what a wonderful smell of roast pork!
DIONYSOS   Keep quiet, and you'll get a sausage.

* * *

INITIATES (A2)   Light up the fiery torches in your
        hands!   340
    You're coming, Iakchos, Iakchos,
    shining star of our nocturnal rite.
    The meadow gleams with flames;
    even the old men dance.
    They shake off cares and all their years
    when they worship the god.
    O blessed one, light up the way! Lead your   350
     young worshipers out to the flowering,
    marshy plain where we can dance.
                    * * *

1 INITIATE   Avoid ill-omened speech, and stand apart
        from our dance,
    all who are ignorant of what we say, or have an
        impure mind,
    or haven't seen or danced the Muses' noble mysteries,
    and aren't word-perfect in the rites of comedy,
    or enjoy nasty jokes said out of season,
    nurture factions and are spiteful to their fellow-citizens,
    stirring strife and fanning it through greed for
        private gain,   360
    or take bribes when the city's tossed by storms,
    or betray a fort or naval vessel, or who smuggle
        contraband
    from Aigina (like Thorykion the corrupt customs officer
    who shipped our oar-pads, flax, and tar to Athens's
        enemies)
    or persuade somebody to subsidize the Spartan navy,
    or shit upon a shrine when singing solo for the choral
        dance,
    and politicians who bite off the comic poets' pay, when
        we've
    made fun of them in these time-honored celebrations
        of the god.

I tell such people once, I tell them twice, I tell them
   one more time
to stand apart from mystic dances; let us now begin
   the song   370
and all-night vigil that this festival demands.
* * *

INITIATES (A1)   Let everyone now boldly step
   out to the flowery hills
   and dales; stamp with your feet,
   and jeer, and mock;
   we've all had quite enough to eat.
* * *

(A2)   Go on your way, and make sure that
   you nobly praise
   the Savior-goddess in your song,
   who's vowed she will preserve this land   380
   for evermore—
   despite Thorykion!
* * *

1 INITIATE   Come now, sing another, special song, adorned
   with sacred melody, to Queen Demeter,
     harvest-goddess.
* * *

INITIATES (B1)   Demeter, mistress of our sacred rites,
   stand by us and keep safe
   your dancing worshipers;
   grant I may play and dance
   this day unharmed.
* * *

(B2)   And may I sing both many jokes
   and much that's serious, and may my play and jest   390
   be worthy of your festival, so I
   will take the victor's crown.
* * *

1 INITIATE   Come now,
   you must also summon by your song

the graceful god, who's our companion on the road.
                              * * *

INITIATES (C1)   Iakchos, most honored god, who first
              composed
        sweet melodies for feasts, accompany us as we go
        to worship Demeter,   400
        and show us how you travel far and wide
        but show no sign of weariness.
        Iakchos, lover of the dance, be with me now.
                              * * *

    (C2)   You made me wear these worn-out sandals
        and these tattered clothes
        for fun—and for economy;
        you've found out how to make us joke
        and dance for very little cash.
        Iakchos, lover of the dance, be with me now.
                              * * *

    (C3)   Yes! I stole a sidelong glance just now
        and saw a very pretty girl,   410
        a partner in our festal dance.
        Her little dress was torn; her lovely tit
        peeked out.
        Iakchos, lover of the dance, be with me now.
                              * * *

DIONYSOS   I've always loved processions, and I'd like
    to sport and dance with her.
XANTHIAS   Me too.
1 INITIATE   Would you like it if we hurl abuse
        at Archedemos, who became long in the tooth
        before he was accepted as a citizen?
1 INITIATE   Now he rants and raves
        among the dead men up above,   420
        and he's the top man there for wickedness.
1 INITIATE   I also hear that The Queen's bum
        was in the cemetery plucking out its hairs
        and tearing at its cheeks;

1 INITIATE   he bent over and struck his head
        and wept and moaned
        for his great squeeze from Erektos.
1 INITIATE   They also say great Kallias, the son of Horsefuck,
        fights the cunts at sea
        dressed in a lionskin.   430
DIONYSOS   Excuse me, could you tell us
        where the house of Plouton is?
        We're strangers, only just arrived.
1 INITIATE   Do not go further, and
        do not ask us again;
        know you have come right to his door.
DIONYSOS   Slave, lift the bags once more.
XANTHIAS   What's this? We're going to do
        another stupid bedbug joke?
                        * * *

1 INITIATE   Go now   440
        into the sacred circle of the goddess, to her
            flower grove,
        and celebrate, all who share in this festival.
        Myself, I'm going with the girls and women where
        they'll spend the night in worship; I will raise my
            sacred torch!
                        * * *

INITIATES (A1)   Yes, we will go into the rose-filled
        flowery meadows, and we'll
        celebrate in our own way—   450
        with lovely dances which
        the blessed Fates convene.
                        * * *

   (A2)   For us alone in Haides' there's
        a sun, and sacred light, because
        we were initiated and
        were always gentle in
        our treatment of both foreigners
        and poor people.

Scene 3

DIONYSOS   Now then, how shall I knock on the door,
     d'you think?   460
   How do the locals do it here?
XANTHIAS   Don't waste time, just give it a good whack;
   remember you are Herakles—at least, you look like him.
DIONYSOS   *(knocking)* Slave, slave!
(Enter DOORKEEPER from the skēnē.*)*
DOORKEEPER   Who's this?
DIONYSOS   Herakles the brave.
DOORKEEPER   You shameless, arrogant bastard!
   Scum, double scum, and triple scum!!
   You took our dog, our Kerberos,
   you grabbed him by the throat and ran away;
   I was responsible for him. Now I've got you!
   Yes, the black-hearted rock of Styx   470
   and crag of Acheron that drips with blood
   will hold you fast, and running dogs of Kokytos,
   and the hundred-headed snake, who'll tear your guts
   to pieces, and the moray eel from Tartessos,
   which will attack your lungs, while ugly hags
   from the next suburb rip apart
   your bloodstained balls and guts—
   so I'll just run and get them now.
(Exit DOORKEEPER into the skēnē. *DIONYSOS has collapsed.)*
XANTHIAS   Hey, you, what have you done?
DIONYSOS   I've shat myself; hail to the gods.
XANTHIAS   Get up, you stupid idiot, before   480
   one of the neighbors sees you.
DIONYSOS   No, I'm fainting.
   Grab a sponge and lay it on my chest.
XANTHIAS   Here, take this, put it on.
DIONYSOS   Where is it?
XANTHIAS   Gods of gold,
   is that where you keep your heart?

DIONYSOS   Yes—in my fear
   it crept down to the bottom of my bowel.
XANTHIAS   You're the biggest coward of all gods and men.
DIONYSOS   Me?
   How could I be? I asked you for a sponge;
   that's not the thing a coward would have done.
XANTHIAS   Yes?
DIONYSOS   He would have just stayed lying in his shit;
   but I stood up and cleaned myself.   490
XANTHIAS   Heroic, by Poseidon.
DIONYSOS   Yes, by Zeus.
   So tell me; you weren't scared by all those noisy words
   and threats?
XANTHIAS   No, didn't give it a thought.
DIONYSOS   Well then, since you're so brave and love
   bold deeds, you can be me and take this club
   and lionskin, seeing your guts are free from fear;
   I will be you and carry all the luggage in my turn.
XANTHIAS   OK, let's do it quickly; I have to obey.
(He puts on the lionskin and takes the club.)
   Now look at me—Herakloxanthias;
   see if I'll be a coward like you were.   500
DIONYSOS   Not a chance; you look like Kallias with all
     his tats.
   OK, I'll take the luggage.
(Enter a SERVANT from the skēnē.*)*
SERVANT   My dearest Herakles, you're here! Come in at
     once.
   The Queen, as soon as she heard you were here,
   began to bake some bread, got two or three large pots
   of pea-soup on the boil, and charcoal-broiled an entire
     cow,
   cooked honey-cakes and special breads. Do come on in.
XANTHIAS   No, I'll be right.
SERVANT   By Apollo, I daren't

let you stay; she's actually steaming
bird-meat, and she's cooked up some   510
desserts, and has decanted a delicious wine.
So please come with me.
XANTHIAS   No, I really can't.
SERVANT   You must be mad;
I will not let you stay. We've got a flute-girl
in here who is very beautiful, and two
or three dancing-girls.
XANTHIAS   Did you say dancing-girls?
SERVANT   They're nice and young; and they have been
    Brazilian waxed.
So please go in; the chef was just about
to serve the seafood entrée, and the table has been set.
XANTHIAS Right, then; first tell those dancing-girls in there
    that I, the mighty Herakles, am coming.   520
(Exit SERVANT into the skēnē.*)*
Boy, bring those bags and follow me.
DIONYSOS   Hang on, you!! You can't be serious;
I only dressed you up as Herakles for fun.
Stop this nonsense, Xanthias,
and pick the luggage up again.
XANTHIAS   What? You can't plan to take from me
what you yourself have given?
DIONYSOS   I'm not planning to; I'm doing it.
Take off the lionskin.
XANTHIAS   I call for witnesses, and beg
the gods to help me.
DIONYSOS   What d'you mean, gods?
You are a human and a slave; it's sheer stupidity   530
for you to think you could be Herakles.
XANTHIAS   Never mind, it's OK. Here then.
(He hands back the lionskin and club.)
Perhaps some time
the god will make you need me once again.

* * *

1 INITIATE   I'll tell you the mark
    of a sensible man
    who's sailed around a bit—
    he always rolls onto
    the comfortable side,
    and doesn't stay fixed like
    a statue in one pose;
    you've got to choose
    the softest option like
    a clever bloke,   540
    a born Theramenes.
DIONYSOS   Wouldn't it be a lovely joke
    if Xanthias, my slave,
    lay on a soft wool blanket
    having it off with a
    dancing-girl, and asked
    me for a chamber pot, while I
    was watching him
    and jerking off—and then
    the bastard sees me, slams me
    on the jaw, and knocks out
    my front teeth!

* * *

(Enter INNKEEPER from the skēnē, *with a slave.)*
INNKEEPER   Plathane, Plathane, come here! It's that bastard
    who once came to the inn,   550
    and ate up sixteen loaves of bread.
(Enter PLATHANE from the skēnē, *with a slave.)*
PLATHANE   Yes, by Zeus,
    it's him.
XANTHIAS   Here's trouble for someone.
PLATHANE   He also ate up twenty bowls of stew
    worth fifteen dollars each!
XANTHIAS   Someone will pay for that.
INNKEEPER   And all those cloves of garlic.

DIONYSOS   Woman, you are mad;
   you don't know what you're saying.
INNKEEPER   I hope you didn't think
   I wouldn't recognize you with those slippers?
   And . . . ! I haven't mentioned all the pickled fish.
PLATHANE   You poor thing, what about the green
     cheese, which
   he ate together with its wrapping-paper?   560
INNKEEPER   Then, when I asked him to pay,
   he growled and gave me filthy looks.
XANTHIAS   That's absolutely typical! He does that
     everywhere.
PLATHANE   And then he drew his sword and went ballistic.
XANTHIAS   Oh, you poor thing!
PLATHANE   We were terrified; I think
   we hid up in the storage loft.
   He stole our rush-mats and then disappeared.
XANTHIAS   Absolutely typical as well.
INNKEEPER   We need to do something.
   You, go and get Kleon; he'll protect my rights.
PLATHANE   And you, see if you can find Hyperbolos
     for me,   570
   so we can utterly destroy this man.
(Exeunt slaves, left and right.)
INNKEEPER   You miserable glutton,
   I would gladly get a stone and bash
   those teeth in, which you used to eat up all my food.
PLATHANE   I'd like to throw you in the execution pit.
INNKEEPER I'd like to take a hatchet and cut out
   that throat which gobbled up my sausages.
   I'm going to find Kleon myself; he'll summon him to
     court
   this very day, and have his guts for garters.
(Exeunt INNKEEPER and PLATHANE, left and right.)
DIONYSOS   May I die miserably, if I don't love Xanthias.
XANTHIAS   I know what you're up to; forget it.   580

No way will I be Herakles again.
DIONYSOS   Oh please,
    dear Xanthy-wanthy.
XANTHIAS   And just how could I
    be Herakles, seeing that I'm a mortal—and a slave?
DIONYSOS   I know you're angry, and that's fair enough;
    so even if you hit me, I would not complain.
    I swear that if I ever take them from you,
    may I be utterly destroyed, together with my wife
    and children, and with blear-eyed Archedemos.
XANTHIAS   I will accept your oath; on these conditions
        I will do it.
(He puts on the lionskin and takes the club.)
1 INITIATE   Now it's your duty, since   590
        you've taken back the costume
        that you had before,
        to be a hero once again,
        look terrifying, and
        remember which god you
        are trying to resemble.
        If you step out of role
        and speak too nicely, then
        you'll have to take
        the luggage once again.
XANTHIAS   That's good advice, my friends,
        but I just happen to
        have had the same idea.
        I know full well that if he could
        get something out of it, he'll try
        to take them back from me.   600
        But still, I'll show I have
        full manly courage, and can flash
        a glance like red-hot chili.
        And I think I'll need to,
        since I hear the door right now!
                                * * *

(Enter DOORKEEPER from the skēnē, *with three POLICEMEN.)*

DOORKEEPER Tie that dog-thief up at once,
  so we can punish him; get a move on!

DIONYSOS   Here's trouble for someone.

XANTHIAS Go to hell! Stay away from me.

DOORKEEPER   O-oh! Resisting arrest, are you?
  Two-Humps, Baboon, Farter,
  come here and arrest this man!

DIONYSOS Isn't it just terrible, a thief like him   610
  hitting a policeman?

DOORKEEPER   Absolutely scandalous.

DIONYSOS It is disgusting and—just terrible.

XANTHIAS   Look here, by Zeus,
  if I ever came here before, I'm willing to die,
  or if I stole a thing of yours that's worth a cent.
  And I'll make you an offer, like the noble man I am.
  Take my slave here and torture him,
  and if you find I'm guilty, you can kill me straightaway.

DOORKEEPER What kind of torture may I use?

XANTHIAS   Oh, any kind you like; hang
  him from a ladder, flay him, skin him,
  stretch him on the rack, pour vinegar into his
    nostrils,   620
  pile bricks on him, and all the rest—except you must
  not hit him with a leek-stalk or young onions.

DOORKEEPER Fair enough; and if I cripple your slave
  when I beat him, I'll give you a refund.

XANTHIAS Don't worry about that; just take him away
    and torture him.

DOORKEEPER No; I'll do it right here, so you can see
    what he says.
  You! Put down that baggage straightaway; make sure
  you speak nothing but truth.

DIONYSOS   I warn you not
  to torture me, since I'm immortal; if you do,
  you'll be responsible.

DOORKEEPER   What are you saying?   630
DIONYSOS   I say I am a god—Dionysos, son of Zeus—
   and he's the slave.
DOORKEEPER   Do you hear that?
XANTHIAS   Yes, I'll say!
   All the more reason why he should be whipped;
   if he's a god, he won't feel anything.
DIONYSOS   Oh well, since you too say you are a god,
   why don't you let him whip you equal strokes to mine?
XANTHIAS That's fair enough; whichever one of us you see
   first bursting into tears or showing a reaction to
   the whipping, you know he is not a god.
DOORKEEPER   You are a perfect nobleman;   640
   you positively look for justice. Strip off, then.
XANTHIAS   How will you torture us fairly?
DOORKEEPER   That is easy.
   One lash each, in turn.
XANTHIAS   That's fair enough.
   OK. Now see if I flinch.
   Have you hit me yet?
DOORKEEPER   No, by Zeus. *(whips XANTHIAS)*
XANTHIAS   No, I didn't think so.
DOORKEEPER   I'll go and hit this one. *(whips DIONYSOS)*
DIONYSOS   When?
DOORKEEPER   I've already hit you.
DIONYSOS   Then why didn't I sneeze?
DOORKEEPER   I don't know. I'll try the other one again.
XANTHIAS Get on with it. *(DOORKEEPER whips him)* O . . . h!
DOORKEEPER   What's that noise for?
   Did you feel some pain?
XANTHIAS   No, by Zeus, I just   650
   thought suddenly about the festival of Herakles.
DOORKEEPER   The man's a saint. Let's try the other one
   again.
   (whips DIONYSOS)

DIONYSOS   Ow! Ow!
DOORKEEPER   What is it?
DIONYSOS   I see some horsemen.
DOORKEEPER   So why are you crying?
DIONYSOS   I can smell onions.
DOORKEEPER   Of course, you didn't feel anything?
DIONYSOS   No, not at all.
DOORKEEPER   Oh, well, back to the other one.
(whips XANTHIAS)
XANTHIAS   A . . . h!
DOORKEEPER   What?
XANTHIAS   Please pull out this thorn.
DOORKEEPER   What's going on? Back to the other one
    again.
(whips DIONYSOS)
DIONYSOS   Apollo! . . . er, "god who dwells in Delos or in
    Delphi . . ."
XANTHIAS   He felt that! Didn't you hear?
DIONYSOS   Certainly not—   660
    I was just remembering a poem by Hipponax.
XANTHIAS   You're getting nowhere; hit him on the flanks.
DOORKEEPER   No, by Zeus; hey, you, stick out that belly!
(whips DIONYSOS on his potbelly)
DIONYSOS   Poseidon!!
XANTHIAS   Someone felt some pain.
DIONYSOS   ". . . lord of Cape Aigai, you rule
    in the grey sea's depths."
DOORKEEPER   By Demeter, I can't find out
    which of you is a god. Go inside;
    my master will sort you out himself,   670
    and lady Persephone, seeing they're both gods.
DIONYSOS   Good idea; I only wish you'd thought
    of it before that whipping.
*(Exeunt DOORKEEPER, DIONYSOS, XANTHIAS, and POLICEMEN
into the* skēnē.)

Choros 3 (Parabasis)

INITIATES   [Muses, join this sacred dance
         and make my song delightful.
         Look at this crowd of people; here
         are thousands more courageous
         and more dignified than
         Kleophon with his funny
         accent. On his lips
         a Thrakian swallow screeches horribly,   680
         perched on a foreign leaf.
         It sings the nightingale's lament
         that he is going to die
         even if he's not found guilty.]
                            * * *

1 INITIATE   The sacred *choros* has to give the city good
         advice
      and good instruction. First we think you must
      give equal rights to all the citizens and take away their
         fears.
      If some people went wrong, deceived by Phrynichos's
         clever tricks,
      I say that those who slipped must have a chance   690
      to get rid of the charge against them and be free from
         past mistakes.
      And next I say that nobody should be disfranchised in
         this city.
      It's disgraceful if men who fought in one sea-battle
      are suddenly all citizens and masters now instead of
         slaves.
      I am not saying that this was a bad idea;
      no, I approve it. It's the one good thing you've done.
      But it is also right that you forgive this one mistake
      to men who beg you, men who've fought beside you
      many times (so did their fathers), and are all your kindred.
      You are by nature very wise; so let your anger go,   700

and let us count *all* those who fight
at sea with us as kin, and as full citizens.
But if we swell with pride and think we are too grand
    for this
—especially now the city's tossed by storms—then in
the future men will see that we were wrong.

* * *

INITIATES   [If I am able to predict about a man
        and how he's going to suffer,
        then this monkey who now irritates us,
        little Kleigenes
        —the very worst of all the bathhouse-keepers   710
        who use stirred-up ash
        and washing-soda (watered down)
        and fuller's earth—
        will not be with us long; and, now he's got
        the message, he's become aggressive. He's afraid
        that if he doesn't take a stick
        he will be mugged and stripped
        when he is pissed.]

* * *

1 INITIATE   We've often thought this city's suffering
   the same regarding all our better citizens
   as with the ancient silver coinage and the recent
      gold.   720
   They were all of sterling quality, the very best
   (as all agree) of currencies,
   coins struck precisely right, sound as a bell,
   accepted everywhere by Greeks and foreigners—
   but we don't use them; we just use this wretched bronze,
   minted just recently and very badly coined.
   Similarly, citizens we know to be well born
   and wise, and just, and good, and fair,
   trained in the wrestling-school, music, and dance—
   we mistreat them; for everything we use base
      bronze   730

—slaves, migrants, criminals, and men from families of
    criminals,
Johnny-come-latelies, people whom in time now past
this city wouldn't gladly even use as scapegoats!
Stop being so stupid, change your ways,
and use your best men once again. If all goes well,
you will be praised; if things go slightly wrong, wise
    men
will say at least that you were hanged from a good tree.

Scene 4

(Enter SLAVE and XANTHIAS from the skēnē.)
SLAVE   By Zeus our Savior, he's a gentleman,
    your master.
XANTHIAS   How could he not be?
    He can only do two things, drinking and fucking.   740
SLAVE   He didn't beat you after you'd been caught,
    when you, the slave, said that you were the master.
XANTHIAS   He'd have suffered if he had.
SLAVE   There you are—
    first-class slave behavior up front, just the sort I like.
XANTHIAS What do you like? Tell me.
SLAVE   I feel supreme delight
    when I can curse and swear about my master secretly.
XANTHIA What about grumbling, when you've been
    beaten
    many times and finally get out?
SLAVE   I like that too.
XANTHIAS   And minding other people's business?
SLAVE   Nothing like it.
XANTHIAS   You're a blood brother, by Zeus! And
    eavesdropping   750
    on the masters when they're talking freely?
SLAVE   Just fantastic.

XANTHIAS Passing on the goss to friends outside?

SLAVE   Who? Me?
   That's not just pleasure; then, I cream myself.

XANTHIAS By lord Apollo, give me your right hand,
   and let's kiss cheeks. Now tell me by Zeus,
   the god who oversees all us whipped slaves,
   what's that commotion, shouting, and abuse
   inside?

SLAVE Aischylos and Euripides.

XANTHIAS Aha!

SLAVE A big dispute's being stirred up—yes, very big
   among the dead, with mighty strife.   760

XANTHIAS Why?

SLAVE There's a law down here that from the arts—
   all the sublime ones, which require real skill—
   the best creator, who's superior to all his fellow-
   craftsmen, gets free food at State expense
   and a throne next to Plouton's—

XANTHIAS   Ah, I see.

SLAVE —until another comes who's better
   at that art; then he must yield his place.

XANTHIAS I understand; but what has upset Aischylos?

SLAVE He held the throne for tragedy
   because he was the best.

XANTHIAS   And now who is?   770

SLAVE When Euripides came down, he showed off
   to all the clothes-stealers and cutpurses
   and father-beaters, and the burglars
   (you get a lot of them in Haides'). When they heard
   his clever arguments and twists and turns
   they went completely mad and hailed him as the
     cleverest;
   then he got so excited he just claimed the throne
   where Aischylos had previously sat.

XANTHIAS   No one threw things at him?

SLAVE No, by Zeus! The crowd all shouted out

that there should be a contest who was better.   780
XANTHIAS   All those thieves?
SLAVE   Their cries rose up to heaven.
XANTHIAS   Aischylos had no support?
SLAVE   Haides' has few good people *(gesture to audience)*—
     just like here.
XANTHIAS   So what is Plouton going to do?
SLAVE   He's going to run a competition straightaway
     to judge and find out which of them is better.
XANTHIAS   But why
     did Sophokles not claim the throne?
SLAVE   No way! When he came down here
     he kissed Aischylos and shook him by the hand;
     and he refused to claim the throne from him.   790
     Now he's going, as Kleidemides once said,
     to sit out on the fence. If Aischylos wins,
     he'll stay where he is; if not, he says that he
     will fight against Euripides down to the bitter end.
XANTHIAS   And this will actually happen?
SLAVE   Very soon.
     Strange things are going to happen—right here, too.
     They're going to put poetry on the scales—
XANTHIAS   What? Weighing tragedy like lamb?
SLAVE   —and bring out rulers and tape measures,
     folding frames—   800
XANTHIAS   —for making bricks?
SLAVE   —set-squares and wedges. Euripides has said
     he's going to test tragedies word for word.
XANTHIAS   I suppose Aischylos took this badly.
SLAVE   He flashed a glance like a charging bull.
XANTHIAS   Who's going to be the judge?
SLAVE   That was difficult.
     There's a shortage of wise men down here.
     Aischylos didn't get on with the Athenians—
XANTHIAS   Too many criminals for him, I suppose?

SLAVE —and he thought everybody else is stupid
   when it comes to judging poets. Finally they   810
   asked your master, since he knows a bit about the art.
   But let's go in; when masters get excited,
   that means trouble for us slaves.
(Exeunt SLAVE and XANTHIAS into the skēnē.*)*
(Set three thrones toward the back of the playing space and also a
lyre: and an altar at C, with voting pebbles on it.)

Choros 4

INITIATES Terrible will be the rage in the heart of the
      mighty
   thunderer, when he sees his rival sharpening
   his piercing and loquacious tooth; his furious eyes
      will roam
   from side to side.
                           * * *

Horse-hair crested words and slivers of linchpins
   will join in flashing-helmet strife, when the craftsman
   of fine carving fights off the horse-charging speech   820
   of the mind-builder.
                           * * *

Bristling the shaggy-necked hair of his mane
   and frowning ferociously, Aischylos will bellow out
   bolt-fastened words, tearing them off like planks
   with a gigantic blast.
                           * * *

And then Euripides' tongue will be unfurled—the
      mouth-craftsman,
   worn smooth by testing words, champing at the bit
      of envy;
   with a phrase for everything it will reduce to ashes
   all the work of Aischylos' lungs.

Scene 5

(Enter PLOUTON, DIONYSOS, EURIPIDES, and AISCHYLOS from
the skēnē. *PLOUTON sits on one of the thrones, DIONYSOS on a*
second; EURIPIDES pushes AISCHYLOS aside and takes the third.)
EURIPIDES I won't get off the throne; don't tell me what
    to do!   830
  I say I am the better playwright.
DIONYSOS   Aischylos, why so quiet? You hear what he
    says.
EURIPIDES   He's doing the arrogant silence bit to start
    with—
  it's a trick he pulled in all his tragedies.
(DIONYSOS leads EURIPIDES away from the throne.)
DIONYSOS   Look here, my friend, a little less big-mouth.
EURIPIDES   I saw through him and got his number long
    ago;
  the man writes violent and reckless verse,
  his mouth's unbridled, uncontrolled, unstoppable,
  incapable of fluent speech, boast-bundle-full.
AISCHYLOS   Is that the truth, son of the fresh fruit
    goddess?   840
  Do *you* say that to me, gossip-collector,
  beggar-maker, rag-stitcher?
  You'll regret it.
DIONYSOS   Steady, Aischylos;
  "do not let rage disturb your inner calm."
AISCHYLOS   No, I won't stop until I have shown up
  this cripple-creator as the braggart that he is.
DIONYSOS   Quick, quick, slaves, bring a black lamb out;
  a whirlwind's getting ready to explode.
AISCHYLOS   You pick up dirty Kretan striptease songs
  and put incestuous relationships onstage—   850
DIONYSOS   Hang on a moment, oh most honored
    Aischylos:
  and you, my poor Euripides, if you are wise

keep well out of this hailstorm's way;
we don't want him to hurl a crowning phrase onto
your head and make you lose your Telephos.
Restrain your rage, Aischylos; let us have
discussion, proof and argument. Tragic poets
should not hurl abuse like fishwives; you began
to roar as quickly as a holm oak set on fire.
EURIPIDES   For my part I am ready; I'm not trying to
    escape   860
from taking a bite—or he can go first, if he likes—
at the dialogue, the lyrics, the very sinews of tragedy;
and yes, by Zeus, he can attack my *Peleus,* my *Aiolos,*
my *Meleagros,* and especially my *Telephos.*
DIONYSOS   What do you want to do? Speak, Aischylos.
AISCHYLOS   I'd rather not have had a contest here;
we're not competing on a level playing field.
DIONYSOS   Why's that?
AISCHYLOS   Because my dramas did not die with me,
but his did, so he's got them here to quote;
however, if it's what you want, I must.   870
DIONYSOS   Slaves! Incense and a fire, so I
can pray, before their subtleties begin,
to judge this contest most artistically;
and you, invoke the Muses while I pray.
*(Slaves bring out incense and a bowl of fire; DIONYSOS burns
incense and prays silently.)*

(Choros 5)

INITIATES   O nine virgins, daughters of Zeus, holy
    Muses, who look down on the subtle minds
    of men who coin opinions, when they fight
    debates with keenly studied, tricky wrestling-throws,
    come now, and watch their two
    ingenious tongues, which have the power   880

to cut up words and turn them into sawdust.
The great contest of wisdom
will happen right now!

* * *

DIONYSOS   Now you must pray before you start reciting.
AISCHYLOS   Demeter, you nurtured my mind when I was
    young;
  may I be worthy of your holy mysteries.
DIONYSOS   And you, take incense and burn it.
EURIPIDES   No thanks;
  my gods are different.
DIONYSOS   Private gods of your own, new-minted?
EURIPIDES   Yes, actually.   890
DIONYSOS   All right, pray to your private gods.
EURIPIDES   Ether, my pasture, Linchpin of my Tongue,
  Intelligence, keen-scented Nostrils, grant
  I may demolish accurately all his bad ideas.

(Choros 6, part one)

INITIATES (A1)   We're burning with desire
              to hear the dancing words
              of these two clever men.
              Go on the road to war!
              Their tongues are savage,
              they are bold,
              their minds are agile.
              We expect Euripides   900
              to say some clever,
              finely polished things;
              but Aischylos will uproot mighty arguments
              like trees, and charge, and scatter
              all the dust left by the broken words.

* * *

1 INITIATE   Begin right now. Make sure that what you say's

sophisticated; nothing personal, and no clichés.

EURIPIDES   I'll tell you later on what kind of dramatist
I am: but first I will expose this man—he's just
a self-promoting fraud; I'll show you how he tricked
the audience of morons he inherited from
    Phrynichos.   910
He'd start with someone sitting down, completely
    covered by a veil—
Achilleus, perhaps, or Niobe; pretentious
    window-dressing
for a tragedy, not uttering a sound.

DIONYSOS   That's right, they didn't.

EURIPIDES   Then the *choros* thumped down four
great slabs of lyric in a row; the actor still stayed silent.

DIONYSOS   I rather liked the silence, and it pleased me
    just as much
as all the smooth talk nowadays.

EURIPIDES   Back then you were
    very naive.

DIONYSOS   I think so too, now. But why did he do it?

EURIPIDES   Sheer pretentiousness. The audience would sit
    and wait for Niobe
to speak. Meanwhile the drama just went on—and
    on.   920

DIONYSOS   Bloody outrageous! He completely took me in.
Why are you fidgeting and fuming?

EURIPIDES   I am showing him for what he is.
Then after all this nonsense, with the drama
halfway through, he'd throw in half a dozen oxlike
    words
with fierce eyebrows and crests, terrible things with
    bogey-faces,
which the audience had never heard.

AISCHYLOS   Ah me! Ai-yai-yai!

DIONYSOS   Shut up.

EURIPIDES   He'd never say a simple word—

DIONYSOS   Don't grind your teeth.

EURIPIDES   —just Skamanders or trenches, or else
  bronze-engraved
  hook-eagles on shields, and horse-cliffed words
  that nobody could understand.

DIONYSOS   Yes, by the gods, I once   930
  spent half a night lying awake and wondering
  what kind of bird a tawny horsecock is.

AISCHYLOS   You ignorant fool, it was the sign on a ship's
  stern.

DIONYSOS   [And I thought it was Philoxenos's son, the
  glutton.]

EURIPIDES   But did you have to put a cock into your
  tragedies?

AISCHYLOS   You enemy of the gods, what kinds of things
  did *you* put in?

EURIPIDES   No horsecocks, by Zeus, or goat-deer like you,
  the kind the Persians weave on tapestries.
  When I inherited the art from you, at first she was
  all swollen up with bombast and with heavy
    phrases,   940
  so I put her on a diet and took off her weight
  with light verse, exercise, and white beetroot,
  and gave her babble juice, squeezed out of books.
  Then I restored her health with monodies—

DIONYSOS   —and a dash of Kephisophon.

EURIPIDES   I didn't just charge in and say whatever
  rubbish I'd thought up.
  No; right away the first actor explained for me the
    story's
  pedigree.

AISCHYLOS   By Zeus, it was usually better than your own!

EURIPIDES   Then from the first words I gave everyone
  something to do; the wives had speeches, even slaves,
  masters, and girls, old women.

AISCHYLOS   Shouldn't you   950 have suffered death for doing that?

EURIPIDES   No, by Apollo;
    it was a very democratic move.

DIONYSOS   I'd leave that line alone,
    my friend; it really isn't one of your strong points.

EURIPIDES   Then I taught the Athenians free speech—

AISCHYLOS   I'll say you did—before that,
    you should have been cut in two!

EURIPIDES   I taught them subtle rules, verbal insertions,
      squaring off,
    thinking, seeing, understanding, twisting, loving,
      scheming,
    suspecting the worst, and being too clever all the time.

AISCHYLOS   I'll say!

EURIPIDES   I brought in everyday things that we know
      and love
    —so I could not have fooled them; audiences
      understood,   960
    and could have criticized my art. I never made great
      outbursts
    with my brains in neutral, and I didn't try to shock them
    with Kyknoses and Memnons and their horses'
      harness-bells.
    You can tell his pupils from mine; he's got
    Phormisios and Megairetos the loser,
    trumpet-spear-and-beard men, bent-pine-flesh-tearers,
    while I have Kleitophon and smart Theramenes.

DIONYSOS   Theramenes? He's terribly clever, and
    if he gets into trouble and too close to danger,
    he throws a double six and turns up trumps.   970

* * *

EURIPIDES   I helped the audience
      to learn things
      (I brought reason and inquiry
      into drama); now they all
      know everything, and really

understand—especially
the modern way to run
a household—asking:
"What is this? Where is my
so-and-so? Who's taken that?"

DIONYSOS   Yes, by the gods, now every   980
Athenian gets home
and yells out to his slaves:
"Where's the jug?
Who's bitten off the head
of that sardine? And last year's
soup-bowl's died on me!
Where is the garlic I had yesterday, and who
has nibbled at the olives?"
Before that they were stupid,
gaping mummy's darlings,
halfwits.   990

(Choros 6, part two)

INITIATES (A2)   Do you see this, mighty Achilleus?
How will you reply?
Just do not let
your temper carry you
off course; he has made
terrible accusations.
My noble friend, do not
respond with rage; reef in,
and use a shortened sail,   1000
then gradually gather speed
and wait until you get
a gentle, steady breeze.
                                              * * *

1 INITIATE   You were the first to build up solemn speeches,
and give order

to the crazy words of tragedy; be brave, pour out a
    stream of words.

AISCHYLOS   I'm angry, and my guts are all churned up,
    to have to answer *him*; but, so he cannot say I'm at a loss,
    tell me—what should we look for in a dramatist?

EURIPIDES   Intelligence and good advice, because we make
    men in the cities better.

AISCHYLOS   And if you did not do this,   1010
    but made once good and noble men depraved,
    what d'you think you deserve?

DIONYSOS   Death; do not even ask him.

AISCHYLOS Look at the audience that he inherited from me
    —noble, upstanding; no draft-dodgers,
    loafers, con men, villains like today's,
    but breathing spears and javelins, white-crested casques,
    helmets and greaves, brave as their armored shields.

DIONYSOS   This is getting bad; he will destroy me with his
    helmet-making.

EURIPIDES   So, how did you make them noble?

DIONYSOS   Speak, Aischylos; don't keep on being proud
    and stubborn.   1020

AISCHYLOS   I made a tragedy brimful of War.

DIONYSOS   Which one?

AISCHYLOS   *Seven against Thebes*;
    every man who saw it fell in love with bravery.

DIONYSOS   That was bad; you made our enemies the
    Thebans
    more courageous; one strike against you.

AISCHYLOS   You could have practiced what I preached; you
                             simply didn't bother.
    Then I presented *Persians*, and I showed how you can
    always
    beat your enemies, when I immortalized that splendid
    victory.

DIONYSOS   Yes; I liked it when they listened to Dareios's
    ghost,

and then the *choros* clapped their hands like this and
    wailed "I-au-oi!"
AISCHYLOS   These are the things poets should do.
    Just think   1030
how useful all the best poets have been.
Orpheus showed us mysteries and how to value life,
Mousaios taught healing and oracles, and Hesiod
working the land, seasons for crops, and ploughing—
    while
we honor godlike Homer for the useful things he taught;
tactics and military power, men in uniform.
DIONYSOS   Well, he didn't teach
that clumsy Pantokles! The other day, when he was
    marching in procession,
he tried to first put on his helmet, then attach the crest.
AISCHYLOS   He taught a lot of other fine men, like the
    hero Lamachos.
Thanks to Homer, I exhibited great soldiers—   1040
Patroklos, and Teukros Lionheart; so I inspired each
    citizen
to measure up to them, when the war-trumpet sounds.
By Zeus, I never showed them sluts like Phaidra,
    Sthenoboia;
No one caught me exhibiting a sex-mad woman.
EURIPIDES   No, by Zeus, the love-goddess was never close
    to you.
AISCHYLOS   Thank god!
But she had all too much to do with you and yours;
indeed, she caused your downfall.
DIONYSOS   That she did!
The things you showed those other women doing all
    caught up with you.
EURIPIDES   You bastard, what harm did my Sthenoboias
    do the city?
AISCHYLOS   You made the noble wives of noble men
    drink hemlock,   1050

shamed by their love for men like your Bellerophon.
EURIPIDES   Do you say I invented Phaidra's story?
AISCHYLOS   No, it existed—but the playwright must hide evil, not show
and teach it to the audience. Boys have schoolteachers
to explain things to them; young men have the playwrights.
That's why we have to teach what's right.
EURIPIDES   So if you spout great words
as tall as mountains, that is teaching what is right?
Poets should talk like real people.
AISCHYLOS   No! Miserable man, great thoughts
and concepts must give birth to words of no less size.
Besides, it's natural demigods should utter mighty words,   1060
just as they wear more splendid clothing than our own.
I showed them as they truly are—and you defiled them.
EURIPIDES   How?
AISCHYLOS   You clothed your kings in rags, to make them seem
more pitiful.
EURIPIDES   What was the harm in that?
AISCHYLOS   Not one rich man is now prepared to sponsor naval ships;
each wraps himself in rags and cries poor mouth—
DIONYSOS   —wearing thick woolen underwear so he stays warm.
And if he gets away with it, he pops up in the most expensive sushi-bar.
AISCHYLOS   Next you taught them how to chatter and make small talk.
This emptied wrestling-schools and softened up the firm   1070
round arses of the boys; also, it made the crew of *Paralos*
start answering back to their officers; men who in my time

only knew how to ask for barley-bread and shout out
        "Yo-ho-ho!"
DIONYSOS   Yes, by Apollo—and fart in the faces of the
        lower row, and shit
    upon their messmates, and go ashore and mug someone;
        now they
    all answer back and will not row; the ship goes
        everywhere!

                          * * *

AISCHYLOS   Is there a single evil he's not caused?
        He put procurers in our plays
        and women who give birth in temples,   1080
        screw their brothers, and say that
        to live is not to live!
        That's why our city's been filled up
        with petty bureaucrats and with
        big-talking monkey-demagogues
        who trick the citizens;
        now no one's left who's fit enough
        to run the torch-race.
DIONYSOS   You're quite right! At the last
        Panathenian, I died laughing at   1090
        a slow guy with his head bent down—
        pale, fat, left far behind
        and doing badly; the people in
        the Kerameikos gates slapped at
        his belly, ribs, his flanks and arse;
        all their blows made him fart, so he
        blew on his torch and tried to get away.

Choros 7

INITIATES (A1)   A great affair, a bitter strife, fierce battle's
        being done.
        It's hard to see who'll win,   1100

   since one puts out such mighty energy, while his
      opponent
   wheels around and thrusts back powerfully.
   Don't just sit tight;
   there are all sorts of new, clever attacks.
   Whenever there's a chance to make a point,
   speak out, attack, lay bare
   both old ideas and new.
   Be brave; speak subtle, clever words.

                              * * *

(A2)   And if you fear the audience
   might be a little ignorant, and will   1110
   not recognize your subtle points,
   don't be afraid! They aren't like that, not anymore.
   Each one's seen active service, and has got
   at least one book; they understand clever ideas.
   Nature made them the strongest of mankind
   and now they're very sharp.
   Fear nothing and try everything;
   this audience is really wise.

Scene 6

EURIPIDES   Right! Now I shall turn to your prologues,
   so I'll test first the very first part   1120
   of this clever bastard's tragedies.
   His expositions weren't exactly clear.
DIONYSOS   Which one will you test?
EURIPIDES   Lots of them.
   First give me the famous prologue from the *Oresteia*.
DIONYSOS   Quiet, everyone. Aischylos, recite.
AISCHYLOS   "Hermes! God below the earth, protector of a
      father's power,
   become my savior, fight beside me as I ask you now.
   For I have come back to this land; I'm home once more."

DIONYSOS   Any problems so far?

EURIPIDES   Oh, a dozen or more.

DIONYSOS   But it's only three lines.   1130

EURIPIDES   Yes, with twenty faults in each.

DIONYSOS   Aischylos, I advise you to be quiet; if not,
    I'll have to fine you more than just three lines.

AISCHYLOS   Must *I* be quiet for *him*?

DIONYSOS   If you take my advice.

EURIPIDES   Right at the start he made a huge mistake.

AISCHYLOS   You're mad.

EURIPIDES   See if I care.

AISCHYLOS   What's the mistake?

EURIPIDES   Give us the first line again.

AISCHYLOS   "Hermes! God below the earth, protector of a
    father's power."

EURIPIDES   Isn't Orestes saying this
    at his dead father's tomb?

AISCHYLOS   Yes.   1140

EURIPIDES   Then why—seeing that his father died
    by violence, at a woman's hand, by treachery—
    does he call Hermes the protector of a father's power?

AISCHYLOS   He didn't mean that; he called on Hermes as
    the god
    below the earth who brings good luck—and made this
    clear
    by saying he inherited the function from his father.

EURIPIDES   That's an even bigger mistake; for if Hermes got
    his power below the earth from his father—

DIONYSOS   —he's a tomb-robber, authorized by Zeus.

AISCHYLOS   Dionysos, you drink lousy wine.   1150

DIONYSOS   Recite another verse; and you, watch out for
    faults.

AISCHYLOS   ". . . become my savior, fight beside me as I
    ask you now.
    For I have come back to this land; I'm home once more."

EURIPIDES   Clever Aischylos has said the same thing twice.

DIONYSOS   What?

EURIPIDES   Look at the verse; I'll show you.
   He says "I have come back to this land; I'm home once
      more."
   But coming back is the same thing as coming home.

DIONYSOS   Yes, it's just as if you asked your neighbor,
      "please,
   lend me a kneading-trough; or, if you like, a trough for
      kneading."

AISCHYLOS   It's not at all the same, you silly little
      man;   1160
   this is a really good line.

EURIPIDES   Explain, then; show me why.

AISCHYLOS   A man who lives in his native land simply
   "returns," since there's no complication; but
   an exile "comes back" *and* he's "home once more."

DIONYSOS   Very good, by Apollo. What do you say,
      Euripides?

EURIPIDES   I say Orestes didn't "come back home once
      more";
   he crossed the border secretly, without permission.

DIONYSOS   Very good, by Hermes; I don't understand a
      word.

EURIPIDES   Get on to the next bit.

DIONYSOS   Yes, next bit,   1170
   Aischylos, and hurry up; you, look out for faults.

AISCHYLOS   ". . . and here upon his burial mound I call
      out to my father;
   hear me! Listen!"

EURIPIDES   Look, he's saying something twice again;
   "Hear me! Listen!"—obviously the same.

DIONYSOS   He's talking to the dead, you idiot, who do
   not hear us even if we pray three times.
   What kind of prologues do *you* create?

EURIPIDES   I'll show you.
   And if I ever say the same thing twice, or put in any

irrelevant padding, just spit on me.

DIONYSOS   Give me a sample; I'm just going to have   1180
to check how well you word your prologues.

EURIPIDES   "Oidipous, at first, was favored by the gods—"

AISCHYLOS   Nonsense! He was ill favored by his ancestry;
even before his birth, Apollo said that he
would kill his father—yes, before he was conceived;
how could he be considered fortunate at first?

EURIPIDES   "—and then became most wretched of all
mortal men."

AISCHYLOS   Nonsense! He'd never stopped!
How? When he was first born
he was exposed in a jar in midwinter,   1190
so he wouldn't grow up to kill his father.
He went painfully, limping, to live with Polybos;
then he married a woman old enough to be his mother
—and then found out she actually was his mother!
After that he blinded himself.

DIONYSOS   So he really was lucky—
providing he was executed later on.

EURIPIDES   You are crazy; I make excellent prologues.

AISCHYLOS   OK! By Zeus, I won't just scratch your phrases
word by word; with the gods' help
I will destroy your prologues with a tiny flask of
oil.   1200

EURIPIDES   My prologues with a flask of oil?

AISCHYLOS   Yes, one will be enough.
The way you make your verses anything
fits on—a little fleece, a prick-shaped flask,
a tiny bag of balls; and I will prove it right away.

EURIPIDES   What, you'll prove it?

AISCHYLOS   Yes.

EURIPIDES   OK; I will recite.
"Aigyptos, as the best-known story tells,
sailed in a ship with fifty sons;
landing at Argos, he—"

AISCHYLOS   —lost his flask of oil.

DIONYSOS   What's the point of this oil flask? Is it safe?
   Recite another prologue; let him try again.   1210

EURIPIDES   "Dionysos, bearing the bakchic wand and
      clothed
   in fawnskin, dancing, leaping down
   Parnassos—"

                     AISCHYLOS   —lost his flask of oil.

DIONYSOS   Oh dear! Once more a mortal blow struck by
      the flask.

EURIPIDES   No worries! Here's a prologue
   he can't stick his oil flask on.
   "No mortal man can ever be completely happy;
   either he's of noble birth but poor, or else,
   being of humble stock, he's—"

AISCHYLOS   —lost his flask of oil.

DIONYSOS   Euripides!

EURIPIDES   What?

DIONYSOS   Lower your sails a bit.   1220
   This little flask is blowing up a gale.

EURIPIDES   No, by Demeter, I don't think so; this
   will knock it from his hand right now.

DIONYSOS   Give us another, then—and keep clear of the
      oil flask.

EURIPIDES   "Kadmos, son of Agenor, when he left
   Sidon's fair city—"

AISCHYLOS   —lost his flask of oil.

DIONYSOS   My good friend, buy the oil flask,
   or he will ruin all our prologues.

EURIPIDES   What?
   I've got to buy it?

DIONYSOS   Yes—take my advice.

EURIPIDES   No way! I've got a whole lot more
      prologues,   1230
   which are oil-flask proof.
   "Pelops the son of Tantalos, coming to Pisa

with swift horses—"
AISCHYLOS   —lost his flask of oil.
DIONYSOS   D'you see? He stuck the oil flask on again.
   My friend, do everything you can to buy it off him;
   it's in good nick, and it will only cost a buck or so.
EURIPIDES   No, by Zeus! I've still got lots.
   "Oineus once, leaving home—"
AISCHYLOS   —lost his flask of oil.
EURIPIDES   At least let me say one whole verse!
   "Oineus once, leaving home with a rich crop of
        grain   1240
   and offering the first-fruits—"
AISCHYLOS   —lost his flask of oil.
DIONYSOS   In the middle of a sacrifice? Who stole it?
EURIPIDES   Relax, my friend; let him fit it on *this*.
   "Zeus, as is told in legends old and true—"
DIONYSOS   Stop!! He's going to say Zeus lost his flask
        of oil.
   That little flask clings to your verses like
   styes on the eyes.
   Change the subject; turn to his lyrics.
EURIPIDES   Good! I can show he was a bad composer and
   always repeated himself.   1250

(Choros 8)

Either 405 version
INITIATES   [What's going to happen now?   1251
        I am amazed that he   1257
        is going to criticize
        the king of bakchic song;
        I am afraid he'll fail.]   1260

Or 404 version

INITIATES   What's going to happen now?   1251
   I can't think how he
   could criticize the man
   who wrote the best songs we
   have ever heard.   1256

* * *

EURIPIDES   Yes—bloody crazy lyrics, as you'll see.
   I can give you all his songs condensed in one.
DIONYSOS   All right—I'll take these pebbles and keep
   count.

* * *

EURIPIDES   Phthian Achilleus, why, when you can hear
     man-slaughtering
   —ah!!—blows—do you not go to help?
   We live beside the lake and worship Hermes as our
     ancestor
   —ah!!—blows—do you not go to help?
DIONYSOS   Two strikes against you, Aischylos, so far.   1270
EURIPIDES   Noblest Achaian, king of kings, learn from me,
     son of Atreus
   —ah!!—blows—do you not go to help?
DIONYSOS   That's three strikes, Aischylos.
EURIPIDES   Be silent. Beekeepers are near, to open
     Artemis's sanctuary
   —ah!!—blows—do you not go to help?
   I have authority to tell the power of young men in
     their prime
   —ah!!—blows—do you not go to help?

* * *

DIONYSOS   O Zeus our lord, so many heavy blows!
   I need to go to the bathhouse—all these blows
   have made my kidneys swell.   1280
EURIPIDES   Hang on! You've got to hear another set
   constructed from his pieces with a lyre accompaniment.
DIONYSOS   Go on, and don't add any blows.

* * *

EURIPIDES   How the twin-throned power of the Achaians,
of the youth of Greece, *(he strums his lyre between verses)*
phlattothrattophlattotthrat
sends out the Sphinx, the bitch presiding over evil days,
phlattothrattophlattotthrat
a fierce, warlike bird-omen with spear and avenging
     hand,
phlattothrattophlattotthrat   1290
granting his body to the bold air-ranging hounds
phlattothrattophlattotthrat
and the united force surrounding Aias
phlattothrattophlattotthrat.

* * *

DIONYSOS   What's this *phlattothratt?* Where did you get
these rope-hauler songs? From Marathon?
AISCHYLOS   I took my music from a good source, and I
     made it be
a thing of beauty; no one could say I gathered honey in
those meadows of the Muses Phrynichos had
     roamed.   1300
Euripides gets honey anywhere—whores' tunes,
Meletos's drinking-songs, and Karian flute-melodies,
laments, and choral dances. I will show you
     straightaway.
Someone bring me a lyre. On second thought
who needs a lyre for this? Where is that woman who
beats time on castanets? Muse of Euripides, come here—
you are the right accompanist for songs like these.
(Enter an ugly OLD WOMAN from the skēnē, *with castanets.)*
DIONYSOS   *She* never sang good lyrics or gave head—no
     way.
AISCHYLOS   *(dancing to the woman's castanet accompaniment)*
Halcyons, who gossip as they fly
over the ocean's ever-flowing waves   1310
and wet their wings

with moist drops;
spiders, you who in the rafter-corners
w-i-i-i-ind
the threads for stretching on the loom,
creating the sweet music of the shuttle,
where dolphins, the song-lovers,
leapt to the ships' dark prows—
oracles and racecourses.
Delight of the wine's flowering, curl   1320
of the grape-cluster which cures woes,
embrace me, child!

                * * *

[D'you see that foot?
EURIPIDES   I see.
AISCHYLOS   What?! Well, do you see *this* one?
DIONYSOS   I see.]
AISCHYLOS   So you make stuff like that
    and dare to criticize my lyrics,
    when you make yours all fit one of
    a prize whore's twelve positions?

                * * *

So much for your lyrics. Now I want
to demonstrate the style of a Euripidean monody.   1330
(*Exit OLD WOMAN.*)
    Black-shining darkness of the Night,
    what is this frightful dream
    you've sent me from the depths of Haides',
    soul without a soul,
    horrible daughter of black Night,
    a terrifying sight,
    black-corpse-clothed,
    looking awful, awful,
    and with great long nails?
    My handmaids, light a torch,
    get water in your buckets from the river,
    heat it up, so I

can wash away this nightmare sent by gods.   1340
O Lord of the Ocean,
that's it! Neighbors,
see these portents. Glyke's snitched
my cockerel and done a bunk.
Nymphs of the mountains, and
Mania, you must catch her.
I, ill-fated one,
was concentrating on my work
and wi-i-i-inding in my hands
a spindle full of wool   1350
to make a skein, so I
could go down early to the marketplace
and sell it.
Then he soared, he soared into the sky
flapping his wing-tips;
me he left in grief, in grief—
I cried, I cried in misery
tears, many tears.
Oh Kretans, children of Mount Ida,
bring your arrows to my aid
and swiftly ply your limbs;
surround the house.
Oh holy goddess Artemis, please come
with all your little hunting-dogs
and search these halls.   1360
Hekate, Zeus's daughter,
bring your piercing torches,
light my way to Glyke's place,
so I can search for stolen property.
                              * * *

DIONYSOS   That's enough lyrics.
AISCHYLOS   I agree.
   I'm going to take him to the scales,
   the only true test of our poetry.

That will compel us to reveal our words' true weight.
DIONYSOS   Come here then, if I really have to do this too—
   weighing poetic skill like cheese.
(Attendants bring out a giant pair of scales.)

(Choros 9)

INITIATES   Clever poets do work hard!   1370
   This is another new idea
   —and pretty crazy; who else
   would have thought of it?
   If someone had met me
   and told me this, I wouldn't have
   believed it, but I'd think
   that he was mad.

                         * * *

DIONYSOS   Right, stand by the scale-pans.
AISCHYLOS/EURIPIDES   OK.
DIONYSOS   Grasp them firmly, speak a verse,
   and then let go before I call "cuckoo."   1380
AISCHYLOS/EURIPIDES   We've got them.
DIONYSOS   Speak your verse into the scales.
EURIPIDES   "If only Argo hadn't flown right through . . ."
AISCHYLOS   "Spercheios, river rich in cattle-grazing land."
DIONYSOS   Cuckoo.
AISCHYLOS/EURIPIDES   We've let go.
DIONYSOS   The scale falls
   much further down on his side.
EURIPIDES   Why?
DIONYSOS   He put in a river, like a wool-salesman
   who's pouring water on the fleece,
   while you put in a wingèd word.
EURIPIDES   Let him recite another verse and weigh it
   against mine.

DIONYSOS   Take hold again.
AISCHYLOS/EURIPIDES   OK.
DIONYSOS   Now speak.   1390
EURIPIDES   "Persuasion has no other shrine except the
     word."
AISCHYLOS   "Alone among the gods, Death loves no gifts."
DIONYSOS   Let go.
AISCHYLOS/EURIPIDES   We have.
DIONYSOS   Down on his side again;
     he put in Death, the heaviest of evil things.
EURIPIDES   But I put in Persuasion, and spoke a most
     noble phrase.
DIONYSOS   Persuasion is an empty, foolish thing.
     Try to find a really heavy verse,
     which will weigh in your favor—strong and big.
EURIPIDES   Now, where would I find something like that?
DIONYSOS   Try this;
     "Achilleus threw two sixes and a four."   1400
     Say something; this is your last chance at weighing.
EURIPIDES   "In his right hand he took a club, heavy as iron."
AISCHYLOS   "Chariot piled on chariot, and corpse on
     corpse."
DIONYSOS   He's beaten you again.
EURIPIDES   How?
DIONYSOS   He put in two chariots and two corpses,
     which a hundred Aigyptians couldn't lift.
AISCHYLOS   Stop going verse for verse; let him get in
     the scales himself, his children, wife, Kephisophon,
     and sit with all his books—
     and I'll recite just two of my own verses.   1410
DIONYSOS *(to PLOUTON)* These men are friends of mine.
     I won't decide;
     then I won't upset either one.
     I think one's very clever, and I do enjoy the other.
PLOUTON   So! You won't do what you came here for?

DIONYSOS   And if I do decide?

PLOUTON   You can take back
   the one you choose, so you won't waste your trip down
      here.

DIONYSOS   Thanks for your kindness. OK, listen to me.
   I came here for a poet. Why? So Athens
   will survive and keep my drama festival.
   I'm going to take the one of you   1420
   who's going to give the city good advice.
   First, then, both tell me what you think about
   Alkibiades. The city's in hard labor.

AISCHYLOS   What do the people think of him?

DIONYSOS   What?
   They love him, hate him, want to have him.
   Now tell me what you think.

EURIPIDES   I hate that citizen, who's slow to help
   his native land, but quick to do great harm,
   most helpful to himself, but useless to his city.

DIONYSOS   Good, by Poseidon. And *your* view?   1430

AISCHYLOS   A city should not rear a lion-cub;
   but if you do, accept all its demands.

DIONYSOS   By Zeus our savior, I cannot decide;
   he spoke so cleverly, and *he* so clearly.
   OK; each of you must tell me how
   the city can escape her troubles.

Either 405 version

[EURIPIDES   Suppose that someone stuck a tall, thin bloke
      as wings
   on a big fatso, and the breezes wafted them across the
      sea—

DIONYSOS   It would look stupid; what's the point?

EURIPIDES   In a sea-battle, they could carry vinegar   1440
   and pour it down into the eyes of enemies—   1441

DIONYSOS   Wonderful, Palamedes, cleverest of men!   1451
     Did you think that up for yourself, or did Kephisophon?
EURIPIDES I did—he only had the idea of the vinegar.]

or 404 version

EURIPIDES   I know, and want to say.
DIONYSOS   Go on.   1442
EURIPIDES   When we trust those we now distrust,
     and call what we now trust untrustworthy—
DIONYSOS   What? I don't understand.
     Say something that's less learned and more clear.
EURIPIDES   If we no longer trust those citizens in whom
     we trust at present, and we use those men
     whom we don't use, perhaps we might be saved.
DIONYSOS   We are so badly off right now that we're
     bound to be saved, if we reverse our course.   1450

[DIONYSOS]   OK; what do *you* think?
AISCHYLOS   First tell me whom the city   1454
     uses nowadays as leaders; all the better people?
DIONYSOS   Not at all!
     Everyone hates them.
AISCHYLOS   So they prefer the worthless men?
DIONYSOS   No—but they use them; there's no choice.
AISCHYLOS   How could one ever save a city that
     doesn't like a good, warm cloak or blanket?
DIONYSOS   You've got to find out how, to go back up
     again.   1460
AISCHYLOS   I would speak there; I do not want to say
     down here.
DIONYSOS   No; you must send up good advice from here.
AISCHYLOS   They must realize that enemy land is theirs
     and their own land is now the enemy's; the ships
     must be their riches—other wealth is worthless.
DIONYSOS   Great—but the jury-men drink all the city's
     wealth.

PLOUTON   Make your decision!

DIONYSOS   This will be my judgment;
    I will take the one my heart desires.

EURIPIDES   Remember, when you choose your friends,
    the gods
    by whom you swore to take me home with you!   1470

DIONYSOS   "It was my tongue that swore . . . ," but I
    choose Aischylos.

EURIPIDES   What have you done, oh most accursed of men?

DIONYSOS   I?
    I have decided Aischylos has won. Why should I not?

EURIPIDES Can you look me straight in the eye, after this
    shameful deed?

DIONYSOS   "What deed is shameful, if it does not seem so
    to . . ." the audience?

EURIPIDES   You bastard, will you really leave me here—
    still dead?

(Exit EURIPIDES, right.)

DIONYSOS   Who knows if life may not be death,
    or breathing eating, sleep a fleecy blanket?

PLOUTON   Dionysos, come inside.

DIONYSOS   Why?

PLOUTON   So I can entertain you two before you leave.

DIONYSOS   Well said, 1480
    by Zeus; that's not a bad idea.

(Exeunt PLOUTON, DIONYSOS, and AISCHYLOS into the skēnē.*)*

Finale

INITIATES   Happy indeed is he
    whose mind is finely tuned.
    You can learn this in many ways.
    Here is a man who showed good sense
    and now he'll go back home;
    he will do good to his whole city,

good to all
his kinsmen and his friends
because he is so wise.   1490

* * *

The best thing's not to sit
with Sokrates and spout philosophy,
abandoning good music
and the greatest strengths
of tragic poetry.
Wasting your time
on pompous words and petty quibbles,
signifying nothing, shows
you're going crazy.
(Reenter PLOUTON, DIONYSOS, and AISCHYLOS from the skēnē.)
PLOUTON   Aischylos, farewell!   1500
     And save our city with your wise
     advice. Do try to educate the fools;
     there are so many of them.
(He hands AISCHYLOS a sword, several nooses, and a bunch of
hemlock.)
     Give this to Kleophon,
     these to the tax-officers
     and Myrmex and Nikomachos,
     and this to Archenomos; tell them they
     must come down here to me
     with no delay; if they do not,   1510
     I'll have them branded and chained up
     with Adeimantos, son of the White Crest,
     and I will send them quickly underground.
AISCHYLOS   With pleasure! And please give
     my throne to Sophokles to guard
     and to preserve, in case
     I ever come back here. I judge him
     second in ability.
     Just make sure that crim   1520
     and lying wanker never

sits upon my throne,
not even by mistake.

* * *

PLOUTON   *(to the INITIATES)*
Light sacred torches for him,
and escort him on his way; celebrate
him with his own
lyrics and songs.

* * *

INITIATES   First grant safe journey to this poet who departs
and rises up toward the light, gods of the underworld,
and give the city good ideas, which will bring
many blessings!   1530
Then we could find release from all our sufferings
and ghastly battles. Kleophon can fight, and anybody
else who wants to, back in their own native lands!
(Exeunt AISCHYLOS, DIONYSOS, and INITIATES, left; exit PLOU-
TON into the skēnē.)

Theatrical Commentary

The Theater of Dionysos at Athens in the Fifth Century B.C.E.

Key: B = Back C = Center E = Extreme F = Front L = Left R = Right

Theatron; audience seating

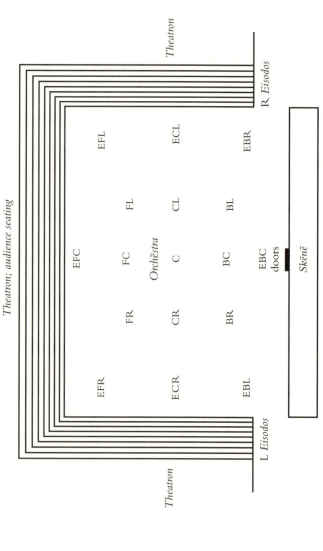

This schematic drawing shows the various positions in the *Orchēstra*, as indicated by the key. The audience sat in raked seating; the first five rows were marble, and the rows above were wooden benches on earth.

Lysistrata

Acting Style, Lysistrata

Lysistrata is a special character. She is intelligent, has learned much, and can hold firm when all around her are weakening.[1] Her part even employs stagecraft tactics that echo the role of Klytaimestra in Aischylos's *Agamemnon*.[2] But she is far from being just a foil for other characters' comic ripostes. Lysistrata uses sexually explicit language (149ff., 212ff., 715ff., etc.); when Kinesias arrives she helps "to work him up / and get him on heat" (843–44); and she is not above a sexual double entendre even in her moment of victory (1183). So this is a complex role; she is not merely one of Aristophanes' most determined and serious protagonists, but also a woman who has no inhibitions about using a four-letter word and entering fully into the world created by her sex strike. The modern actress must therefore portray a born leader, concentrate upon bringing out the full power of her serious sociopolitical case against the warmongering men—and also be alert and alive to the comic possibilities that Aristophanes has built into the character of Lysistrata. Even by the standards of other heroes (such as Dikaiopolis in *Acharnians*) who also have to make lightning changes of mood,[3] hers is an exceptionally demanding part. And this play is, of course, also the first time that Aristophanes made a woman, rather than a man, his principal figure.

1. Cf. especially scene 4 and 1124ff.
2. Below, footnotes 18 and 21.
3. For Dikaiopolis, cf. my commentary in *Aristophanes:* Acharnians, Knights, *and* Peace (forthcoming).

Scene 1

Eight of Aristophanes' eleven surviving comedies[4] begin with a scene in which an angry or suffering hero (in *Lysistrata* and *Assemblywomen*, a heroine) divulges his or her dissatisfaction with the current state of the polis, reveals the plan by which he or she proposes to solve it, and takes the first steps toward doing so—using means that are impossible in real life, but whose effectiveness is taken for granted in the world of the comedy. The choice of characters for this opening scene emphasizes the Panhellenic nature of the sex strike right from the start, and Lampito's strong support for Lysistrata prefigures the appearance of Spartan delegates as fellow sufferers with the Athenian males from scene 6 to the end.

Location

It has often been claimed that for this opening scene there were two side doors into the *skēnē*, apart from the central pair of doors; that these were used for the entrances of Lysistrata and Kalonike, and that the scene at the start of scene 1 is a street in downtown Athens.[5] However, the use of such extra doors here would be confusing; before the end of the scene the central double doors clearly represent the Propylaia, the entrance into the Akropolis (as they do for the rest of the drama), and Aristophanes does not normally alter the location of action without clear dialogue indicating that the *skēnē* doors now represent a new location (which does not happen anywhere in this scene).[6] So the scene must from

4. *Acharnians, Clouds, Peace, Birds, Lysistrata, The Women's Festival, Frogs, Assemblywomen.*

5. E.g., Sommerstein 1990, 15; Henderson 1996, 43, and 2000, 267; and Revermann 2006, 246ff.

6. Cf. especially the travels of Dionysos and Xanthias in *Frogs*, between the early scene where the *skēnē* represents Herakles' house (35ff.) and the point where the location settles in front of the house of Plouton and Persephone at the start of scene 3 (460ff.). Similarly, in *Acharnians* the scene is clearly changed three times, finally settling in front of the hero's own house at the end of scene 2.

the outset be set in front of the Akropolis; the *skēnē* facade would have had panels representing the Propylaia;[7] and first Lysistrata and then Kalonike should arrive in the regular way for people who have come from their homes downtown to the place represented by the *skēnē* facade—through the left *eisodos*. This also avoids having to posit unnecessary extra doors toward the sides of the facade.[8]

Props

The scene requires someone[9] to produce, quickly, a large bottle and a large wine-mixing bowl at 199.[10] She could go in through the *skēnē* doors to fetch these objects, but this would spoil by anticipation the big moment when, after the older women have captured the Akropolis, Lysistrata and her fellow conspirators enter the Propylaia at the end of the scene. So it is better if they are preset unobtrusively just outside the perimeter of the *orchēstra*, near the doors, before the play begins. If this is done, it is also worthwhile to preset there the stool and basket of wool, which will be needed in scene 3. Then both sets of objects can be brought into play rapidly, as the script requires (see 199–201 and 535ff.).[11]

Acting Style, the Other Women

It is fascinating to note how Aristophanes provides few clues—but just enough—to enable a production to create contrasts within the group of women, both in casting and in

7. For the use of scenic panels from Aischylos onward, see Ley 1989.

8. Against side doors, cf. further introduction, Performance. At *Ach* 1070ff. and *Clouds* 120ff. and 1471ff., the central double doors lead in to two separate but adjacent locations; Dearden 1976, 20ff., argues convincingly against the theory that these scenes required two separate doors into the *skēnē*.

9. Either one of the conspirators or the Skythian slave girl.

10. On the outsize props in this scene, cf. Revermann 2006, 244–46.

11. Similarly the series of gifts to Demos at *Knights* 781ff. should also be preset near the *skēnē* doors; see my commentary in *Aristophanes:* Acharnians, Knights, *and* Peace (forthcoming).

costume. Kalonike is feisty and full of energy; Myrrhine and the Athenian woman who enters left with her are fashionable and well dressed (see below, blocking, 66–67); the two other Athenians, who come from "the stinky swamp," are country girls (see below, note 12); Lampito is athletic and sporty (78ff.); the Korinthian is well built and voluptuous (86ff.); while the Boiotian is exquisite in her see-through dress (90ff.). As with all nonlead roles in Aristophanes, each of these characterizations is one-dimensional; but the one dimension is there to be built on and made theatrically alive by directors and actresses today.

Blocking

The two-person scene between Lysistrata and Kalonike needs to be focused around the center line (CL–CR), but Lysistrata can circle as she outlines her grand plan at 29ff., and Kalonike can break out toward the periphery to express her excitement at 50ff. (returning unhappily at 55).

* * *

66–67: These lines indicate that Myrrhine and one Athenian come in from one direction and two Athenians come in from the other direction. Myrrhine, who in the Kinesias scene represents an ideal of perfumed, coiffed, and cultivated urban femininity, cannot be one of the people from the stinky swamp, whose body odor repels both Kalonike and Lysistrata. To play on the prejudices of sophisticated Athenians against country peasants, it is best to have Myrrhine and her companion (Athenian Woman 1) enter L and position the "stinky swamp" out of town by having the two unfortunate rural women (Athenian Women 2 and 3) enter R.[12]

12. In the original text, Aristophanes named the swamp-ridden village of Anagyrous. This was in reality in the southeast of Attika, well on the way to Anaphlystos and Cape Sounion, so their entry from the right *eisodos* will have been geographically correct.

* * *

77–183: The effective playing of this part of the scene requires initial positions as follows: Kalonike and Lysistrata are still to either side of C (or just behind the center point); Myrrhine and one Athenian are to their left; the two Athenians from the "stinky swamp" are BR, having retreated there in an angry huff after Kalonike's insults. Then there is plenty of playing space for the three visitors from other cities to take up position FR, ready for Lysistrata to advance from C and greet Lampito; she is followed by Kalonike, who darts forward and gets physical with each of them in turn.

Lysistrata needs to hold the dominant position throughout most of her exposition; she can break away to expand on her views at 108ff. but must definitely be at C from 120 to 125.

Whom does Lysistrata address in 121ff.? All the other women turn away from her, but the ones best positioned to look as if they are going to leave are the two rural Athenians BR, who are near the R *eisodos*. So the second half of 125 should be addressed to them, and "Your skin's turned pale, you're crying" (127) is best addressed to Kalonike in view of the subsequent dialogue with her. Therefore the people in 126 who purse their lips (literally impossible, of course, in the Greek masked theater) and shake their heads (definitely possible) are the first Athenian woman, Myrrhine, and the Korinthian and Boiotian women. Lysistrata can then effectively round on Myrrhine (CL) at 131–32 before crossing FR to appeal to Lampito at 140. She can then move through FL and CL back to C during 148ff., a typical "circling" speech designed to reinvolve all the other characters in her plan.

* * *

184–90: The slave girl either must have come in with Lysistrata and taken up a position EBC, or must now enter very fast, perhaps from the left *eisodos*, and come to C on the cue of 184. She can then either be silently dismissed by Lysistrata after 190 or fetch the bottle and bowl when Lysistrata orders them to be produced at 199ff.[13] This brief subscene requires an additional actor, a large shield, and a military costume for less than ten lines. It is not particularly funny today, since it simply depends on racist and sexist humor at the expense of the Thrakian "girl soldier"; cutting it from modern performance is recommended.[14]

* * *

199ff.: When one of the other women—if the slave girl is cut, perhaps one of the two rural Athenians already BR—brings the bottle and bowl to Lysistrata, the women need to form a loose circle with its center at C,[15] and Lysistrata needs to be at the middle of the circle's back segment for dominance. Myrrhine and Kalonike fight for possession of the bowl; Lysistrata induces them to place their hands instead upon the "victim"—the bottle (200). So Kalonike is at her side, holding the bottle with Lysistrata, when she pours the offering; another woman, on the other side of Lysistrata, holds up the bowl. Myrrhine makes a grab for the bowl at 207; Lysistrata firmly reimposes order at 209. Now the women should all be in a close-knit circle, each with one hand on the bowl except Lysistrata, who holds it firmly with two. Especially in a modern theater with a relatively small rake, it is desirable for sight lines that all the women kneel other than Lysistrata, Kalonike, and perhaps the person next to Lysistrata on the other side of Kalonike (for symmetry). Then Kalonike's "breakout"—at the end of 215, where she feels "weak at the knees" and should let go of the rim for a moment, only for Lysistrata to reinstall her hand in its correct position at 217—will be clearly visible to all spectators.

13. If she stays to do this, she must of course not be part of the circle of oath takers but must stand aside.

14. Cf. appendix 1.

15. Revermann (2006, 244) supports this positioning but wrongly follows Rehm's view (1988) that the stage altar was permanently located at C. The center point is frequently needed for actors to take position there for maximum effect (cf., e.g., Ewans 1995, 144, on Agamemnon's entry in Aischylos, *Agamemnon*), and sometimes props need to be placed there (e.g., the sword

Continuing his stream of jibes at women's love of alcohol,[16] Aristophanes makes his heroine behave no better than Myrrhine; as soon as the oath taking is over, Lysistrata makes a grab for a drink (238), only to be restrained by Kalonike. However, the principal characters forget the bowl and bottle as soon as the victorious cries from inside the *skēnē* (made by the female members of the *choros*, who will appear via the left *eisodos* at 319) are heard after 239; it is up to the director to dispose of these objects humorously.

Exit Sequence

A possible improvement on the fairly conservative stage direction printed in the text would be for the Athenian Women (including Myrrhine), the Boiotian, and the Korinthian to exit into the *skēnē* on 245–46; this leaves Kalonike and Lysistrata to complete the dialogue, bid farewell to Lampito (hugs or high fives!), and end the scene alone as they began it.

Significance of the Exit

The women barricade themselves inside the doors of the Akropolis, where, in deference to the virgin goddess who presides over the hill, neither sexual intercourse nor childbearing can take place.[17] Since "doors" was a slang expression for the vagina, the men have both literally and metaphorically to break down the doors if they want to possess their wives' bodies again. In this way Aristophanes uses the threshold of the *skēnē* doors, and the dominance of Lysistrata over who

---

and corpse of Aias in Sophokles; Ewans, with Ley and McCart, 1999, 191ff.), so the altar must have been removable—and removed when not needed in a performance. It is not needed at all in *Lysistrata*, as it is, for example, throughout *TWF* and from scene 5 to the end of *Frogs*.

16. Cf. *TWF* 394, 630ff., and 733ff.

17. Hence the brilliance of the exit stratagem created by the Third Woman at 742ff.

may cross it and when, as a powerful spatial realization of the main theme of the play.[18]

Choros 1

Aristophanes now deploys one of the central and original features of *Lysistrata*—a gender-divided *choros*. The men enter first, played by only twelve of the twenty-four *choros* members.

The dramatic technique needed to convey a long journey is for the travelers to complete a slow circuit of the *orchēstra* perimeter.[19] The entrance to the Akropolis (represented by the *skēnē* doors) is imagined to be a long way away from, and above, the place represented by the mouth of the left *eisodos*, and the choreography for the male *choros* must reflect this distance. They must mime both weariness and the comic difficulties that their old bodies find with climbing the imaginary "steep path" (cf. 287–88) up to the entrance. It takes them from 254 to 307 to get there, passing via ECL, EFC, and ECR.

For the B2 stanzas, they gather together (ECR?) and blow on their torches; they only arrive near the doors, at EBR, as the lyrics end. Then action takes place during the spoken dialogue; they put their logs down near the doors (not precisely in front of them!)[20] and start pouring coals out of the bucket ready to light them.

The Old Women now enter. They do not look at the *skēnē* building, but turn their faces to their left as they panic

18. Cf. Revermann 2006, 246ff. The technique is reminiscent of Klytaimestra's dominance over who shall cross the threshold, when and under what conditions, in Aischylos's *Agamemnon*—a play that Aristophanes clearly knew well (cf. note 21).

19. Cf. *Frogs* scene 1, opening, and Xanthias's circuit of the perimeter while Charon conveys Dionysos across the Styx in his boat (190ff.).

20. The logs must not block the rapid entries of Lysistrata and the Three Women in scene 3.

about the smoke and haze. They scurry round the perimeter, following the imaginary path up which the old men have climbed, right round the front of the *orchēstra*, and only "see" the Old Men thirty lines after they first entered the playing space—at the start of scene 2.

Scene 2

Now the Old Women are approximately EFR; they scuttle to ECR when they see the Old Men. The text indicates that they put their pitchers down there at 358–59, ready for a head-on confrontation, which ensues at once in the BR segment of the *orchēstra*. The women go back to get their pitchers at 370, throw a first shower of water over the men at the end of 381, and launch a second in the middle of 383. After their defeat, the Old Men retreat round to EFL; as the Bureaucrat enters for scene 3, the victorious Old Women traverse the shorter distance to the symmetrical position at EFR. The *choros* is now "parked," ready for the next scene, which is primarily for solo actors.

Scene 3

The Bureaucrat enters for the *agōn*, which in this comedy with no real *parabasis* becomes the most important serious scene. The Policemen should stand just inside the perimeter at EBL, ready for the physical confrontation with the Three Women who subsequently enter from the *skēnē*; this leaves the Bureaucrat with the power positions BC/C/FC to range around during his exposition at 403ff. (which consistently misses the point). It turns out to be the only section of the scene in which he is able to dominate.

Lysistrata now shows that she shares the uncanny ability of Aischylos's Klytaimestra[21] to enter from the *skēnē* precisely when she is needed. It is a stark demonstration of her power, before she has uttered a word in the contest.

The traditional stage direction is for all three of the Women to enter after 438 (or perhaps to enter with Lysistrata at 430, so each of the protagonists has three people ready for physical backup); but we found it more effective to bring in each Woman as needed to stop successive Policemen from trying to grab first Lysistrata then each of their predecessors.[22] Aristophanes could easily have achieved this effect simply by leaving the *skēnē* doors open after Lysistrata enters.

* * *

451ff.: Does the Bureaucrat have extra "troops" at his disposal, apart from the Policemen? If so, they don't do anything, and there is no indication in the text of the presence of more troops apart from the three Policemen who have entered. Nor is it essential that extra women enter to match Lysistrata's stream of rhetorical compound words at 456ff. The entry and subsequent exit of two groups of supernumeraries would slow the action down, at a moment when it needs to be exciting and fast paced. It is therefore better to take 451 as exhorting the Policemen to be brave and re-form; we can then stage a three-against-three confrontation, followed after 460 by an all-in fight, in the BL segment. When the Policemen are on the ground and thoroughly humiliated, Lysistrata calls her three Women off and the Policemen run away, their tails between their legs.

The ensuing addresses to the Bureaucrat by an Old Man and Old Woman (467ff.) give a chance to calm the emotional temperature after the physical confrontation, in readiness for the verbal *agōn*.[23] Then a short stanza (choros 2, stanza A1;

21. *Agamemnon* 587, 851; cf. later *Lys* 1106.
22. So too Sommerstein 1990, 61.
23. NB that Lysistrata, her forces having won, still has the Three Women at her disposal for further physical action, and they make a menacing presence

N.B. 476ff.) and an exhortation to the Bureaucrat from one of the Old Men (484–85) formally introduce the *agōn*.

Like any other Aristophanic *agōn* (e.g., that between Aischylos and Euripides in *Frogs*), this should begin with the two antagonists in equally powerful positions, BCL and BCR or CL and CR; but this *agōn* starts lopsided, as the Bureaucrat does not begin with a set speech but tries to live up to an Old Man's exhortation to "interrogate, do not give in, ask probing questions" (484). And Lysistrata almost immediately puts him on the defensive, so she should be at C around 489ff. By 503 he is ready to resort to violence; in our production, he raised his fist to strike Lysistrata. The interventions of first one and then another Old Woman (505, 515) are designed to pull the Bureaucrat forward, away from the center and toward FR; this allows Lysistrata to dominate during the sequence of three crucial speeches at 507ff. She can circle during the first speech at 507ff. but must be back at C for the climactic speech at 522ff.

* * *

531ff.: The Bureaucrat undergoes his first transformation—into a woman, with veil and basket of wool; during these lines the women need to escort him to a seat in the position of minimum power, which is EFC. (In our production the Old Woman supplied him with a small stool to sit on, as well as his basket.)[24]

Formally, choros 2 stanza A2 introduces the part of the *agōn* in which Lysistrata speaks and the Bureaucrat responds, but she has already won the Bureaucrat's half, so we expect her to dominate completely in this second part. She does indeed; the Bureaucrat's responses are first pompous (559), then simply incredulous (571–72, 574).

---

at the back of the *orchēstra*, while the Bureaucrat is now gender isolated but for the impotent Old Men, who are, of course, more than counterbalanced by the Old Women, who have recently been victorious over them.

24. As noted above, it works well if these props are preset just inside the perimeter, near the *skēnē* doors.

Meanwhile Lysistrata elaborates her program, with the famous simile that the polis is like a knotted skein of wool. An obvious way to direct this is for her to take a skein of wool out of the Bureaucrat's basket at 566. He will have abandoned his humiliating stool and gone back to confront her on 555 or at latest 559, so if he brings his basket with him this is easily achieved.

Lysistrata's program is Aristophanes' program.[25] The first and most important element is getting rid of conspirators and cliques—prophetic words, when performed in January 411—and Lysistrata has already (490) named Peisandros, the future leader of the coup that was to establish the regime of the Four Hundred. The second element is widening the franchise, a theme to which Aristophanes was to return in the *parabasis* of *Frogs*.[26]

Finally Lysistrata completes the scene by returning to the special sufferings of women, a theme already touched on in the first part of the *agōn* (507ff.). 588ff. are a passionate depiction of the different consequences of the war for women and for men. When the Bureaucrat pompously demonstrates his utter indifference to women's suffering with 598, Lysistrata begins his second and final transformation; already costumed as a woman, the Bureaucrat now becomes a corpse, as she places her garland around his neck and two of the other women complete his adornment. He leaves, not to be seen again—and he is not even given the dignity of an unchallenged exit couplet; Lysistrata has the last word in the scene.

Choros 3

At the midpoint of the play, Aristophanes creates a choros whose form resembles that of the *parabasis* which normally occurs here; four danced lyric stanzas (two pairs)

25. See introduction, Comedy and Politics: *Lysistrata*.
26. *Frogs* 686ff. The finale of *Lysistrata* will add the third and least attainable of Aristophanes' ideals: a return to past glory through a joint hegemony of Athens and Sparta, united against the Persians.

are each followed by spoken dialogue between individual *choros* members. In both the A and B sets of stanzas, the Old Men begin with a stanza and a speech, then the Old Women respond with a stanza and a speech of their own. Each A stanza is introduced by a pair of spoken lines.

The Old Men stand up, leave their "parked" position at EFL, and take possession of the left half of the *orchêstra* to perform the first quarter of the choros. They begin by addressing themselves to the situation that the plot has reached; they do not address the city, as the *choros* character normally does in the *parabasis*, on issues of importance. It is not necessary, in this comedy where Lysistrata has recently done just that and will do so again in the finale. And in any case the Old Men rapidly prove that they are in no position to provide useful advice; their repeated accusation (620, 630) that the women are aiming at tyranny is not justified by anything they have seen or heard, and when they claim to be as tough as the tyrannicides of the sixth century, a single threat from one of the women (636) is enough to quash them.

The Old Women now leave their position at EFR and take possession of the entire right half of the *orchêstra*. In A2 and the following spoken lines, they bring choros 3 back toward its proper function; *their* section of the choros is indeed a (mini-)*parabasis* (638–58). They pick up one of Lysistrata's most compelling arguments against the men of Athens—"we've borne you sons"—who've died defending the city (658; cf. 588ff.) The men's contribution, they allege, has by contrast simply been to squander the city's wealth.

First the Old Men (617) and then the Old Women (637) took off their cloaks ready for the action of this ode; now the Old Men take off their shirts as well and call each other to battle stations (B1). The stanza effectively admits that the men cannot reply in rational words to the women's argument. In response, the women threaten to strip for action too (689–90)—even though they do not actually do so[27]—and dare

27. Like the Old Men, they have already taken off their cloaks (637), but in scene 6 they are clearly dressed, while the Old Men are not—pace Dearden

the men to attack them (an offer that the men do *not* take up!). As B2 begins, the two sides are arraigned against each other as for the start of a football match, facing off across the central line EFC-C-EBC.

Choros 3 is punctuated by three threats of a physical attack:

1. 634–35 from the Old Men, which one firm counter-threat (636) is enough to prevent, allowing the women to start their mini-*parabasis*.

2. At 65758 one of the Women makes a threat in the place parallel to the Old Men (at the end of the speech that follows their lyric); the men evade her kick by moving into their second lyric stanza.

3. 681–82: Again the spoken section ends with a threat of violence, and this time it provokes a defiant and powerful counterchallenge from the women. The conflict has now escalated, since in this final quarter delivered by the women, a threat of violence concludes the lyric stanza as well as the subsequent speech. And the men, for all their fine words, do not have the guts to counterattack. Both 694–95 and 704–705 therefore give an opportunity for a vigorous mime in the choreography, which leaves the Old Women in the ascendant and the Old Men scared and defeated. The women should use these two passages to invade the Old Men's half of the *orchēstra*, pursue them back to their normal position EFL, and then return in triumph to *their* normal position EFR, ready for the next scene.

Scene 4

Several of Aristophanes' comedies[28] settle down after the *parabasis* into a sequence where the hero repels several freeloaders, who try to exploit the profits they can see in

---

1967, 167, Sommerstein 1990, 87 and 192, and 2009, 240–41, and Henderson 2000, 361. Aristophanes deliberately (and naturally, given Greek social customs and expectations) made his Old Women more modest than his Old Men.

28. Cf. especially *Acharnians, Birds*.

the hero's "great idea." This scene and the next are an ingenious variant on that traditional sequence; the freeloaders (the four Women and Kinesias) seek not to take advantage of Lysistrata's sex strike but to break it.

A tragic heroine enters the playing space and treads the doleful path from EBC to C, interrogated by a member of the *choros*.[29] But when she drops her pose and comes down to earth with a four-letter word (715), Lysistrata abandons her central position as well as her elevated language, as she rages colloquially against the frailty of the sisterhood and comes forward to address the Old Women. When the individual wives start to try to escape, she strides back toward BC to intercept them. The first one tries to tiptoe toward the L *eisodos* unobserved, but the others more boldly advance toward the center of the *orchēstra* and try to justify their wish to leave. After Lysistrata has refused permission, she needs to "park" each successive delinquent at EBL (or EBR). Then she can deliver the oracle from C, with the women coming forward to gather round her while she reads it. After that they all exeunt back into the *skēnē*.

Choros 4

The banter between the Old Men and the Old Women continues. Once again the Old Men take possession of their dancing space—the left half of the *orchēstra*—first; but the Old Women must move early toward the center line to match them. After each side has sung a short stanza—about two legendary recluses, one who hated and one who loved women—there is a dialogue sequence implying that at least the speakers of 797 and 821 are on or over the borderline.

The two warring sides of the *choros* will be reconciled in choros 5, and a tentative move toward this may perhaps be seen when one of the Old Men wants to kiss one of the Old

29. For the technique (in reverse, the heroine moving from C to the *skēnē* doors), cf. Aischylos, *Agamemnon* 1290ff.

Women at 797. However, he is roundly rebuffed; and since
the Old Men have shed their outer garments (during choros
3), the argument descends at the close of each stanza to pubic
hair. That of the Old Men would be visible under their short
chitons, together with their phalluses, if they dance too vigor-
ously; it is thick and (they hope) black. The Old Women
counter by asserting that their own is neatly trimmed (*without*
showing it; once again the women are, naturally, more deco-
rous than the men). As the next scene begins, the whole *choros*
retreats to "parked" positions EFC and EFR.

Scene 5

Aischylos was the first to use the flat roof of the *skēnē* as
a practicable part of the mise-en-scène; *Agamemnon*, the very
first tragedy to survive dating from after the erection of a
skēnē building, begins with a speech from a Watchman on
the roof of the house of Atreus. Here the roof represents the
parapet of the walls above the entrance to the Akropolis, and
placing the start of scene 5 up there enables Aristophanes to
set up what is going to happen in the Kinesias/Myrrhine
scene before Kinesias arrives in the *orchēstra*, while the actor
is still moving up the left *eisodos*.

Aristophanes now begins to bring his comedy to its
climax by exploiting a logical consequence of his subject
matter, combined with the comic convention that actors
playing men wore a large artificial phallus; from now until
the finale, all the men who appear in the play do so with
massively erect, stiff phalluses, ill concealed by their dis-
tended clothing. Lysistrata provides a prelude to the most
famous cock-teasing scene in all drama by speaking seduc-
tively to Kinesias and helping "to work him up / and get him
on heat" (843–44); her miniscene with Kinesias whets the
audience's appetite for what Myrrhine herself will actually

do to him.[30] At the end of the scene Kinesias offers Lysistrata his erect prick as a bribe, but she clearly disdains this.[31]

Then comes a surprise. Lysistrata promises to call Myrrhine out (864) and leaves Kinesias marooned in agony at the center of the *orchêstra* (865ff.), but instead of coming out to him, Myrrhine extends his torments by reappearing on the *skēnē* roof; only reluctantly (and mock-sententiously, 884) does she agree to come down.[32] When she finally does so, the scene proceeds exactly as scripted by Lysistrata at 839ff.—"make him burn, torment him, / cheat him, make love but not make love, / and give him everything except what we swore we wouldn't." Myrrhine first says she will not lie down with Kinesias but then deliberately spurs him on with "but I'm not saying I don't love you" (905). Then she prevaricates about where they might do it, but suddenly she appears to give in and is apparently prepared to make love in the center of the *orchēstra*, just as if the *choros* was not there (915–16).[33]

As with some other extended comic scenes in Aristophanes, this one begins with verbal humor alone (870–915) and then introduces props (916ff.).[34] After that point, the rest

30. If Aristophanes followed his general practice in earlier comedies, the heroine, having achieved her grand design, should defend it herself (cf. especially *Acharnians, Birds),* but the playwright is treading a fine line here. Lysistrata can certainly tease Kinesias from the battlements, but for this heroine to actually play an extended cock-teasing scene with *her* husband would compromise the dignity and authority she needs for the finale.

31. Sommerstein (1990, 201) and Henderson (2000, 185) suggested that he then throws her up a purse, after 863. This is not necessary.

32. The end of this subsection leaves only three lines for Myrrhine to descend the ladder from the *skēnē* roof and come out through the doors. This timing is very tight, especially if a modern-dress Myrrhine is wearing high heels!

33. This scene of sexual teasing does *not* take place "in the grotto of Pan" as supposed by Revermann 2006, 251. The idea that it should do so is just an offhand suggestion by Kinesias (911), which Myrrhine rejects.

34. Cf. *Lys* scene 4, *Frogs* scene 3, and especially the contest between the tragedians in *Frogs*, which begins with verbal exchanges and later introduces an extra (the castanet-playing "Muse of Euripides," 1305ff.) and a substantial prop (the scales for weighing poetry, 1370ff.).

of the scene proceeds with a sense of pace and comic timing that are a gift to actors, as Myrrhine "remembers" no less than five other "necessary" sex aids to fetch from the *skēnē* before finally producing the climactic, phallic-shaped perfume bottle. Her sudden, final exit follows immediately. After that, his desolation and agony force Kinesias onto the heightened plane of a lyric interaction with the Old Men.[35]

Scene 6

Kinesias now encounters his double—a Spartan Herald who is trying without success to conceal *his* massive erection.[36] In order to do this, the Herald turns away from Kinesias at 986 (addressing the Old Men or Women in 988); but Kinesias comes round him and confronts him at 990. Then the Herald tells his story, walking around hunched up to illustrate 1003–1004. At the completion of the dialogue, the two characters leave in opposite directions.

After scene 2, the confrontation between the Old Men and the Old Women has been conducted primarily in lyric meters. Aristophanes therefore uses the "cooler" medium of dialogue to dramatize their reconciliation (which is placed here to prefigure the larger reconciliation between warring states that will resolve the action of the play). Once again, props are key symbols of what is taking place. The first one is visible to the audience—the shirt that the Old Woman picks up and puts back on the Old Man (followed during the subsequent dialogue by some of the other Old Women, so that all the Old Men are fully dressed again for *choros* 5).

35. This lyric section, danced in the front half of the *orchēstra*, provides "cover" for stagehands to quickly remove the bed, mattress, and other props back into the *skēnē*.

36. Against the traditional view that this scene was played not by Kinesias but by an Athenian official, cf. Henderson 1987, 185.

So too is the ring, but the insect and the tears were, of course, left to the audience's imagination.

Choros 5

The *choros* now promise to abandon one of their core functions in comedy for the remainder of this play; there will be no more abuse of their fellow citizens (1043–45). And they keep their promise.

This first performance by the *choros* as a united whole consists of a simple joke repeated with variation: the Old Men, and then the Old Women, appear to promise rich rewards to the audience—but then present a compelling obstacle in the last line of each stanza. Aristophanes must have thought that his audience would be fond of this trope, because he repeats it again in choros 6. In modern performance it is hard to make it really funny enough to sustain two choroses.

In performance both choros 5 and choros 6 require the entire *choros* to suddenly adopt a formation that takes possession of the entire *orchēstra*, dance two stanzas from this position, and then retreat back to the front perimeter.

Scene 7

Scene 7 begins with dialogues between individual *choros* members and the two sets of ambassadors; during this, the other *choros* members move away from the center. These two dialogues take place at opposite sides of the *orchēstra*; one group from the *choros* engages with the Spartans R/BR as they arrive; another group then engages with the Athenians L/BL. The Old Men and Old Women are now intermingled, so Aristophanes writes choral dialogue first with the Spartans and then with the Athenians that can best be performed by

a combination of *choros* characters of both genders. 1072ff. are
clearly a woman's lines, while the sympathetic 1089 is best
played by a fellow male. So 1072ff. and 1082ff., the announce-
ment speeches, should be assigned, as in this script, to two
Old Women. Similarly, 1078–79 and 1088–89 should be
assigned to two Old Men.

The whole *choros*, persons of both sexes intermingled
from here to the end, completes the process of retreat to
EFL/C/R after 1094. The Spartans and the Athenians meet
and greet each other around C at 1097. They determine to
call out Lysistrata—but once again (cf. 430) Aristophanes'
heroine shows her Klytaimestra-like ability to enter precisely
when she is needed.

Events are moving very fast in this scene, and it is fascinating to see that Aristophanes now chooses to slow them
down slightly; one of the Old Women detaches herself from
the *choros* and makes a verbose and comical salutation to
Lysistrata.[37] This allows a sufficient pause between Lysistrata's own entry and the comedy's climactic surprise—the
personification, as a naked girl, of the spirit of Reconciliation, whom the Athenians have just invoked (1004). They
said that only Lysistrata could bring them Reconciliation,
and nine lines later she *literally* does just that.[38]

Lysistrata's entry from the *skēnē* upstaged both the
Spartan and the Athenian ambassadors; accordingly, her
entry obliged them to move apart in deference to her, considerably away from the center line, to BR and BL respectively. Reconciliation takes up a position next to Lysistrata
at BC, and Lysistrata immediately orders her to bring the
ambassadors closer to her, setting the Spartans close beside

37. Revermann (2006, 241) supposes that this salutation could "perhaps more
attractively" be spoken by one Old Man and one Old Woman in unison. Having
experimented with unison speaking in Greek drama, I doubt this very much.

38. For the role of Reconciliation and how to play it in a modern production,
see introduction, Performance.

her on her right and the Athenians a little further away on her left (by 1123).

The position at BC between the two embassies is very good for Reconciliation—every line that the ambassadors speak from here to 1174 is based on a direct and close contemplation of her sexual assets; but it is not so good for Lysistrata, who has serious things to say to the ambassadors and needs space, not confinement, to say them. So she should break away forward down the center line at 1124 and then turn back at C on 1128 to face both groups when she delivers her rebuke.[39] She clearly then moves a little R (i.e., to her left), toward the Spartans, at 1137, and a little L (to her right), toward the Athenians, at 1149.

The cue to take her back nearer to the ambassadors is 1159ff., in which her questions indicate her frustration. She needs to be directly in front of Reconciliation, facing both pairs of ambassadors, during the immediately following sequence, in which she negotiates with each side in turn.

When the reconciliation is achieved, Lysistrata needs on and after 1175 to be back between the ambassadors BC, facing forward and addressing both pairs as at the start of the scene. The most effective way to achieve this is to make Reconciliation depart instantly the moment Lysistrata no longer requires her services, that is, after 1173–74, in which the ambassadors are effectively agreed and are about to commit sexual assault on Reconciliation from front and rear. Reconciliation should therefore retreat hastily into the *skēnē* to avoid this undesirable consummation, and Lysistrata

---

39. This is one of several scenes in tragedy and comedy that can only be effectively played if the director has confidence that in the Greek theater shape a principal character can turn his or her back to a large part of the audience, provided that (1) the character is in a position of power, and (2) the audience can see the faces (or masks) of the characters whom she is addressing and so can relate to the dialogue. The *skēnē* facade acts as a sounding board to direct the voice back to the audience in the *theatron*. Cf., e.g., Sophokles *Antigone*, 441ff., with notes at Ewans, with Ley and McCart, 1999, 219.

then takes up Reconciliation's previous position BC, now facing forward.[40]

The rest of the scene plays itself. Note that the joyful exit of the reconciled Ambassadors is so hasty that Lysistrata has to go into the *skēnē* last; her solemn exit, closing the scene, can be most effective.

Choros 6

Once again, as in choros 5, the *choros* rapidly possess the center of the playing space and deliver two stanzas; in this case the first is more suited to delivery by a woman/the old women, the second to a man/the old men. They then retreat to the perimeter during the banter that follows.

Finale

The finale opens with an episode that includes a threatened assault on some slaves (it is unclear whose slaves they are and when they came on); Aristophanes freely admits (1218–20) that this was an old and tired comic routine. Today it is likely to be simply offensive, since we do not share the Athenian assumption that slaves deserved any suffering that free men chose to inflict upon them. Cutting two sets of lines here can dispose of a section of the play that it is hard to make funny for a modern audience, dispenses with the need for two to three extras to play the slaves, and moves us on more swiftly into the main section of the finale. The opening episode then simply consists of the two Athenians, rolling drunk, staggering to the center full of bonhomie.

40. Editors and commentators have tended to leave Reconciliation on until 1188, not realizing how important it is for Lysistrata to regain the BC position for herself alone after 1174, when Reconciliation has completed her task (N.B. the wording of 1175).

The first Spartan Ambassador joins them, and here Aristophanes would have considerably surprised his audience. Given the recurrent human habit of demonizing the culture of our opponents, it is unlikely that much Spartan art, music, or dance was on display at Athens during the Peloponnesian War. In a brilliant stroke, which would have truly impressed the Athenian audience with the depth of the reconciliation and peace that have now been achieved in the play, Aristophanes (and/or his producer, Kallistratos) trained one of their lead actors to sing Spartan songs and lead the dance. Every word of the Ambassador's two songs was composed in the Doric dialect spoken at Sparta, and the people who enter just before 1246 all dance in Lakonian style.[41] This is like scheduling a Wagner concert in England during the Second World War!

Lysistrata should enter dramatically for 1273, and she should declaim the final spoken words of the play. It has been her play, and she has been the one who admonished both the Spartans and the Athenians. It is right that she arranges the dancers in couples for the final dance; and she—the woman who has demonstrated more political ability (by far) than any man in this play—should deliver the final admonition: "Let us make sure / we never make the same mistakes again" (1277–78).[42]

Now the *choros* invoke the gods and perform the exit song (1279–93). 1291–93 are unmistakably "closing lines"— but as M. Neuburg correctly perceived,[43] the general exodus is halted by the first Athenian Ambassador's drunken call

41. Some editions do not bring the couples on until after 1272, so the Spartan Ambassador can have a solo song and dance from 1246 to 1272. It is, however, vastly preferable to bring them on earlier. Then Lysistrata can make a powerful entry, at 1273, alone—or perhaps attended by her two leading fellow conspirators, Kalonike and Myrrhine—rather than as part of a large crowd.

42. Further arguments in favor of Lysistrata as the speaker will be found at Sommerstein 1990, 221–22, and 2009, 244–46 and 252–53. The only other candidate, the first Athenian Ambassador, is at this stage too drunk to speak these powerful lines. (But contra Henderson 1987, 214, and 2000, 437).

43. Neuburg 1992, 85–88.

for an encore. Aristophanes decided to break the exit convention and give the audience one more surprise, with a
second song from his gifted actor who could perform Spartan
monody. This stirring encore concludes the play.[44]

44. Revermann (2006, 257ff.) reports a conjecture by Taplin (1993, 98 note
7) that this encore was added for a performance in a Spartan colony in Sicily
or southern Italy in the fourth century. This is obviously unprovable, and I
think it is unlikely. The sheer extent of Lysistrata's triumph is shown in this
closing part of the *kōmos* by the spectacle of Athenian characters willingly joining
in Spartan song and dance.

The Women's Festival

Acting Style, Euripides

There are two complementary sides to Euripides' persona: the sophist, through whom Aristophanes parodies contemporary movements in philosophy (15ff.), and the tragedian.[1] Most of the role is to be acted as a parody of a professional tragedian, able to slip into role and ham it up whenever the language becomes quasi tragic. For example, the actor must convey his character's melodramatic style with over-the-top movements and gestures (e.g., 71ff.); but the fact that this is all a performance is given away at 209ff., where Euripides is almost groveling on the floor in agony with 209 and 211 but recovers instantly at 213. This subsection, like 71ff., requires the ability to change form and style instantly, which is typical of several of Aristophanes' leading roles.[2]

In the second half of the play, Euripides' role is to parody two of his own recent tragic heroes. This translation does not resort to the hackneyed device of using obvious archaisms, let alone pseudo–Shakespearian English, to represent the Euripidean verses, and parodistic adaptations of them, in the Menelaos and Perseus episodes. The two plays that Aristophanes parodies, *Helen* and *Andromeda*, had both been produced the previous year, and the idiom of Euripidean tragedy was as contemporary as that of Aristophanic comedy, making due allowance for the differences between the two media. So I have provided an elevated but still contemporary idiom for the tragic and quasi-tragic passages of text. In the

1. Cf. Silk 2000, 242–43.
2. Cf. Lysistrata (above, Theatrical Commentary, Acting Style: Lysistrata), and especially Dikaiopolis in *Acharnians*.

first production my very talented "Euripides," decked out in rags and bits of seaweed, found that this text enabled him to provide an effective, over-the-top impersonation of a tragic hero lost at sea and dumbfounded by meeting his wife in Egypt. A few props—a winged helmet and sandals, a heroic costume and cape—enable Perseus's few lines to be delivered in a similarly mock-heroic manner. The actor must then be able to remind us of the scheming, ingenious Euripides for whom the In-Law hoped (271) with the five lines in his own character at the conclusion of the scene (1128ff.).

Euripides' final impersonation is a comic one. The best way to play scene 6 is for Euripides to come on carrying a long cloak and a longhaired grey wig (plus optional walking stick). He makes his deal with the Women in character as Euripides and then puts on the cloak and wig after 1172. A senile, high-pitched delivery follows, which is dropped instantly after 1201.

Acting Style, In-Law

This is one of the most challenging roles in Aristophanes' surviving comedies; the In-Law has some of the funniest lines and finds himself caught in some of the most bizarre situations of any Aristophanic hero. He begins as Aristophanes' ideal frank-speaking man in the street (cf. esp. Dikaiopolis in *Acharnians*). He is not game to abuse his relative Euripides openly (even though what the playwright says is quite beyond his understanding), but he is both willing and able to puncture the pretensions of the Servant with his interventions at 45ff., which become obscene at 50 (but note the subtle retreat from obscenity to delicate parody with "the windless air," at 52). Agathon himself naturally suffers even more of the same treatment (130ff. and esp. 200–201—but notice the generous gesture at 206–207).

The actor must be capable of a sustained falsetto once he has been costumed as a woman. This could start with "I will do my best" at 268 and is required throughout the festival assembly scene, especially in his long speech at 466ff. However, he could well anticipate the moment when his true gender is revealed (650) by dropping back into the male register for his asides at 604–605. Another opportunity for the audience to be reminded that the In-Law is playing a role (with difficulty) is for him to copy Mika and clear his throat before the big speech—but first cough low like a man and only suddenly recover the female character he is supposed to be playing, repeating the cough falsetto. There should also be much gawkiness in his physical impersonation of a woman (which must convey great effort to do, e.g., the correct pelvic swing, but with little success). As for his female costume, a fine line must be drawn. The In-Law's disguise must be far from convincing for the audience—though, comically, it *is* apparently good enough to deceive the women at the festival completely, until he fails to answer Kritylla's questions (628ff.).

He resumes a female voice at 855ff., for the role of Helen, and only loses it at 914 (together with his composure). Then the Andromeda monologue (1015ff.) involves a complex interplay between "in-character" monody as the unfortunate virgin and lapses into his own character as an old man chained to the plank. To assist the actor, these passages are marked **A** for Andromeda and **I** for In-Law in this script.

The Echo scene begins with the In-Law in character as Andromeda, but his exasperation with Echo leads him to lapse at 1073. The rest of the part is straightforward.

Presets

A central altar was not a permanent feature in the *orchēstra*.[3] Most surviving tragedies and comedies do not need

3. Pace Rehm 1988.

one, and it is invaluable for an actor to be able to stand at
the exact C position, since it is the point of focus, and therefore of dominance, in the Greek playing space. However,
when there is an altar in a play, the action frequently centers
around it (cf., e.g., Euripides' *Andromache, Helen, Herakles,
Suppliants*), and the central position is therefore normally
the right place for it.[4] This is also the case in *The Women's
Festival*. A knife for 679ff. and votive tablets for 773ff. need
to be preset behind the altar.

Change of Scene

The location for scene 1 is in front of Agathon's house;
at 39ff. the Servant emerges from what has been established
as Agathon's door and uses the altar, so that it represents
an altar in front of Agathon's house. The *skēnē* building
continues to represent Agathon's house until 265. There is a
substantial lapse of time before the *skēnē* building is used
after the change of scene; after 730, it represents an uniden-
tified building in the festival precinct. Meanwhile the location
has been changed by the normal Aristophanic method—the
In-Law circles around the *orchēstra* perimeter during 279ff.[5]
This sequence is quite brief; the scene has changed from in
front of Agathon's house to the festival precinct by 286ff.,
when the In-Law delivers a prayer to the two goddesses of
the festival, which is best delivered from C, immediately
behind the altar. In this way the altar is immediately rede-
fined as part of the new scene, at the Thesmophoria; and
this impression can be cemented by centering around it the
choreography for the invocations to the gods in choros 1. This
then prepares for the intensive use of the altar, in parodies of

4. An exception is Sophokles' *Oidipous the King*, in which the altar plays a
less central role and is therefore better placed at FC. Cf. McCart's note at Ewans,
with Ley and McCart 1999, 269.

5. Cf. the opening scene of *Frogs* and *Acharnians* 175ff.

the suppliant-refuge scenes from *Telephos* and *Helen*, after the In-Law seizes Mika's "baby" from Mania at 688.

Scene 1

The Warm-up

Two travelers arrive via the left *eisodos*, the second weary and limping in one leg (25). The opening parody of sophistry includes a pretentious speech from Euripides at 14ff.; its style is best brought out in performance by an expansive circling movement in the *orchêstra*. Then the focus turns to the *skēnē* door (26ff.). This dialogue needs to be played not directly in front of the door but beside it (i.e., BL/EBL), both to give space for gestures toward the door during the dialogue, and also so the Servant does not collide with Euripides and the In-Law as he enters.

The Servant

The In-Law and Euripides retreat to the mouth of the L *eisodos*, sheltering behind the retaining wall, which holds up the end of the theatron.[6] The Servant advances to C, bearing burning frankincense and myrtle twigs, which he places on the altar before beginning his invocation. He should be ornately, almost ridiculously costumed—but as a man, so as not to upstage Agathon.

---

6. This strategy was used once in the surviving plays by each tragic play-wright—Aischylos, *Libation Bearers* 10ff.; Euripides, *Elektra* 107ff.; and Sophokles, *Oidipous at Kolonos* 111ff. (where, however, the retreat is into the *skēnē* building). Pace Austin and Olson 2004, 64, and Olson 2002, 141, I think it unlikely that the whole *choros* retreated into the *eisodos* at *Acharnians* 239ff., but there are parallels in Aristophanes at *Peace* 232ff., where Trygaios hides from War, and at the end of *Frogs* scene 2, where Dionysos and Xanthias conceal themselves behind the retaining wall as the procession of Initiates arrives.

As in the parallel scene in *Frogs,* the two half-concealed characters step back into the *orchēstra* to comment, once they have the sense of what the newly arrived character is saying. The In-Law objects to the Servant's pretentious poetic language (which is designed as a foretaste of his master's lyric performance). The Servant ignores the first two interjections, notices the third ("who spoke?," 51) but resumes anyway, and is only finally stopped by "—and sucks some cocks" (57). He moves a little left toward the In-Law on 58, but the In-Law closes in on him, adding action to words as he turns the Servant around and mimes buggering him. The Servant gets free with difficulty, and Euripides comes over to stand between them.

The Plot Revealed (in Part)

The moment the Servant has gone inside, Euripides launches into totally over-the-top tragic despair, collapsing at least to his knees at 71. The melodramatic action continues, and Euripides needs to move energetically to convey his extreme agitation during much of the dialogue down to 84. Only then does he settle down, and indeed there is a total contrast to what has gone before; the final mood is upbeat.

Agathon

The In-Law and Euripides once again retreat to the side as the *skēnē* doors are opened and Agathon is wheeled out on the *ekkuklēma* to BC. Here begins the comedy's complex sequence of different ways in which men impersonate women:

1. Agathon: A male actor plays a man who impersonates women effectively (though rather extravagantly), because he wants to feel like a female to help write his plays—and also because he dresses up as a woman to go out at night, sexually available to anyone (200–201, 206).

2. The In–Law: A male actor plays a man who attempts to impersonate a woman, but precariously, incompetently, and with lapses, which constantly remind the audience that he is indeed male (and elderly).

3. Kritylla, Mika, Mania, Garland-Seller, *Choros*, Fawn: In the original production male actors took these parts, directly impersonating women with great competence. Since credibility is crucial, in modern performance it is normal for actresses to take these roles, because modern audiences are not accustomed to effective illusionist, noncamp impersonation of women by men.[7]

4. The Queen (Kleisthenes): A man plays the role of a man who, as a passive homosexual, chooses to dress in female clothes. This must be an extravagant, high-camp transvestite performance.

The nuances of these four different kinds of impersonation of females need to be brought out by costume and acting style. In scene 1, Agathon must look like a male who has effectively transformed himself into an imitation of a woman—but a rather over-the-top one; his wig, dress, and makeup should at least partially justify the In-Law's accusation that he looks like Kyrene the whore (98). He must be clean shaven (legs as well, if visible beneath his dress), fully made up with a wig, and wearing femininely styled (but large, n.b. 263) sandals.

Agathon's solo is the first of Aristophanes' brilliant parodies of tragedy in *The Women's Festival*. The actor's performance needs to be camped up and extremely effeminate, with the high degree of emotional involvement in the alternate roles of soloist and *choros* ("immersion") that we soon discover is Agathon's artistic credo (149).[8] In our production,

---

7. Though in recent years there have been successful all-male productions of Shakespeare, who in his own productions, like Aristophanes, used only male actors.

8. Euripides claims this was his practice as well, when he was young (174–75), and in *Acharnians* he is displayed composing in a beggar's rags—presumably those of the role he is working on (*Ach* 410ff.). This scene hints

we made comic business out of Agathon's need to change roles from soloist to *choros* and back again, and he became more and more exhausted as his performance progressed, until at the end he collapsed on the floor.

The In-Law inspects the exhausted performer with disdain, noting that he fails to be either male or female—in particular, he apparently lacks a phallus.[9] Agathon rises above the abuse and returns to his couch during 146ff.; this enables Euripides to kneel before him in supplication at 179 (but he quits the suppliant posture and tone suddenly at 185). His appeals are useless; Agathon has a touch of bitchiness about him (as well as sententiousness)—see 195ff., which must be delivered nastily enough to at least partially justify the In-Law's furious outburst at 200.

When Agathon refuses, the In-Law consents to do what Euripides wants. Note how the major comic absurdity of the play—the fantasy idea that underlies the rest of the plot (that the In-Law can impersonate a woman as well as Agathon could)—is simply introduced in a couple of lines and taken for granted (211–13) from then onward. At Euripides' bidding, the In-Law strips naked—and in modern productions, where the ancient comic convention that all actors playing male parts should wear visible phalluses is not elsewhere being followed, this should be the moment to shock and/or titillate the audience (in our production a splendid purple fake penis with a red tip was revealed).

The shaving scene does not take place at the end of Agathon's couch,[10] but with the In-Law seated on the altar.

---

toward the role immersion that Euripides himself will adopt as Menelaos and Perseus in the second half of the play. Though Aristophanes enjoys making fun of it by comic exaggeration, Agathon's method of creating female roles is not too far removed from that recommended seriously by Aristotle himself; see *Poetics* chap. 17, 55a29ff.

9. This would not have been obvious in the original production, since Agathon is wearing a female dress, which would cover the phallus normally worn by actors playing male roles. Perhaps at 172 the In-Law lifts Agathon's dress to see if he can find out whether he has castrated himself.

10. Austin and Olson 2004, 167.

This makes it much easier for Euripides to shave first one cheek and then the other, as well as making sense of the script's requirement for successive props to be *fetched* from Agathon, whose couch is BC. The absolutely central position also highlights the indignity of the treatment, so for the singeing the In-Law should stand—and bend over—just to one side of the altar. Euripides fetches first the mirror, then the belt and wig; the In-Law gets the scarf and sandals himself; and Agathon is wheeled back into the *skēnē*.

The Plot (continued)

The In-Law experiments with his costume, posture, and walk and (I strongly suggest) tries out his falsetto for the first time at "I will do my best" (268). Now Aristophanes reveals how the plot of the second half of the comedy will be generated. The In-Law makes Euripides swear to rescue him "with all your skill" (271), and the importance of this oath is emphasized both by one more glance back to Euripides the sophist (when he tries to swear by the Ether) and by one to the danger of false oaths; and the In-Law refers at 275–76 to the infamous defense of perjury in Euripides' *Hippolytos* (612)—which Aristophanes was to mock twice more, in *Frogs*.[11]

The Scene Changes

The women are now seen in the distance coming from the city (i.e., via the left *eisodos*), so Euripides exits right to avoid them. In the original production, unless five actors were used (which is unlikely), Actor 2 would have had to change mask and costume quickly in order to reenter from the opposite direction as the Garland-Seller. This would have

11. At *Frogs* 101–102, where the line is very loosely and clumsily paraphrased over two lines, and when Dionysos makes his climactic decision to change his mind and take Aischylos instead of Euripides back to Athens (1471).

been difficult but not impossible, as it would be in character for the Garland-Seller to be late.[12]

The In-Law circles the *orchēstra*, followed by an imaginary slave, and makes his way to just behind the central altar before delivering 286. The circling, together with the entry of the *choros*, creates the change of scene to the sacred site of the festival of the Thesmophoria. The women should enter L and divide into two groups, which process counterclockwise and clockwise around the perimeter until they reach their positions, spaced around the perimeter from EBL via EFC to EBR. The future solo speakers, Mika and the Garland-Seller, should be intermixed with choros members—and at 292 the In-Law finds himself a place in the circle as well.

In our production we found it useful for a stagehand to set a chair near the perimeter BR, during the arrival of the women. It gave Kritylla a place to retreat to, as chairperson, during the women's speeches; and it could be used by the Policeman to sleep in, during scenes 5 and 6, rather than the mat specified at 1007. Its great advantage then is that Fawn can dance a highly erotic lap dance for the Policeman in scene 6, if he is seated in a chair rather than on a mat.

Kritylla

The high priestess is not necessarily old—896 could be simple comic abuse, and she still enjoys the sight of a handsome penis (644). It is better for her to be middle aged, an executive type who takes her role as high priestess and chairperson very seriously. She has only one line designed to get a laugh (644), and her role is otherwise that of the "straight man" (or in this case woman)—especially in the *Helen* parody in scene 4, where she gets "cast" as Theonoe and sent up mercilessly.

---

12. I disagree completely with the allocation of roles proposed by Austin and Olsen (2004), 150, 190–91, and 256–57. In their edition the crucial role of the Priestess and chair of the assembly, which I allocate (following Sommerstein 2001) to Kritylla, is given to a "choros leader/spokesperson" (against this concept

Choros 1

This choros introduces a startling feature of the play.
Unlike in, for example, *Lysistrata*, where the choroses are an
active part of the fun, Aristophanes writes generally solemn
and serious lyrics for the choroses in this play, many of
them—as here—invocations to the gods whose tone would
not be inappropriate in a real religious context. I believe he
made this choice because the extremes of cross-dressing, slapstick, bawdy, and parody in the scenes of this play demand
contrasting points of rest in the choroses that separate them.
We opted for simple but dignified choreography for the two
parts of this choros, accompanied by solemn (Spanish classical) music, creating a mood in total contrast to the farcical
episodes of scene 1.

Scene 2

From 295 onward, the scene is a parody of the Athenian assembly. One part of the humor is highly sexist; to the
Athenian male audience, the very idea of women having a
Council with a president, secretary, motions, and speeches
(372ff.) would have seemed absurd.

This aspect of the humor cannot be translated to a
modern Western culture. However, modern audiences can
delight in the comic world that Aristophanes rapidly establishes, when Kritylla advances to just behind the altar to

---

of one choros spokesperson, cf. Ewans 1995, xxiii–iv). They believe that the
person who speaks 893–94 cannot have been present when the In-Law was
stripped, and they assign to "Kritylla" the role of the Garland-Seller, imagining
rather implausibly that she has come back to the festival again, after plaiting her
garlands, to guard the In-Law during the Helen parody scene. I vastly prefer
Sommerstein's role allocation, which gives Kritylla a real and coherent part as
the priestess who conducts the assembly and also does not envisage an implausible return by the Garland-Seller. The "inconsistency" of 893–94 is a simple
illogicality of a kind frequent in Aristophanes; 862–63 show that Kritylla *was*
present when the In-Law was discovered to be a man.

perform the invocation (331ff.). In the world of this play, negotiating with Euripides (which the women eventually actually do, in scene 6) is as dire a crime as negotiating with the Persians (336–67). This was a serious political issue at the time, since Peisandros and other right-wing politicians had recently set off east to do just that, and soon after the performance of this play, despite failing to come to terms with the Persians, they did in fact "set up a dictatorship" (339).[13] So Aristophanes here combines allusions to the most serious political issues of the time with the comic theme of the next part of the play, which is now defined as "what we should do / to make Euripides suffer, since we all think / he's done wrong" (377–79).

The speeches of Mika and the In-Law are designed as the thesis and response of an *agōn*, with the Garland-Seller's short speech designed as an interlude, a "breather" between the two long ones. Mika lists a large number of increasingly absurd slanders that Euripides has made against women, as well as their consequences; the In-Law responds by trying to demonstrate all the thousands of female tricks that Euripides *does not* know—and he succeeds in this far too well for his own good!

Each speaker takes the garland from Kritylla (who then retreats to the perimeter, in our production sitting in a chair). Following that, the speaker moves to just behind the central altar to begin her/his speech. However, narratives as long as those of Mika and the In-Law cannot be delivered from a static position in Greek drama; the three-sided performance space positively invites movement. Since the assembled women are spaced around the perimeter, it makes sense for the speakers to move first to near one of them and then onward, circling to address others as the rhetoric of the speech unfolds. So, for example, in Mika's part we found a point of

13. Cf. introduction, Comedy and Politics: *The Women's Festival.*

departure from C at 389; then she circled, addressing individual members of the *choros*. We brought her back to the center
for 410–17, and she had further movements, round a smaller
segment of the circle of women, during the storage-room narrative from 418. She must be back at the center for the close,
428ff. At the end of the speech, she returns the garland to
Kritylla and goes back to her own place on the perimeter.

The three post-speech commentaries which comprise
choros 2 are best played in modern performance by solo
choros members; each should detach herself from the perimeter and dance briefly to near the center of the playing space
while delivering her stanza. She should then retreat back to
her place as the second and third speakers cross to the rear to
take the garland from Kritylla and then advance to the center.

The Garland-Seller is an honest "working woman" type
(however, her claim that Euripides' atheism has cut her sales
by over 50 percent is somewhat undermined by the bulk
order that she leaves to fulfill).[14] Like the other speakers, she
has a "take-off point" built into the speech, after which she
should leave the center and engage with the women of the
assembly; in her case this is after line 446. She has a two-line
rhetorical conclusion (455–56), followed by a two-line exit
declaration (457–58).

The In-Law's movements are more complex, as befits a
complex and virtuoso speech. 471–72 are well performed if
he makes an early departure from the altar at this point, as
this is the first idea he wants to "sell" to his audience; but
the full "break-out"—his attempt to engage with the whole
of the audience of women by going to them and circling—is
best delayed until 476 or 477. In the subsequent narrative, the
In-Law needs vigorous gestures to bring the scene in "her"
story alive; in our production the In-Law broke away from
addressing the assembly by the middle of 487 and knelt head

14. Pace Austin and Olson 2004, 194.

down, leaning on the altar, at 488–89 to illustrate the position in which "her" lover fucked "her." The blasphemy of using the onstage altar matches the blasphemy in the narrative, where "she" has sex beside the altar of Apollo, clutching at his sacred laurel bush.

The actor playing Mika had three times to impersonate a male voice (403–404, 406, 413). If this is done in a modern production by an actress lowering her own voice as much as possible, there can be great comic effect in the In-Law's speech if he uses his real male timbre for the husband in 482 and 484, completely discarding the falsetto in which the remainder of the speech is delivered and outdoing Mika in credible "impersonation of a male." The real audience in the *theatron* will enjoy this, and Aristophanes has already established the comic convention that despite the poor quality of his physical impersonation of a woman, the *orchēstra* audience of women do not have the slightest idea that the In-Law is not a real woman until Kritylla interrogates him at 627ff. So there is no dramatic plausibility to be lost, if the husband's words are given a full masculine intonation.

Another important aspect of the In-Law's speech is the style of delivery. Mika should have been played as a fully prepared speaker, who has all her case studies and examples at her fingertips; she must be just as good at public speaking as the Women say she is at 433ff. For maximum contrast, the In-Law should be played as an improviser, desperately trying to think up example after example, until he finally hits upon the imported baby story at 502. This gives him a clear run to the end of the speech—but he gets carried away by the momentum of his narrative (the climax is the croaking, evil voice for the old crone at 514ff., which must be superbly impersonated)—and thereby irrevocably compromises his position with the women.

One of the *choros* expresses her outrage in the third and final commentary stanza; Mika then decides it is time for action. She moves in toward the center to speak 533ff., addressing the women (she is better positioned for this address in front of the altar rather than behind, to indicate that this is an informal speech), and then, when she gets no volunteers from her rather spineless audience, she heads straight across the center of the *orchêstra* toward the In-Law, followed by her slave Mania.[15]

Then the pursuit begins. Mika reaches the In-Law at 543, and the comic potential of the next section depends on the In-Law's retreating around the rear perimeter of the *orchêstra* in fear of the physical menace of Mika, while still uttering verbal defiance, which of course makes Mika even angrier. The pursuit probably ends around EFL, with Mika and the In-Law about to come to blows.[16]

The Queen (Kleisthenes)

Aristophanes now interrupts the climax he does not want (a girlie fistfight), and relaxes the tension for a few moments with The Queen's high-camp speech before proceeding right through to the even greater climax that he does want (the In-Law stripped naked and exposed as a man).

Kritylla and The Queen confer near C; when they agree to search for the impostor, the In-Law starts to tiptoe as "invisibly" as possible around the perimeter from where his fistfight with Mika was about to happen (FL), round past FC, toward the right *eisodos*. Like all "asides" in Greek drama, his cries for help, while The Queen is busying himself with Mika and Mania, (603–604) are addressed to the real audience in the *theatron,* so they can perhaps be delivered in an all-male voice for added effect. None of the women in the *orchêstra* are listening to him; they are all concentrating on The Queen's interrogation of Mika and Mania.

---

15. This section works best if, after their individual speeches, Mika and the In-Law have returned to positions that are opposite each other across the *orchêstra*—in our production Mika was at ECL, the In-Law at ECR on 531.

16. Mania should follow Mika throughout this section, looking as menacing as is possible for a woman carrying a "babe in arms."

Then (610) The Queen spots the In-Law (who has maybe got as far round as ECR) and takes a shortcut across the center to examine him there. Staying CR, The Queen allows the In-Law the "privacy" of going behind the retaining wall into the mouth of the R *eisodos* to pee but soon hauls him back into the playing space, dragging him at 618ff. to where Kritylla is waiting, around C, ready for the climax of this scene: the discovery.

Kritylla banishes The Queen to the rear perimeter at 627,[17] but she calls him back as soon as her questions have exposed the In-Law. The ideal place for the wonderful slapstick in 636–47 is near to or just in front of C, so as many as possible of the spectators, both in the *orchēstra* and in the audience, can see the lead actor's virtuoso manipulation of his artificial phallus as Kritylla and The Queen circle around him.[18]

Choros 3 (part one)

The *choros* members keep the mood of the play upbeat after this memorable discovery sequence, which concludes the assembly (in some disarray). They perform the next dance with lit torches, cloaks off, and skirts hitched up. It is a circular dance, and stanza A1 becomes more and more intense as it unfolds. The increasing frenzy enacted here (and paralleled in the A2 stanza at 707ff.) should prefigure

17. This is the only part of the *orchēstra* not occupied by the assembled women.

18. Note, however, that the dialogue is carefully written so that it is obvious from the text alone where the phallus is at any given time. Aristophanes takes this precaution whenever detailed action is called for in his plays; it allows those spectators to follow the action who are either too far away to see clearly (i.e., in the upper rear parts of the *theatron*) or too near (some seats in the front few rows would have their view blocked either by members of the *choros* or by the circling movements of Kritylla and The Queen, as they move between positions in front of and behind the In-Law).

that of their bakchic dance in the B and C stanzas of choros 5 (970ff.); in our production we used the same music.

Action!

Now Aristophanes embarks on his first parody of Euripidean tragedy in *The Women's Festival*: the In-Law follows the precedent of Telephos,[19] who seized the baby Orestes to improve his bargaining position with the Greeks; races from the altar to Mania; and returns clutching the "baby." Mika rapidly approaches the altar and kneels as suppliant, and she and the In-Law go into high paratragic mode.

Choros 3 (part two)

Now for a surprise. The matching A2 stanza of choros 3 is not just a commentary on the situation sung by the Women alone; instead, it raises the tension still further by being a lyric interplay between the Women, the In-Law, and Mika, in which the Women should circle round the In-Law and end by surrounding him menacingly.

Scene 3

The humor is now raised a further two degrees in intensity; first, while Mika and Mania go off to gather sticks to burn and force him off the altar, the In-Law strips the "baby girl"—and reveals a wine bladder (complete, in the original, with "tiny Persian boots," as seen on the famous Apulian bell krater that illustrates this scene). This discovery gives him the chance for a typically Aristophanic denunciation of

19. Aristophanes had already sent up *Telephos* in *Acharnians* (331ff., "child"-hostage scene, and 409ff., the rags and other accessories of Telephos).

women as sex-mad piss pots, before the rapid reentry of
Mika and Mania.

The In-Law must re-cover the wine bladder, or otherwise conceal it from Mika, for a couple of moments (739–42),
but as soon as the bladder is revealed again at 743, the
humor resumes at a second, higher level of intensity. Mika,
far from abandoning her suppliant role in the parody of
tragedy now that the "baby" has revealed to be (just) a wine-
skin, continues to lament her loss in high tragic mode (apart
from the brief, and amusing because unexpected, change to
a matter-of-fact tone when she answers the In-Law's question at 746). And Mika's hysteria continues until 754, when
she accepts her "child's" fate. But there is one more joke
still to be extracted from this situation: the In-Law is ruthless to the last, and instead of letting the wine flow down
into the bowl, from which Mika could retrieve it to drink
later in the festival, he sprays it all over her (and probably
over Mania as well). On retrieving the now empty skin,
Kritylla gets a couple of lines in the tragic style for herself
(760–61). But Mika has had enough of playing the tragic
victim; now that the joke is over, she resumes her normal
voice for her exit lines (762–64).

Kritylla returns to the perimeter; she and the *choros*
freeze, while the In-Law makes his first attempt at a Euripidean escape, borrowing an idea from *Palamedes*. The messages that Oiax wrote on oar blades in the original tragedy
were probably fairly implausible even in Euripides, and
Aristophanes' parody makes the scene absolutely ludicrous.
The In-Law is given nowhere near enough lines at 776ff. to
carve more than a few syllables on one tablet, given the difficulty he is apparently having with his knife. So instead of
Oiax's oars with full messages on them, floating away on
the ocean, the In-Law throws almost entirely blank tablets
out to various parts of the *orchēstra*, where they will remain
unread and disregarded for the rest of the play.

Choros 4 (Parabasis)

In the difficult political climate at the time when this play was being prepared for performance,[20] Aristophanes almost entirely declined to attack political figures in this *parabasis*[21] or even to acclaim himself (as he often had in earlier plays).[22] There are also no lyric passages, which further limits the entertainment value of this section, in contrast with a normal *parabasis*, which would alternate between ribald abuse, advice to the city, and song-and-dance numbers.[23]

For the first time in the surviving plays, the whole *choros* is comprised of women; *Lysistrata* had a half *choros* of Old Women balanced by a half *choros* of Old Men, but the dynamic is very different now the *choros* characters are all female. And the women defend themselves. For some commentators,[24] "the parabasis has little good to say of women," and the alleged absence of praise for their domestic role and their hard work, or for their roles in cult, is pointed to in support of this view.

This is to fail to take the *parabasis* in the context of the comedy as a whole, which celebrates women's role in one of the principal female cults—the festival of the Thesmophoria, at which the events of the play take place. And it ignores the power of the *parabasis*'s argument, which begins by asserting women's right to have a life and to be free from being perved on and harassed by men—a serious issue to this day.

The next stanza, which is more fanciful, is based on wordplays in the Greek that have very little effect in English, as the Women produce examples of Greek female names that

20. Cf. introduction, Comedy and Politics: *The Women's Festival.*
21. The widely unpopular Kleophon (805) and Hyperbolos (840) do make appearances, together with the recently defeated naval general Charminos (804).
22. Cf. all of his first five surviving comedies. *Birds* is the first surviving play in which the *choros* speak entirely on their own behalf.
23. Cf., e.g., *Frogs* 674ff.
24. Austin and Olsen 2004, 262–63, with references.

demonstrate superiority over men. This is a conceit which does not work in modern performance, and I recommend that the stanza be cut.

At 814 ff. the Women argue through an elegant comparison that women are relatively crime free in comparison to men (a point that modern statistics bear out), and that they conserve their household goods, and thus are superior to men, who often lose their military equipment on campaign. Women's hard work is, therefore, most certainly alluded to—both in 811–13 and in 819ff.

Their final demand is a typical Aristophanic request for the recognition of those who have served Athens well— but, naturally, from a female perspective, since this *choros* plays women. The women accept, as was inevitable in Athenian society, that their own esteem depends on that of their male kindred; so they simply (and forcefully) demand that due recognition should be given to the mothers of those who have served the city well, such as Lamachos (841).[25] At the end of the *parabasis* the *choros*, who are not involved in the next scene, should return to the "parked" position EFR-EFC-EFL and can sit down.

Scene 4

Aristophanes now presents his third parody of a scene from Euripides. This time the In-Law resolves to be Helen, from Euripides' romantic tragedy performed the previous year. *Helen* survives, so it is possible to tell exactly which lines and words are straight quotes from Euripides and which are Aristophanes' pseudo-tragic and comic inventions.[26]

25. Aristophanes here posthumously rehabilitates Lamachos, whom he had caricatured as an extreme warmonger in *Acharnians*. He also refers to him favorably in *Frogs*, 1039.
26. Table in Sommerstein 2001, 212.

Disregarding Kritylla's warning, the In-Law veils his face to play a modest and maltreated queen, launching into the first three lines of *Helen* at 855—with a comic conclusion added by Aristophanes. Kritylla now hovers around near the altar, providing abusive responses to each of the In-Law's tragic outbursts, until Euripides (who has somehow sensed the role he needs to play!) enters in costume and character as Menelaos—dressed in rags and festooned with seaweed. The two men proceed to play out the recognition scene from Euripides (*Helen* 549ff.), with "Menelaos" at CR and "Helen" on the altar. They plow on regardless of Kritylla's intervention between them and her attempts to convince the "shipwrecked gentleman" (whom she apparently takes at face value) of the real situation. She gives up after 899, and this enables Euripides and the In-Law to act out the moment of recognition, with a characteristic Aristophanic obscene substitution ("pussy" for "arms") in the last words. Kritylla has now seen though them—they are a pair of scumbags, "playing sneaky Egyptians" (921–22).[27] So she threatens them with her torch, and the escape attempt is foiled immediately by the arrival from the city of the Executive with his Policeman. Euripides slinks off in the opposite direction to try again.

The Executive enters, comes round to face the In-Law (who is still seated on the altar, but took off his veil after 903) to about CR, and gives his orders. The In-Law approaches the Executive and takes him by the hand for his appeal (936). But as this Executive is incorruptible (especially since the In-Law does not actually *offer* a cash bribe!), the appeal is hopeless. The Policeman drags the In-Law into the *skēnē*, so he can be placed during choros 5 on the punishment plank, which has been erected in advance on the *ekkuklēma*. Meanwhile the

27. Ironically, of course, though they *are* sneaky, this is factually wrong; *she* has been cast as an Egyptian (Theonoe) in the parody, while the In-Law and Euripides play the roles of a Greek hero and heroine (Sommerstein 2001, 216).

Executive exits back to the city, together with Kritylla; neither of them appears again.

Choros 5

The women let their hair down (literally, cf. 947 and 984) and embark on their longest and most exciting dance. It begins as a relatively formal circular dance (953ff.)—but they stop this after three stanzas, at 967–69, and during the B stanzas the dance becomes more and more intense, free flowing, and complex (987), with leaping and twirling (986). In the last two (C) stanzas, the music and choreography must express the full state of *ekstasis* of bakchic dancers— an experience in which the worshipers experience supreme Dionysian joy.

Scene 5

In this scene Aristophanes uses the *ekkuklēma* for the second time in *The Women's Festival*, this time to display the In-Law chained to a vertical plank. And he uses the *mēchanē* as well, for Euripides' appearances as Perseus.[28]

The staging of scene 5 is very straightforward; the Women are not involved and should be seated in the normal position for a "parked" *choros*,[29] watching the action. The action itself centers around the figure of the In-Law, chained to his plank on the *ekkuklēma* at BC.

---

28. Austin and Olsen (2004, 326) strangely assume that although the real Euripidean Perseus must have appeared on the *mēchanē* ("through the middle of the air / I cleave my path with wingèd feet," 1099–1100), Aristophanes' "Perseus" made his entrance on foot. But they give no reason; and as Sommerstein (2001, 229) had already noted, "it is unlikely that Ar. would have turned the most spectacular moment of *Andromeda* into a commonplace pedestrian entry."

29. EFL-EFC-EFR.

Now comes the third, last, and most complex parody of Euripides. As in *Frogs*,[30] the final parody is of a Euripidean speciality, the lyric monologue; here Aristophanes simply alternates between lyrics taken directly from Andromeda's lament and lapses out of character—and out of falsetto—as the In-Law makes his own complaints. (These sections are marked **A** and **I** respectively in the text.)

Echo enters, a mysterious female figure. She probably enters right, to signal that she is a visitor come from far away to meet Andromeda; but she could enter from the *skēnē*, since it is probable that in Euripides' play, Echo sang back to Andromeda from a cave represented by the *skēnē* facade and doors.

Many editors, following the lead of an ancient commentary, cast Euripides as Echo. But there is no good reason for this, and a strong practical reason not to do so: Euripides would have no time to change costume, mount the *mēchanē*, and reenter as Perseus between 1096 and 1098.[31]

The Echo scene is straightforward verbal slapstick. The In-Law makes ever more appalling sounds as he tries to sing more of Andromeda's lyrics; Echo sings back to him, copying and parodying his botched attempt at singing Euripides. Then the Policeman (slowly) catches on, and his

---

30. *Frogs*, 1331ff.

31. So rightly Sommerstein 2001, 226–27. He also notes that Echo speaks of Euripides as a different person and that there are obvious differences between the Echo scene and the Euripides scenes, in particular that Echo makes no attempt to rescue the In-Law. Indeed, she treats him as Andromeda throughout. The difficulties of the traditional belief become very evident in Austin and Olsen (2004, 323); they believe that Echo could retreat behind the *skēnē* doors before her speaking part is over, so the actor can start to change into Perseus's costume while still responding to the Policeman. This is completely undramatic and untheatrical; it is crucial to the climax of the scene that Echo be present right up to her last words, so the Policeman has a visible person to chase. And the actor would still have insufficient time to go round to the right *eisodos* (as Austin and Olson would have it) or to mount the *mēchanē*, ready to make his entry as Euripides/Perseus; there is virtually no time between Echo's last line and Euripides' first.

incompetent pursuit of Echo prefigures the final moments
of the play.

Euripides reappears on the *mēchanē*, lands, and begins to
play a few of Perseus's lines from *Andromeda*. But comic con-
fusion begins when the Policeman assumes that he has in his
sack the head not of the Gorgon but of Gorgos the secretary.
The Policeman is an even less sympathetic stage audience for
romantic tragedy than was Kritylla in the Menelaos-Helen
scene, and Euripides' attempts to pretend that the In-Law is a
beautiful maiden lead to some ribald humor (1110 ff., culmi-
nating in 1123–24). Once again Euripides' bluff is called;
when he says he will take the In-Law away, the Policeman—
like Kritylla—threatens violence, for which Euripides is inad-
equately prepared. Euripides beats his last retreat.

Choros 6

This is a short but intense prayer, first to Athena and
then to Demeter and Persephone, with an overt political
message in the appeal to Athena: "Show yourself—we need
you—enemy of tyranny!" The choreography and music must
be solemn and powerful.

Scene 6

The parodies of Euripides are over, and Aristophanes
now brings the conflict between Euripides and the women,
which has sustained all the fantasy since the opening scene,
to a complete close in ten deft lines (1160–70). *The Women's
Festival* lacks a full closing *kōmos* of comic revelry, but Fawn
takes off her dress and sandals at 1181ff., so—as often in
Aristophanes—a naked woman's sexuality is a symbol for
the joy of a comic finale. But here—unlike the conclusions
of, for example, *Acharnians, Peace,* and *Birds*—the hero is not

victorious, and therefore deserving of wine, women, and song; the conflict between Euripides and the Women has ended in a standoff.

Aristophanes, however, has one problem left before the play can end—the Policeman. Euripides therefore uses Fawn's erotic power on him. In most Aristophanic comedies the hero is to be imagined as eating, drinking, and having sex with his newly acquired nubile female (or females!) only after the play is over. But here, Euripides is able to free the In-Law from his chains, because the Policeman actually goes into the *skēnē* with Fawn to have sex with her during the action.

Staging this scene is straightforward. If, as suggested earlier, the Policeman has been sleeping EBR, then Fawn (who has followed Euripides in left, together with the boy musician Woodworm) waits CL until Euripides has finished negotiating with the Women around C. The *choros* then retreats to the perimeter, Euripides returns to BL, and Fawn crosses to the BR sector to perform her dance. The rest of the scene plays itself, right down to the final section, where various members of the *choros* misdirect the policeman, who then races off in hot pursuit of Euripides and the In-Law— but down the wrong *eisodos*.

And so the play ends—too abruptly, and with an anticlimax? Perhaps, but Aristophanes has richly entertained a war-weary and faction-ridden audience with one of his most hilarious comedies, and so he simply declares, through the mouth of one of the Women, that "we've had enough fun. / It's time for each of us to go / back home" (1227–29).

Frogs

Mise-en-scène for Scenes and Choroses 1 and 2

In a tragedy or comedy with a fixed setting, the left *eisodos* (as seen from the *skēnē* doors) led by convention back to the city nearest to the play's setting (as in actual physical fact it was the path to and from the city of Athens), and the right *eisodos* led to the countryside, the mountains, and other city-states.[1]

In the first two scenes of *Frogs*, Dionysos and Xanthias journey from the earth to Haides'; they arrive in front of Plouton's house at the start of scene 3. Consistent with the convention for fixed scenes, the upper world is always regarded during this journey as being to the left of the action and Haides' as being to the right. So Dionysos, Xanthias, and the Corpse, who are bound from earth to Haides', all enter from the left (and the corpse exits right); Charon, the Frogs, and the Initiates, who all live in or near Haides', enter right.

The journey itself is enacted by two means: by Xanthias and Dionysos's circulating around the *orchēstra*, as in the opening episode, and later, by Xanthias's running around the lake; and in choros 1, by contrary motion. Charon and Dionysos traverse the rear of the playing space from left to right, while the Frogs enter right, dance around the boat, and exeunt left. In this way it is conveyed that his voyage in the ferry has taken Dionysos deeper into Haides'. Finally, the Initiates enter from the right, to convey that they are residents of

1. Rehm 1992, 54.

276

Haides'; however, at the end of the play they will exit left, as a procession escorting Dionysos and Aischylos back to Athens.

Dionysos and Xanthias in Scenes 1–3

The Aristophanic hero or heroine, who—dissatisfied with the state of the world—embarks on a quest in seven of the plays, is usually permitted jokes at the expense of others and is often assailed by freeloaders. But this central character is himself or herself not normally a figure of fun.[2] It is clear from scenes 1–3 that when he wrote *Frogs*, Aristophanes and his producer, Philonides, had two virtuoso actors at their disposal, who could alternate freely between the roles known in modern comedy as "gag man" and "straight man."[3] Dionysos's opening appearance is self-contradictory; he is potbellied (663), and he absurdly wears for his quest the lionskin of the heroic Herakles over a flowing saffron garment suitable for a relaxed and alcoholic evening among friends. This prefigures the contradictions in his character as the first half of the comedy unfolds; he oscillates between his real determination to fulfill the quest (cf. esp. 60–108) and all-too-frequent lapses into cowardice, which become fully evident first in Xanthias's creation of the imaginary Empousa in scene 2 and then in the beautifully crafted comic sequence of scene 3.

Xanthias is an equally fluid character. His overall character in scene 1 is the traditional comic slave, complaining futilely about his hardships; but he is very far from being solely a butt for jokes. His initial position on the donkey, which his master leads, is symbolic of the unslavish character and ability that will emerge later; indeed, he begins to send up Dionysos as early as 41. And Xanthias comes fully into

2. Cf., e.g., Dikaiopolis in *Acharnians*, Trygaios in *Peace*, Pisthetairos in *Birds*, and Lysistrata.
3. Cf. McLeish 1980, 131–33 and 141–43.

his own in scene 2, manipulating Dionysos like a puppet on a string as he punctures his master's false bravado at 279ff. When that sequence ends, he boldly both accuses Dionysos (at this stage, falsely) of shitting himself (308) and mocks his master's love of Euripides (311).

All this is in preparation for the masterly lionskin-swapping sequence of scene 3. In scene 1 Herakles immediately observed the incongruity of Dionysos's appearance, which the audience can plainly see; but now Aristophanes changes the rules. Whichever of Dionysos and Xanthias wears the lionskin is taken by the inhabitants of Haides' to *be* Herakles, and indeed Dionysos can be presumed to be either Herakles or a slave, despite wearing a fifth-century aristocrat's symposium dress throughout. During the Doorkeeper's aggressive verbal attack on "Herakles," Dionysos actually does shit himself (479ff.), and now the role reversal begins. Xanthias accuses him of cowardice and is promptly given the lionskin and club for the first time. But a sexually attractive Servant now emerges with the promise of exotic delights, and Dionysos reasserts his mastery by demanding the Herakles disguise back (522ff.). The importance of this swap is conveyed both by Xanthias's prophetic remark, "perhaps some time / the god will make you need me once again" (532–33), and by the two-stanza lyric interplay between an Initiate and Dionysos, which follows immediately. It will be matched symmetrically with a similar interplay between an Initiate and Xanthias, after the next episode, to mark the parallel between the two characters' assumption of the role of "Herakles."

When the Innkeeper and Plathane appear, Xanthias first utters a sardonic aside ("someone will pay for that," 554) and then participates in the scene with relish, egging on the two wronged and angry hostesses. Dionysos of course begs him to take back the Herakles props after they have left, so when the Doorkeeper reenters with the Policemen, it is payback time; Dionysos first matches Xanthias's earlier aside with "here's trouble for someone" (606) and then encourages the Doorkeeper to arrest Xanthias. But the real slave now reaches the apogee of his power, graciously offering up his "slave" Dionysos for the most severe of tortures. This leads into the climactic pre-*parabasis* episode, in which both Dionysos and Xanthias attempt with diminishing success to disguise the fact that (despite the truth that one is, and the other is pretending to be, a god) they do feel the pain of the whipping.

Throughout scenes 1–3, Aristophanes gained enormous comic mileage from the interplay of Dionysos's alternations between heroic god and cowardly buffoon with Xanthias's emergence from the downtrodden comic porter role to dominance, which is prefigured in scene 1 and seen at its full extent in scenes 2 and 3. It is no wonder that the playwright, unwilling to let the theme go, returns to and stresses Xanthias's bravado at 739–43 in scene 4, which is both the link forward to the playwrights' contest and the last scene in which he appears.

Scene 1

The fact that Dionysos and Xanthias are on a journey is immediately conveyed by the presence of the live donkey (a member of the cast best omitted from modern indoor performances) and the fact that there are thirty-five lines of dialogue before they arrive at the *skēnē* door. The two actors should circle at least EBL>BC>ECR before they begin the dialogue, and they then have ample time to complete a full circuit of the *orchēstra*, back to the *skēnē* doors. This is the case even if we allow for moments when Dionysos brings the donkey to a brief halt (we found this desirable for 6–10; another possible place for a halt is 29–32).

Aristophanes begins the comedy with two visual incongruities. Dionysos is walking and his slave is riding; and Dionysos wears, over his own saffron robe and slippers

(ideal for a symposium rather than a journey), the lionskin
and club of Herakles. The playwright teases the audience
by declining to explain either of these visual puns until he
is ready to do so. Instead he begins with a sequence of jokes
in which the two players are fully aware of themselves as
actors, desperate to entertain their audience; they only
begin to get into their characters for performing *Frogs* at
16ff. Aristophanes chooses to pretend that he is superior to
his rivals; he is above using the "old jokes" about farting
and shitting and the comic cliché of carrying on luggage.
Of course he can only convey this fact by allowing the actor
playing the slave to demonstrate the kind of coarse jokes that
his master proscribes, so we get to hear them anyway, and
then the luggage comes into play. Cliché or not, Aristophanes
exploits it shamelessly, first for the mock-sophistic sequence
at 25ff., then for interjections by Xanthias (87, 159–60), and
finally as the prop to be exchanged for the lionskin and club
in the role reversals of scene 3.

Upon arrival at the *skēnē* door, which for the next few
minutes will represent the door of Herakles' house, Xanthias
stands away from the door (CL/BCL) while Dionysos knocks.
Herakles needs to turn away, that is, to BR, as he is convulsed
by laughter at Dionysos's outlandish appearance (which
Aristophanes now gradually begins to explain, together
with the plot of the play), while Dionysos briefly turns back
toward Xanthias for support, which he does not gain (40–41).
Xanthias is now in position for the "asides," which he inter-
jects into the rest of the Herakles scene; these are of course
addressed openly and directly to the audience.

Dionysos and Herakles interact in the rear half of the
orchēstra: Dionysos moves away in horror on the "Aaaah!"
in 57; the two actors draw closer during 59ff., and in what
follows there are plenty of moments where turning and
moving away from the other protagonist, and later reen-
gaging, are desirable in the large Greek playing space to
physicalize the meaning of the dialogue, which in a more

intimate theater could be supported by small gestures without actual movement. For example, Dionysos can usefully turn away at 86 ("Oh, let him rot"), return toward Herakles at 92, turn away again as he expands on Euripidean phrases at 98ff., and move defiantly toward Herakles as he asserts his independence at 106–108. Then the center point is needed, first by Dionysos as he makes his requests of Herakles (112ff.), then by Herakles, who should displace Dionysos aggressively at 116 ("Rash fool, will you too dare to go?"). Dionysos retreats to FR and moves away from and toward Herakles during the next sequence according to whether his response to what Herakles is saying is scared or excited. If Herakles moves at all, he needs to be at the center once more for 145ff.

As soon as his scene is over, Herakles goes abruptly back into the *skēnē*. Its doors close and will not open again until the journey is complete, when Dionysos and Xanthias arrive in front of Plouton's (and Persephone's) door.[4]

The Corpse enters by the left *eisodos*, and Dionysos intercepts him before he reaches BC. The Corpse stops briefly, then orders his bearers to proceed (174). Dionysos manages to detain him for a few more moments, but then he fails and turns disconsolately back to Xanthias (still CL/FL).

Charon's boat was probably a wooden boat on wheels, propelled by the feet of the actor through holes in the floor. He rows it onstage himself—from the right *eisodos*, as he is coming from Haides'—and comes to rest somewhere in the rear left segment of the *orchēstra*. Dionysos gets onboard; Xanthias, who did not fight at Arginousai and so was not given his freedom, has to go right round the lake, which is of course now represented by the *orchēstra*. He does this during choros 1, while the Frogs engage in their famous song-and-dance battle with Dionysos.

4. As scenes 1–2 portray a journey, no painted scenery panels would have been attached until during choros 2.

Choros 1

Almost incredibly, there are some who believe that the Frogs did not appear in the performing space but were simply heard as voices offstage (i.e., from inside the *skēnē*).[5] This is to disregard the close interplay between song and dance in classical Greek choroses; a performance of the one implied a performance of the other. It is also highly untheatrical. Finally, it diminishes the force of Aristophanes' in-joke. He had created comedies called *Clouds, Wasps,* and *Birds,* in all of which the exotic title was justified; when the *choros* appeared, they were dressed up to play the parts of Clouds, Wasps, and Birds respectively, and their relevance to the plot and action of the play was real and apparent. Now he presents a comedy called *Frogs,* in which the title characters do indeed appear as expected—but only for a single comic sequence lasting 57 lines; they then leave for good, are not the main *choros,* and are irrelevant to the plot![6]

The Frogs are played by the whole *choros* (or, if economy in costume expenditure was really necessary in the straitened circumstances of 405, perhaps by a half *choros* of twelve). They surround the boat as Dionysos attempts to row it from BL to EBR, and they fight a metrical and vocal battle with him, which he eventually wins by adopting their "Brekekekex koax koax" and shouting them down. The Frogs exeunt left, to indicate that by the end of choros 1 Dionysos has crossed the marshy lake, which the *orchēstra* represented during the choros. Meanwhile Charon and his boat disappear into the darkness of Haides', right.

---

5. This view goes back to ancient times; for references and discussions that come to the same conclusion as mine, cf. Macdowell 1972 and Dover 1993, 56–57.

6. This fact has not stopped learned scholars from trying to link the Frogs in some way with the main theme of the second part of the play, the contest between Aischylos and Euripides; for examples and refutation, cf. Campbell 1984, 164. On the Frogs' "liminality," cf. Lada-Richards 1999, 57 note 44.

Scene 2

Dionysos searches for Xanthias in the "darkness" of the *orchēstra*, which now represents the mud of the farther shore of the lake. Xanthias is actually very near him, having completed his circuit of the *orchēstra* during choros 1 (both are BR), but for a couple of minutes as the scene begins they mime that they cannot see, so they grope through the darkness toward the sound of each other's voices. A classic comic sequence now follows, in which Xanthias manipulates Dionysos by the creation of an imaginary monster (a detailed blocking can be found in the introduction).[7] As this episode concludes, music is heard, and the *choros* of Initiates begin to approach the playing area down the right *eisodos*. Dionysos and Xanthias therefore retreat to the mouth of the other *eisodos*, sheltering behind the retaining wall holding up the left end of the *theatron*, to observe the Initiates' entrance and listen to choros 2—but they peek briefly into the playing area for their interjections at 318–22, 337–39, and 417–19.[8]

Choros 2

The *choros* now reenter, clad in the ragged clothes of Initiates in the Eleusinian mysteries. Two stanzas bring them all into the *orchēstra*, then one of them takes the center point for the ritual invocation at 354ff. He remains there to prompt the sequence of festive songs in honor of the gods, which begins at 372. The end of the dance sequence is symbolized

---

7. Introduction, Performance.

8. Cf. *TWF* scene 1. But there is a much closer parallel in tragedy; at Aischylos, *Libation-Bearers* 20ff., two characters retreat to the opposite *eisodos* as the *choros* enters, uncertain who the *choros* are and why they have come. *Libation Bearers*, which is quoted during the contest in scene 6 (1124ff.), may also have been in Aristophanes' mind at the start of scene 3; like Dionysos, Orestes received an unpleasant reception when *he* knocked, on the door of the palace that should be his, at the start of *Libation Bearers* scene 3 (651ff.).

by the breaking of the pattern with the additional stanza (C3) at 409ff.

The Initiates then sing five short stanzas of ritual abuse of prominent citizens.[9] Dionysos enters the playing space and interrupts them. Following this the last sequence of dances ends, with the *choros* going to their "parked" position, EFR-EFC-EFL, out of the way of the next scene, which is predominantly for solo actors.[10] During this choros panels are put in place, which indicate that the *skēnē* now represents the palace of Plouton and Persephone.

Scene 3

Dionysos approaches the door of the *skēnē* from BL and summons a slave. The Doorkeeper enters ferociously,[11] and the actor in the role of Dionysos has a choice between delivering "Herakles the brave" as one last heroic utterance before his comic collapse or stuttering and quaking in his slippers as he endeavors to declare and stay in his heroic role. During the splendid invective that follows, the Doorkeeper should pursue Dionysos round the perimeter of the *orchēstra* into a weak position, so that when he collapses around 475, he is in the front segment and near the perimeter (i.e., FR). After the Doorkeeper leaves, Xanthias—having wisely stood back from the door (BL)—crosses the playing

9. Abuse and ridicule of individuals was "an integral part of various festivals and rituals," including the Eleusinian procession (Dover 1993, 247–48).

10. Two Initiates do step forward to sing and dance the lyric interludes at 534ff. and 590ff., but they resume their place in the *choros* after each of their intrusions.

11. The Doorkeeper was of course, in Aristophanes' conception, a forbiddingly impressive male figure (636); but in one of the best productions I have ever seen, the part changed genders to a Gothic dominatrix in diamond-patterned black pantihose, leather miniskirt and jacket, and a spiked collar, with chains and (of course) a whip.

space to provide Dionysos with assistance. When he takes over the lionskin and club, he needs to be at C to declaim 499–500. Dionysos picks up the luggage, which Xanthias has given him, and retreats to the perimeter.

The Servant episode is best enacted using the center line. She enters and moves forward through BC during her first speech. Xanthias turns to listen to her, and on each of his refusals backs away from her toward FC. The Servant pursues him, arriving at C during the speech beginning at 508 and then starting back toward the *skēnē* with "So please come with me." But he declines once again, and she turns forward again, to tempt him with erotic as well as culinary pleasures. This time Xanthias does not retreat, and he starts moving up the center line toward the *skēnē* at the end of 520, following in a heroic Heraklean fashion as the Servant leaves rapidly. As he passes Dionysos (who is probably, to make this subsection effective, at CR), he orders him to follow; Dionysos has to move to intercept him. Outraged, Xanthias stops going toward the *skēnē* and approaches Dionysos instead (506–507), but he has to give in. Xanthias takes up the baggage and stands aside CR, as did Dionysos in the last scene, while Dionysos moves to the center for the lyric interchange with one of the Initiates.

Once again the *skēnē* door opens to reveal inhabitants aggrieved by Herakles; the Innkeeper and Plathane enter and take up positions near each other BC, with their slaves waiting on either side of the *skēnē* door. Xanthias comments sardonically from the sidelines as the two women advance steadily on Dionysos, near C, during the next phase of the dialogue. Then, on 563, Xanthias leaves the luggage and joins the women in order to sympathize with them and humiliate Dionysos. They turn back toward the *skēnē* to send their slaves off for support from Kleon and Hyperbolos (two politicians who are apparently as willing to prosecute in the underworld as they had been during their lives in Athens). Then they turn forward again and advance on Dionysos, driving him into a weak position (e.g., FL) before their sudden exits.[12]

Dionysos, with some difficulty—and an oath (which he keeps!) that he will never take the lionskin and club from Xanthias again—persuades his slave to once more become Herakles. The positions from the end of the previous episode are now replicated in reverse; after their dialogue Dionysos goes over to the baggage at CR, while Xanthias takes the center point for his lyric interchange with a member of the *choros.*

The Doorkeeper enters, followed by three Policemen who take up position in front of the *skēnē* and advance menacingly when ordered to at 608–609. But Xanthias stands firm (unlike Dionysos in *his* episode with the Doorkeeper); this signals a change of pattern, as Aristophanes moves into the last, climactic episode of the scene. Characteristically, he adds a prop (the Doorkeeper's whip) to climax a sequence of jokes that had previously all been verbal.[13]

Dionysos insinuates himself with the Doorkeeper, just as Xanthias had done with the Innkeeper and Plathane (the role reversal is explicit in Dionysos's echo at 606 of Xanthias's sardonic aside at 552). But Xanthias turns the tables on him, with the idea that his "slave" should be tortured.

Dionysos and Xanthias need to be facing forward, one on each side of the centerline (i.e., CR and CL), for the whipping scene itself. The best way to achieve this is for Dionysos to advance commandingly toward C as he asserts his divinity, 628ff. Then they can take up their exact positions while they take off their outer garments after 641. The episode proceeds,

---

12. Which way do the slaves, and then the Innkeeper and Plathane, go off? If the convention that has governed the play so far is respected, they should all go off R, symbolizing that they are going further into the depths of Haides' to fetch the prosecutors. But I think it can probably be felt that the location has stabilized, now that the *skēnē* represents Plouton's palace. They can therefore go off in opposite directions, imagined now as going to different parts of Haides', "lower/darker" (R) and "upper/lighter" (L); this is theatrically more effective.

13. Cf. the use of scales at the climax of the tragedy contest (1370ff.), the helmet of Athena in *Lysistrata* scene 4, and the use of the *mēchanē* for the third and last tragic parody in *The Women's Festival.*

with the Doorkeeper moving from behind one of the pair to behind the other, until the pattern is broken; improving on Xanthias's suggestion, he (or she) comes round in front of Dionysos on 663 and whips him straight on his potbelly. Even this does not resolve the Doorkeeper's dilemma, so Aristophanes—having made each protagonist cry out more and more, while trying successfully to disguise the fact—simply brings the scene to a halt and clears the playing space of all but the *choros* to signal the end of the first half of the play.

Choros 3 (Parabasis)

The *parabasis* alternates between two danced stanzas of personal abuse (of Kleophon and Kleigenes), which will mean little to a modern audience and are recommended for cutting, and two speeches declaimed by individual Initiates. The first of these pleads for a reconciliation with, and reenfranchisement of, those who were caught on the wrong side, supporting the oligarchs in the coup of 411; the second presents the famous analogy of the coinage, which introduces the theme that Athens, in Aristophanes' view, is neglecting the best, well-born and well-educated (i.e., aristocratic) members of society and seeking its leaders in the wrong place. This crucial idea is picked up again at the climax of the contest in the second part of the play, which turns on the possibility of the recall of Alkibiades (1422ff.). In the 404 revision this is followed up by Euripides' advice, which reinforces the theme of the *parabasis*:

If we no longer trust those citizens in whom
we trust at present, and we use those men
whom we don't use, perhaps we might be saved. (1446ff.)

Aristophanes inserted these lines, which pick up the second theme of the *parabasis*, doubtless because the advice in this *parabasis* was one of the main reasons why the play was selected for revival.

Scene 4

Aristophanes is loath to part with Xanthias, even though he will soon need Actor 2 for the role of Euripides.[14] So he uses him, in dialogue with an anonymous Slave, to set the scene for the contest between Aischylos and Euripides.

This is a straightforward two-actor scene; for most of it the actors should be BL and BR, except when they embrace at 754ff. and during the Slave's two longer speeches 761ff. and 771ff., which are best delivered with a half circle through the front of the *orchēstra*. Smaller movements toward and away from each other need to be included during the question and answer sequence after 778.

Choros 4

In extraordinarily complex poetry, Aristophanes establishes the mood for the contest of the two wordsmiths with four stanzas describing their verbal power, which demand vivid and daring choreography. Meanwhile stagehands preset three thrones in a sideways row BC and bring on an altar to C, on which must be placed a small number of voting pebbles.[15]

14. This is the best reconstruction of the original doublings, given that Euripides' smooth sophistry is not too far from Xanthias's sassy banter. Philonides clearly selected for Actor 3 a commanding figure, who could play the aggressive and/or imposing roles of Herakles, Corpse, Charon, Doorkeeper, Innkeeper—and Aischylos.

15. An altar was a stock prop in the Athenian theatre, used, e.g., for the refuge of the suppliants in Euripides' *Herakles* and *Suppliants* (on which cf. Ley 2006, 46ff.). For theoretical considerations in favor of usually placing the altar at the center of the *orchēstra*, cf. Wiles 1997, 78ff. The practical advantages of this position are obvious once you workshop or perform in a three-sided performing space any scene from tragedy or comedy that involves the use of an altar, and it

Scene 5

There are three thrones—one for Plouton, who will remain silent and solemn on the central one until just before his sudden intervention at 1414;[16] one for Dionysos; and the third the Throne of Tragedy, which Euripides usurps at once as they enter. Aischylos walks away in silence.

It is arbitrary which side of the *orchēstra* is allocated to Euripides and which to Aischylos. A decision has to be made, however, so we placed the Throne of Tragedy as the rightmost of the three thrones;[17] Aischylos accordingly, having failed to gain his seat, moves diagonally forward to BR, and Dionysos, when he has coaxed Euripides off the throne, moves him to BC. After that, when Dionysos has settled down both contestants (851ff.), their general positions for most of the remainder of the contest will be Aischylos on Dionysos's right, CR, and Euripides on his left, CL.

Dionysos has to rise to get Euripides away from the Throne of Tragedy; in 851ff. he is still BC, mediating between the two angry poets. He calls for incense and a fire to light it at 871ff. Extras bring these out and place them on the altar; Dionysos then advances to take up a position immediately behind the altar at C and burns his incense while the Initiates sing and dance choros 5.

---

should be placed at C for all its appearances except that in *Oidipous the King*, where McCart has argued convincingly for FC (Ewans, with Ley and McCart, 2000, 268–69 with note 8).

16. Plouton does not speak until 1414. But there is no acknowledgment of an entry there, or time to get Plouton on (he only intervenes when he hears Dionysos declare his refusal to make a decision, during 1411ff.); cf. Dover 1993, 295–56. It is also a nice conceit if Aristophanes, whose very first attack on Aischylos is for "the arrogant silence bit" (833) exemplified by the characters of Niobe and Achilleus, shamelessly uses this device himself.

17. Dover (1993, 296) assumes this layout without argument. But it is a good touch that the throne for the most *dexios poiētes*—metaphorically the most "clever and creative dramatist" (71), but literally the poet on the right-hand side—should in fact be placed on Plouton's right; and then Aischylos, the eventual victor, i.e., the poet who turns out to be proved the most *dexios* by the contest, will have been on Dionysos's right throughout scenes 5 and 6.

When Dionysos calls on the poets to pray (882), Aischylos willingly approaches the altar and burns incense; Euripides declines and moves away to FL.

The *agōn* now formally begins. Choros 6, part one (894ff.), marks the beginning of the first half, in which Euripides takes the lead; a matching stanza (choros 6, part two, 991ff.), with corresponding dance movements, marks the midpoint, after which Aischylos counterattacks. Not much movement is implied or needed in this *agōn*, which focuses primarily on developing in words the contrast between the two playwrights (who in the first performances were doubtless as contrasted in their costumes and masks as they are in their approaches to the art of tragedy). Aristophanes is careful to avoid monotony; both Euripides' attack and Aischylos's reply develop in intensity to the point where a short song-and-dance number (very like those in scene 3 for first Dionysos, 534ff., and subsequently Xanthias, 590ff.) creates the climax and leads into a choral commentary: 971ff. (Euripides and Dionysos) and 1078ff. (Aischylos and Dionysos).[18]

Euripides begins with an attack on Aischylos's poetic style; it was designed to overawe the audience with pretentiousness and complex language (which Aristophanes has prefigured in choros 4). In his longest speech (which is best delivered while aggressively circling around Aischylos), he images himself as a doctor who found Tragedy to be a seriously ill patient:

> When I inherited the art from you, at first she was
> all swollen up with bombast and with heavy phrases,
> so I put her on a diet and took off her weight
> with light verse, exercise, and white beetroot,

18. Aristophanes develops the competition between the playwrights gradually; his long-term strategy is to raise the emotional temperature slowly. So after the formal *agōn* of scene 5, in scene 6 he first concentrates on prologues, introducing the brilliant oil-flask joke; this is followed by music, in the parodies of song and dance, and finally by the scales for the weighing of tragedy.

and gave her babble juice, squeezed out of books.
Then I restored her health with monodies— (939ff.)

And the fundamental contrast throughout this episode is flat-
tering to the late fifth-century audience; Aischylos could get
away with bombast before the "audience of morons he inherited from Phrynichos" (910); Euripides educated his audience
and "brought reason and inquiry / into drama" (973–74).

In his counterattack (1006ff.), Aischylos does not attempt
a direct response to these arguments, perhaps because to an
audience in 405 B.C.E. the revived productions of his tragedies
(all now more than fifty-three years old) did indeed seem to
be stylistically archaic and sometimes poetically abstruse, in
contrast to the clearer, more everyday, modern, and post-
sophistic style of Euripides (and of Aristophanes himself).[19]
Instead, he shifts the argument to a different plane. Presumably because he expected widespread audience agreement
with this view, Aristophanes makes both playwrights agree
that tragedy has a moral purpose:

[AISCHYLOS] . . . What should we look for in a dramatist?
EURIPIDES   Intelligence and good advice, because we make
    men in the cities better. (1008ff.)

And although the examples are comically exaggerated, the
contrast between the poets is deadly serious; by the end of
the episode, Aischylos has linked himself to a proud Greek
tradition of didactic poetry, seeking special praise for his
examples of successful military valor (doubtless a sore point
in the Athens of 405, which had suffered major defeats in
the Peloponnesian War and in the disastrous expedition to
Sicily and was currently under siege). By contrast, he alleges,
Euripides encourages moral decay, in women as well as in
the armed forces:

---

19. Cf. introduction, Aristophanes and Euripides.

EURIPIDES   Do you say I invented Phaidra's story?
AISCHYLOS   No, it existed—but the playwright must
     hide evil, not show
   and teach it to the audience. Boys have schoolteachers
   to explain things to them; young men have the
     playwrights.
   That's why we have to teach what's right. (1052ff.)

Euripides' rejoinder to this is literalist and frivolous, but Aischylos has gained the moral high ground for tragedy (and
epic), and he maintains this theme right through to the song-
and-dance conclusion of his attack (1079ff.). Comical this may
be, and outrageous from a playwright who had himself exhibited a consummate adulteress and murderess (Klytaimestra in
Agamemnon), but there is no doubt that Aristophanes, here as
in the *parabasis*, is raising the serious issue of what he regards
as the moral decline of Athens. Since the principal excellence
of a man was to fight in defense of his polis, and that of a
woman to be a chaste guardian of the household, Aischylos's
attacks on Euripides, for encouraging military weakness in
males and sexual license in females, address the twin founda-
tions on which Athenian culture should be based—and in
Aristophanes' diagnosis, no longer was. The finale will return
to the twin themes of morality and military superiority, and
Aischylos will win.

Choros 7

The Initiates exhort the contestants to even cleverer and
subtler attacks. They also (on Aristophanes' behalf, as a pre-
cautionary measure) once again flatter the audience (stanza
A2). The flattery is over the top; though there is much debate
about the precise amount of literacy in classical Athens, no
modern scholar has ever assented to the proposition that

every Athenian "has got / at least one book" (1113–14). This flattery is designed to keep the audience involved with the somewhat elevated subject of the second half of *Frogs*, which is in marked contrast to the relatively knockabout activities after the *parabasis* in, for example, *Acharnians, Knights, Birds,* and *Lysistrata*.

Scene 6

The opening section of scene 6—the testing of prologues—is almost entirely verbal humor, with very little implied movement. Things only get physical when the contest turns to lyrics. Greek singing was always accompanied by dance, and Euripides doubtless performed a scathing parody of the old style of choreography to accompany the nonsensical collage of "Aeschylean lyrics," with a refrain that only makes sense as part of the first couplet, which he sings at 1265ff. Then he produces and strums a lyre, adding a further musical dimension to the next collage at 1283ff. Aischylos, however, trumps this; first he brings on the "Muse of Euripides," an old hag who plays the castanets, while he parodies the style of Euripidean choral lyrics,[20] and then he attacks one of the most conspicuous features of the "new" Euripidean drama—solo songs or monodies. This parody is partly conducted through the contrast between the elevated tragic language and the domestic triviality of the situation (an attack to which Euripides laid himself open in scene 5, with 959 and 971ff.). It is also (untranslatably) a parody of Euripidean lyric meters.

20. This passage concludes with a pun between Aischylos's actual foot in his dance movement and the abnormality in the "feet" of the Greek lyric meter that Aischylos tricks Euripides into making. A small cut is recommended in modern performance.

The Old Woman should leave after the parody of choral lyric is completed. The monody demands the services of the *aulos* player, who is already present to play the accompaniment to the comedy's other lyric sections.[21]

After the lyrics, Aristophanes introduces the last and crowning absurdity—the weighing of poetry in scales. As often in his comedies, the final set of jokes is indicated by the introduction of a prop; slaves bring in and set up a giant set of scales during choros 9. The best place for the scales is just in front of the altar at C.

Aischylos wins this phase of the competition hands down, but Dionysos is still undecided. As he expresses his inability to choose between the tragedians, the ominous figure of Plouton rises from his throne, comes forward to stand over Dionysos, and forces him to make a decision. The competition now enters its final phase, turning back to moral issues and addressing the desperate situation that Athens currently faced.[22] It is evident that Dionysos is attracted to Aeschylus's sage advice, rather than either Euripides' fantastic/prophetic plan for aerial warfare (405 version) or his echo of the *parabasis* in the 404 version. Euripides senses this at once, as Dionysos moves toward making his choice (1471); he confronts Dionysos angrily on 1472, moving round in front of him to stare directly at him on 1474.

Now comes an unusual situation; Euripides apparently leaves, unlike almost any other character in tragedy or comedy, without either speaking an exit line/couplet or being acknowledged as leaving by the other characters onstage.[23] However, on closer inspection the stagecraft can be understood. No other character wants to farewell Euripides the loser, and he is furious with Dionysos (1476). So Euripides speaks his angry final line and then storms out at once via

21. So too Dover 1993, 362.
22. Cf. introduction, Comedy and Politics: *Frogs*.
23. Cf. only the exit of Apollo, after he has secured Orestes' acquittal, at Aischylos, *Eumenides* 753. Cf. my commentary on that scene at Ewans 1995, 215.

the right *eisodos*, making Dionysos's next two lines (1476–77) into "lines cast at a departing back"—a way of signaling an exit for which there are several parallels.[24]

Finale

The Initiates sing and dance two stanzas in praise of Aischylos and in opposition to Euripides' new tragic style, which they characterize as overindebted to the sophists (whom once again, as in *Clouds*, Aristophanes attacks in the person of Sokrates). These stanzas summarize the essence of the conflict in the second half of the play.

It is a basic convention of Greek tragedy and comedy that as much time can be deemed to have elapsed during a choral ode as the playwright wishes; so when they reappear, Plouton, Aischylos, and Dionysos have amply wined and dined. Dionysos is silent for the rest of the play, so Plouton and Aischylos must hold strong positions. This however presents a problem, unless the scales have been removed; the dialogue must either be played BC, in which case the scales obstruct the view for spectators in the lower rows of the central blocks, or FC in front of the scales, in which case the left and right wings of the audience cannot see the dialogue and the exchange of props properly.

There is no point before the start of the Finale where the scales can be removed without disrupting the climactic resolution of the play—the advice about politics and Dionysos's choice. It is therefore best for stagehands to remove the scales during the two lyric stanzas. Then the anapaestic (march-rhythm/recitative) dialogue between Plouton and Aischylos can be played BC, just in front of the thrones. This is appropriate, as the right-hand throne is the subject

24. Taplin 1977, 221, citing Aischylos, *Suppliants* 952–53; also *Agamemnon* 351ff., *Libation Bearers* 1063–64.

of Aischylos's closing stanza, and from BR/BC he can easily gesture toward it.

Finally Plouton invites the Initiates to farewell Aischylos; they form into a procession, with Aischylos and Dionysos either at its head or in their midst, and leave as they sing the final exit song. As K. Dover notes, this procession with torches would arouse an echo of the finale of Aischylos's most famous trilogy; at the end of *Eumenides*, women and girls with torches escort the Furies to their new home in Athens.[25]

25. Dover 1993, 384. He conjectures that the Initiates may have sung their last six lines while still in the *orchēstra* and then sang a real lyric by Aischylos, following Plouton's suggestion, as the actual exit song. This is possible, but I prefer to end the play with Aristophanes' own final words, the desperate plea for peace in 1531ff., leaving the audience to imagine that the Initiates would have sung songs by Aischylos as they escorted him on his way, out of sight and hearing of the spectators.

Plouton also asks them to "Light sacred torches for him" (1524). Dionysos claimed at 314 to smell "a whiff of torch-smoke" as the Initiates first approached, and an Initiate refers to his "sacred torch" at 446/47, so it is probable that they entered with torches in their hands, which they would have placed on the ground near the edge of the *orchēstra* at the end of choros 2. However, it is very undramatic to suppose a pause here while they relight their torches or to suppose that slaves rushed out on 1524, pulling focus massively as they hand out twenty-four new lighted torches (Dover 1993, 383). If the Initiates had torches when they first entered, they would pick them up during 1524 ff. and process out with unlit torches, leaving the flame and smoke to the audience's imagination. (Real flame and smoke would not make much impact in any case, in broad daylight in such a large theater.)

APPENDIX 1:
RECOMMENDED CUTS

These names and passages have been included in the translation to represent the whole of what Aristophanes wrote, but I have marked them with square brackets, and I recommend that they be cut from modern performances for the reasons given below.

Lysistrata

62–63	The pun here is untranslatable.
103	Eurykrates is unknown, so it is not worth naming him.
184ff.	This scene needs an extra, in costume and with props, for less than ten lines that are not particularly funny today, so a cut is recommended.
313	The reference to the generals in Samos is too obscure for the modern audience and impossible to rescue by an intruded gloss.
1082	*[attended by SLAVES]* See Theatrical Commentary on the Finale.
1105	Not very funny for a modern audience ignorant of Lysistratos.
1215ff., 1239ff.	
	See Theatrical Commentary on the Finale.

The Women's Festival

135	The reference to the Lykourgos plays is too obscure for a modern audience.

| 734 | Modern wine bladders are not made from the skin of animals and so do not have feet, unlike the original prop for this scene, which is illustrated in the famous Würzburg Apulian bell krater (see illustration in *TWF,* scene 3). |

799ff.   The puns on female names are relatively ineffective.

834–35   The names of these festivals are too obscure for a modern audience.

861   Phrynondas is too obscure for a modern audience.

949ff.   The humor at the expense of Pauson will not mean anything to modern audiences.

Frogs

673ff., 706ff.

The two stanzas of invective mean nothing to a modern audience.

934   Obscure reference.

1257–60   The 404 version is more intelligible to the modern audience.

1323ff.   Untranslatable pun between *foot*—literally, either Aischylos's or the Old Woman's—and *foot,* term used for a subunit in Greek meter.

1461–65   The 404 version is more intelligible to the modern audience.

APPENDIX 2: A RECONSTRUCTION OF ARISTOPHANES' ORIGINAL DOUBLINGS

This appendix indicates how the solo parts in these comedies might originally have been played by a company of between three and five actors, changing costumes and masks as the performance progressed.

Lysistrata

Lysistrata	Actor 1
Kalonike	Actor 2 (in Finale, Silent Face)
Myrrhine	Actor 3 (in Finale, Silent Face)
3 women from Athens	Actor 5 and 2 Silent Faces
Lampito	Actor 4 (in Finale, Silent Face)
Korinthian woman	Silent Face
Boiotian woman	Silent Face
Archer girl	Silent Face
Old Men	Half *Choros*
Old Women	Half *Choros*
Bureaucrat	Actor 2
3 Policemen	Silent Faces
4 escaping women	Actors 2–5
Kinesias	Actor 2
Slave with Baby	Silent Face
Spartan Herald	Actor 3

Spartan Ambassadors (2)   Actors 2 & 5
Athenian Ambassadors (2)   Actors 3 & 4
Reconciliation (a naked girl) Silent Face
Slaves and Revelers   Silent Faces

The Women's Festival

Euripides   Actor 2
In-Law   Actor 1
Servant   Actor 3, then Silent Face
Agathon   Actor 3
Women   *Choros*
Mika   Actor 4
Garland-Seller   Actor 2
Kritylla   Actor 3
The Queen   Actor 2
Council Executive   Actor 2
Policeman   Actor 4
Echo   Actor 3
Mania, Fawn, Woodworm   Silent Faces

Frogs

Dionysos   Actor 1
Xanthias   Actor 2
Herakles   Actor 3
Corpse   Actor 3
Charon   Actor 3
Frogs   *Choros* or Half *Choros*
Initiates   *Choros*
Doorkeeper   Actor 3
Servant of Persephone   Actor 4
Innkeeper   Actor 3
Plathane   Actor 4

Slave	Actor 3
Euripides	Actor 2
Aischylos	Actor 3
Plouton (Haides)	Actor 4

Corpse-bearers, Slaves, Policemen, Old Woman; Silent Faces

Glossary of Proper Names

Achaian. In fifth-century B.C.E. drama, as in Homer, this word is used as a synonym for Greek, reflecting the preeminence of Achaia, especially throughout the Peloponnese, during the Trojan War period, in which most Athenian tragedies were set.

Acharnai. A large village in Attika, around twenty kilometers north of Athens.

Acheron. A lake in the underworld.

Achilleus. Son of Peleus and the nymph Thetis, from Phthia in Thessaly. His quarrel with Agamemnon, leader of the expedition against Troy, is the central strand in the plot of Homer's *Iliad*. In the *Iliad* and in Aischylos's Achilleus trilogy, he slew the Trojan hero Hektor in revenge for the death of his friend and companion, Patroklos; but this brought about his own death at the hands of Paris. Achilleus's notorious silence in Aischylos's play presumably occurred when he was grieving for Patroklos.

Adeimantos. Alkibiades' cousin, one of the generals of 406/405; he was widely regarded as a traitor, responsible for the disastrous defeat at Aigispotamoi in that year.

Adonis. A beautiful young man, loved by the goddess of love, Aphrodite herself. She grieved so much at his death that Haides permitted him to spend six months of the year in the world above with her. His cult included an annual celebration by women, probably in the spring, since the Adonis myth allegorizes the death of nature in the autumn and its revival in the spring.

Agathon. The most celebrated Athenian tragic playwright of the next generation after Sophokles and Euripides; his first victory was in 417/16. Like Euripides before him, he accepted an invitation to the court of King Archelaos of Makedon, between the productions of *The Women's Festival* and *Frogs*.

Agenor. Son of the sea god Poseidon, king of Phoinikia and father of Kadmos and Europa.

Aigai. The location of this cape is unknown, but other references to it make it likely that it was on the island of Euboia.

Aigina. Island in the Saronic Gulf, due south of Athens's port of Peiraios.

Aigyptos. Eponymous king of Aigyptos, modern Egypt; he and his
fifty sons pursued his brother, Danaos, and his fifty daughters to
Argos; after some resistance, they married Danaos's daughters—
but all except one were murdered by their brides on the wedding
night. (See Aischylos, *Suppliants.*)

Aiolos. The king of Thessaly who founded the Aeolic branch of the
Greek nation. Euripides' drama was infamous for its portrayal
of consensual brother-sister incest, and *Frogs* 1474 parodies the
outrageous line "what deed is shameful, if it does not seem so
to those doing it?"

Aischylos (525/24–456/65). The first great Athenian tragic dramatist.
Six of his tragedies survive; *Persians, Seven against Thebes, Sup-
pliants,* and the *Oresteia* trilogy of 458. He fought the Persians at
Marathon in 490 and probably also at Salamis in 480.

Akropolis. The rock that commands the city of Athens; site of the great
temple of Athena, the Parthenon, and other sacred buildings.

Alkaios. Lyric poet, of Mytilene in Lesbos, c. 600.

Alkibiades. The most controversial figure in Athenian politics toward
the end of the Peloponnesian War. His military talent was as
undoubted as his dissolute private life and willingness to change
sides. He was appointed in 415 to be one of the generals in
charge of the Sikilian expedition, but while the preparations for
departure were taking place, he was suspected of being the ring-
leader of an attempt to overthrow the democracy at the time of
the mutilation of the Hermai (referred to at *Lys* 1093ff.). He
demanded an investigation before leaving but was refused; soon
after landing in Sicily, he was recalled to stand trial. He escaped
on his way back to Athens and went to Sparta, where he advised
the Spartans how to conduct the war against Athens. But he was
opposed by one of the kings of Sparta and took refuge with Tissaphernes, the Persian governor of southwest Asia Minor, in 412. He
attempted to persuade Tissaphernes to change his support from
the Spartans to the oligarchic Athenians based in Samos. After the
fall of the Four Hundred he remained in Ionia, assisting the Athenians in a number of victories there; he returned to Athens and
was elected a general in 407. When the Athenians removed him
from his generalship after the defeat of Athenian forces under
his lieutenant at Notion later in 407, however, Alkibiades went
into voluntary exile at a castle he had built on the Thrakian coast,
which is where he was at the time of both performances of *Frogs*.
In between the two performances he gave good advice, which
was ignored, to the Athenian generals before the disastrous battle

of Aigispotamoi, which took place in the Hellespont near his
castle. He was not again recalled to Athens. After the fall of
Athens in 404, a Persian governor murdered him.

Amazons. A mythical race of warrior women who lived on the Black
Sea. They allegedly cut off their right breasts to enable them to
draw bows effectively. They invaded Attika during the reign of
Theseus, who defeated them and married their queen.

Ameipsias. A comic poet contemporary with Aristophanes.

Anakreon. A lyric poet, celebrated for his love songs, from Teos on
the Asian coast but subsequently residing in Samos and finally
at Athens, and active in the late sixth century.

Andromeda. Daughter of Kepheus, king of Ethiopia. Her mother
boasted that she was more beautiful than the Nereids; angered
by this, Poseidon sent a sea monster to ravage the country. The
oracle of Ammon promised that Ethiopia would be delivered if
Andromeda was given up to the monster; Kepheus chained her
to a rock near the sea. Euripides' play began with Andromeda's
laments, repeated by the echo from a nearby cave; Andromeda
was then joined by a *choros* of girls from the neighborhood.
Perseus rescued her, quarreled with Kepheus, and won the right
to marry her; at the end of the play, the gods promised her that
she would become a constellation.

Aphrodite. Goddess of love. See *Kypros, Kythera, Paphos*.

Apollo. Son of Zeus and Leto; a major god, worshiped especially at
Delos and Delphi. He was the god of archery, music and painting,
purification, healing from disease, and prophecy.

Archedemos. A leading politician at the time of *Frogs*, who prosecuted one of the defeated generals of the battle of Arginousai
for embezzlement.

Archenomos. Otherwise unknown.

Argo. The swift boat used by the Argonauts, the heroes led by Iason
who brought back the Golden Fleece from Kolchis.

Argos. One of the most important cities in the Peloponnese, it is located
on a level, fertile plain in the northeast of the peninsula.

Artemis. Sister of Apollo; a virgin goddess, imaged as a huntress. As
a female counterpart to Apollo, she could both inflict and cure
diseases in women.

Artemisia. See **Karia**.

Athena. Virgin goddess of wisdom, sprung fully armed from the head
of her father, Zeus. Patron goddess of Athens, but also worshiped
at Sparta. Her magnificent temple, the Parthenon, with the state
treasury of Athens, was located on the Akropolis.

Bakchos. Cult-title of **Dionysos**, q.v.

Bellerophon. Son of the Korinthian king Glaukos; after committing murder in his native city, he fled to the court of Proitos, king of Argos, whose wife, Sthenoboia, fell in love with the young man—and, when he rejected her offers, falsely accused him to her husband of having propositioned her. In Euripides' version of the story, Bellerophon killed her; in other versions, she killed herself like Phaidra.

Boiotia. The league of small states, whose capital was Thebes, to the north of Attika. Boiotia was on the Peloponnesian side in the war, and this deprived the Athenians of the Boiotian delicacy, eels from Lake Kopais. Aristophanes framed a comic scene around this deprivation in *Acharnians*.

Charminos. Athenian general who lost six ships in battle against a superior Peloponnesian force at Syme early in 411.

Charon. The ferryman of the underworld.

Chloe. The shrine of the goddess Demeter Chloe (the earth mother as patroness of the young green shoots of corn and grass) was located in the southwest approaches to the Akropolis.

Dareios. The king of Persia from 521 to 485, who, after successfully expanding his empire into Thrakia and Makedonia, sent an expedition against Greece, which the Athenians defeated at Marathon in 490. In Aischylos's *Persians* (472), his ghost commiserates with the Elders of Persia over the defeat of his son, Xerxes, at Salamis in 480.

Delos. The smallest of the Kyklades group of islands, in the Aigeian Sea. It was a sacred island and a central site for the worship of Apollo.

Delphi. Town in Phokis, on the slopes of Mount Parnassos, site of the principal oracle of Apollo.

Demeter. The goddess of agriculture, protectress of all the fruits of the earth, and mother of Persephone. The Athenians celebrated her with a great festival at Eleusis, in Attic territory northwest of the capital and near the frontier with Megara.

Demostratos. A speaker lampooned by other comic poets as angry, loud, and almost crazy in his delivery. The reference in *Lys* is to the several assemblies held at Athens prior to the decision to send an expedition to Sicily, to besiege Syracuse, in 415.

Diagoras. Composer of lyrics from Melos; a militant atheist who was prosecuted before 414 for divulging the secrets of the Eleusinian mysteries. Aristophanes' purpose in mentioning him at *Frogs* 320 is to show that he is not mocking the mysteries themselves, but the kind of version of them that Diagoras might have composed.

Dionysos. Son of Zeus and Semele; god of ecstatic possession, fertility, and the life force, both creative and destructive—especially as manifested through liquids: the sap of young trees, the blood of young animals and humans, and wine. Tragedy and comedy became attached to his festivals, because they involve both creativity and impersonation. *Frogs* shows that even this god, whom Euripides had recently portrayed in all his terrifying power in his last tragedy, *Bakchai*, could be mercilessly ridiculed in comedy.

Empousa. A monstrous creature, believed to devour human beings, and able to change her shape at will.

Eros. The boy god of love, son of Aphrodite. He inflicted love on mortals and gods by shooting them with arrows from a golden quiver.

Euios. Cult title of **Dionysos**, q.v.

Euripides. The leading tragic playwright of Aristophanes' time. Nineteen of his tragedies survive, from *Alkestis* (438) to *Bakchai* (406). Some of his earlier dramas, including *Hippolytos* and *Melanippe*, portrayed adulterous wives and prompted Aristophanes' running joke, taken to its climax in *The Women's Festival*, that his tragedies denounce the immorality of women. By 411 he was branching out into more romantic territory, with plays such as *Iphigeneia among the Taurians*, *Andromeda*, and *Helen*.

Eurykrates. Several Athenians of this name are known; it is not possible to identify which one Kalonike's husband is guarding.

Furies (Erinyes). Female *daimones* of the underworld, who spring from the spilt blood of murder victims and pursue vengeance.

Gorgon. Medusa, whose hair was changed into serpents by Athena; her head was then so fearful that the sight of her changed people into stone. After Perseus succeeded in killing her, Athena placed Medusa's head in the center of her shield.

Gorgos. Clearly the secretary to one of the state bodies, perhaps the Council; otherwise unknown.

Haides. Brother of Zeus and Poseidon, husband of Persephone; also called Plouton. Zeus's counterpart below the earth, the ruler of the underworld to which human souls pass after death. His kingdom is often called Haides', abbreviated from "Haides' halls."

Hegelochos. The tragic actor who committed an unfortunate error when playing Orestes in Euripides' tragedy in 408 (*Frogs* 302–304;

in the original Greek, he mispronounced *galen*, which with different accents means "calm" and "weasel"). Aristophanes was not the only comic playwright who made fun of the mistake.

Hekate. A formidable goddess of the underworld, associated with witchcraft and sorcery. She is frequently imaged as bearing two torches.

Helen. Daughter of Zeus and Leda; wife of Menelaos, king of Sparta. Her elopement with Paris caused the ten-year Trojan War. She successfully begged her husband to spare her life after the fall of Troy; Euripides added the detail that she bared her breasts during this appeal (*Andromache* 629ff.). In *Helen* he dramatized the legend that a replica of Helen, created by the gods, was responsible for the Trojan War; the real Helen was transported to Egypt, where at the start of the play she is being pressured by Theoklymenos, king of Egypt, to marry her. Menelaos, her husband, is cast ashore after suffering many hardships since the fall of Troy; they recognize each other and escape.

Hera. Wife of Zeus and goddess of marriage; the most powerful goddess.

Herakles. Son of Zeus by Alkmene; the greatest Greek hero. Zeus ordered him to serve Eurystheus, king of Tiryns, for twelve years. The Labors of Herakles are the superhuman feats that Eurystheus demanded of him. They included bringing the dog Kerberos up from Haides'.

Hermes. Son of Zeus and Maia; herald and messenger of the gods. He was the god who escorted travelers and conducted souls between the worlds of the living and the dead; also the guardian of paternal rights and the god of deception and trickery. Images of Hermes with an erect phallus stood outside the front door of Athenian houses.

Hesiod. A Boiotian, one of the earliest Greek poets, author of *Works and Days,* which contains agricultural, economic, ethical, and political advice. He also created *Theogony*, an account of the origin of the world and the birth of the gods.

Hipponax. Of Ephesos, a Greek poet of the late sixth century renowned for the bitterness of his satire.

Homer. Creator of the *Iliad* and the *Odyssey*, to whom numerous other epic poems were also ascribed. "Aischylos" celebrates him in *Frogs* for the heroic feats of combat that are described in the many battles of the *Iliad*.

Hyperbolos. An Athenian politician of lowborn origin who was ostracized in 416 and was murdered by the oligarchic faction in

Samos in 411. Like **Kleon** (q.v.), he is imagined in *Frogs* to be as keen on prosecution and character assassination in the underworld as he had been in real life.

Iakchos. The son of Zeus and Demeter, worshiped solemnly at the Eleusinian mysteries and imagined in *Frogs* as dwelling in the underworld.

Ibykos. Lyric poet from Rhegion in Sicily, who spent most of his life at Samos. Active in the late sixth century.

Ida. A mountain in central Krete.

Ionia. The west coast of modern Turkey, site of several major Greek cities.

Iophon. Sophokles' son, a productive and successful tragic playwright. His works are lost.

Kadmos. Son of Agenor, founder of the city of Thebes, capital of Boiotia.

Kallias. In reality the son of Hipponikos ("victorious with horses"); a distinguished, wealthy Athenian and a patron of intellectuals—but also with a reputation as a womanizer.

Karia. Artemisia, Queen of Halikarnassos in Karia (southwest Asia Minor) led her fleet in support of Xerxes' invasion and had a lucky escape in the battle of Salamis (Herodotos, *Histories* 7.99 and 8.87–88).

Kepheus. King of Ethiopia, father of **Andromeda**, q.v.

Kephisophon. A collaborator with Euripides on some of his tragedies.

Kerameikos. The northwest gate of Athens.

Kerberians. Otherwise unknown inhabitants of Haides'.

Kerberos. The three-headed dog that guarded the entrance to Haides', brought up to earth by Herakles as one of his labors.

Kimolos. One of the Kyklades group of islands in the Aigeian, famous for its fine white earth.

Kimon. The greatest general of the previous generation, frequently in command of Athenian offensives against the Persians, especially the sea and land battles at Eurymedon in 466. His assistance to the Spartans against the revolt of their slaves, the helots, in 464 was not quite the success that Lysistrata claims; his assault on the helot stronghold of Mount Ithome failed, and the Spartans dismissed him ignominiously. This was the end of both his career and his policy of a joint hegemony between Athens and Sparta, which Lysistrata's speech suggests should be revived.

Kinesias. The composer of dithyrambic poetry and music, referred to three times in *Frogs*, was physically weak and chronically ill; he is almost certainly not to be identified with Myrrhine's extremely virile husband in *Lysistrata,* who is given this name because it echoes his main asset—"Prick."

Kithairon. A mountain on the borders of Attika and Boiotia.

Kleidemides. Cannot be identified with certainty.

Kleigenes. A bathhouse proprietor, who might possibly be identified with the first secretary of the Athenian Council in 410/9.

Kleisthenes ("The Queen"). Athens's most notorious homosexual.

Kleitophon. An associate of the sophist Thrasymachos.

Kleomenes. King of Sparta from 520 to his death in 491. In 510 he commanded the Spartan army, which helped the Athenians to expel the tyrant Hippias, who was supported by foreign troops from Thessaly. But later he intervened in Athenian politics on the side of the aristocrats who opposed the democratic reforms of Kleisthenes and was defeated by the democrats.

Kleon. A notorious Athenian politician, who had been dead since 422 and is invoked by the Innkeeper because of his fondness for prosecutions.

Kleonymos. A significant politician, probably a member of the Council in the year when *Acharnians* was first performed. He is satirized in every surviving play of Aristophanes from *Acharnians* to *Birds* for gluttony and cowardice—allegedly for running away in battle and discarding his shield.

Kleophon. An ambitious and bellicose man, who became Athens's leading politician in 410 and intransigently opposed negotiations with Sparta. He was condemned to death and executed at the prompting of the right-wing (oligarchic) faction in 404, just before the revival of *Frogs*.

Kokytos. A river of the underworld, flowing into Lake Acheron.

Korinth. City commanding the Isthmus that unites the Peloponnese with the Greek mainland; an ally of Sparta in the war.

Krete. One of the largest islands in the Mediterranean; its inhabitants were sometimes alleged to be morally degenerate.

Kyknos. Either the son of Ares who robbed travelers on the road to Delphi and was killed by Herakles, or the son of Tithonos who was killed by Achilleus at Troy. No play about him is listed in the catalog of Aischylos's works.

Kypros. Modern Cyprus, birthplace of Aphrodite (but see **Kythera**).

Kyrene/ian. A woman/women notorious for sexual versatility.

Kythera. An island off the south coast of the Peloponnese, celebrated for the worship of Aphrodite and claimed by some to be her birthplace.

Lamachos. A successful general in the earliest years of the Peloponnesian War (but ridiculed in 425 in Aristophanes' first surviving comedy, *Acharnians*). He died attempting a heroic exploit during the siege of Syracuse in 414; after his death, Aristophanes treats him with respect in *TWF* (841) and in *Frogs*.

Leonidas. King of Sparta 491–80, who made a heroic stand against Xerxes' invading land army at the pass of Thermopylai in Lokris and died together with his three hundred Spartans and some of their allies.

Leto. Mother of Apollo and Artemis.

Lykis. A comic playwright contemporary with Aristophanes.

Lykon. Lykon's wife was Rhodia; he himself was a prominent citizen, ridiculed in comedies by Eupolis and Kratinos.

Lykourgos. King of the Edones in Thrace; he persecuted Dionysos and his worshipers and was punished with death by the god. He was the subject of a lost trilogy by Aischylos.

Lysistrata. The name of Aristophanes' heroine means "disbander of armies," deliberately echoing that of Lysimache ("dissolver of battles"), who in 411 was the long-serving priestess of Athena Polias.

Lysistratos. Perhaps the passive homosexual Lysistratos, of Amphitrope.

Malian Gulf. The gulf between Malis in southern Thessaly and Lokris, closed in by the northwest end of the island of Euboia. Following the pun between the name of the city of Echinos at the top end of the Malian Gulf and the sea urchin (Echinos, in this translation the Hedgehog—i.e., in this context, Reconciliation's pubic hair), Aristophanes now puns on the fact that Greek *kolpos,* which in geography meant gulf, was also used to describe the vulva.

Marathon. Site of the Athenian victory over Dareios's invading Persian army in 490; forty-two kilometers northeast of Athens on the east coast of Attika.

Megairetos. Unknown.

Megara. The city-state adjacent to Athens on the west. The Megarians fought on the Peloponnesian side in the war. The "legs of Megara" were the long walls connecting Megara to its port of Nisaia, which in 411 was still occupied by Athenian forces. The walls had actually been demolished in 424/23, but this does not deter Aristophanes from pursuing his pun.

Melanion. A legendary figure, taught to hunt by the *kentaur* Cheiron, who hunted in the forests of Arkadia.

Melanippe. Daughter of Aiolos, falsely accused of unchastity when she had in fact been raped by Poseidon.

Meleagros. Son of Oineus, king of Kalydon, and Althaia. When Meleagros was born, the Fates prophesied that he would live no longer than a brand then burning on the fire; she snatched it from the flames and kept it. As an adult Meleagros slew the Kalydonian boar and gave the hide to the woman he loved, Atalanta, but his mother's brothers took it from her, and Meleagros slaughtered them in revenge. Hearing of this, Althaia deliberately burned the brand and so killed her son.

Meletos. Composer of erotica and drinking songs.

Memnon. King of the Ethiopians, son of Tithonos and the dawn goddess, Eos; he came to help the Trojans toward the end of the Trojan War. Achilleus killed him, but to soothe Eos's grief Zeus made him immortal.

Menelaos. King of Sparta, brother of Agamemnon, husband of Helen. When he married her, the unsuccessful suitors swore an oath to come to his defense if she was abducted. Helen's elopement with Paris therefore caused the Trojan War. His adventures after the war, as imagined by Euripides in *Helen* (q.v.), are parodied in *The Women's Festival*.

Mikon. One of the leading painters of the generation before Aristophanes. His mural of the Amazons was in the Peisianakteion, later known as the Stoa Poikile.

Miletos. Greek city in Ionia, on the southwest coast of Asia Minor, it had defected to the Spartan side in 412. Greece's leading manufacturer of dildos.

Morsimos. A tragic playwright.

Mousaios. A legendary resident of Eleusis, famous for poems of various kinds, but in particular for a compilation of oracles.

Muses. The nine goddesses whom creative writers invoked as the inspiring goddesses of song. Places sacred to them were Mount Helicon and Mount Parnassos, both in Boiotia.

Myrmex. Not otherwise known.

Myronides. An Athenian general in the previous generation; he defeated the Korinthians at Megara in 459 and the Boiotians at Oinophyta in 457.

Myrrhine. A contemporary priestess was named Myrrhine, but Aristophanes chose the name more for what it evokes; it is related to the word "myrtle," which was slang for the female genitals.

Nikomachos. He had been entrusted in 410 with the codification and public inscription of laws. Lysias wrote a speech prosecuting him in 399/98.

Niobe. Daughter of Tantalos and wife of Amphion, king of Thebes. She boasted that she was a better mother than Leto, because she had more children. In revenge, Apollo and Artemis killed her children (this scene was actually dramatized in some remarkable surviving fragments of Sophokles' *Niobe*; Ewans 2000, 169–70). Aischylos clearly began his *Niobe* after the killings, with Niobe sitting shrouded, silent in her grief. She wasted away and gradually turned into stone.

Nysa. Legendary scene of the childhood of Dionysos, located by Sophokles on the island of Euboia.

Oidipous. Son of Laios and Iokaste, exposed on a mountainside but rescued and brought up as their son by Polybos and Merope; ruler of Thebes after he rid the city of the Sphinx, until he discovered that his wife was his own mother and he had killed his real father. He then blinded himself.

Oineus. King of Kalydon, husband of Althaia and father of **Meleagros**, q.v.

Olympos. Mountain in northern Greece, legendary residence of the gods and goddesses.

Orestes. The only son of Agamemnon and Klytaimestra, sent into exile as a child by Klytaimestra after she and her lover, Aigisthos, had murdered Agamemnon. When he came of age, he returned to Argos to avenge his father's death by killing Klytaimestra and Aigisthos. The opening lines of the play by Aischylos in which he did this, *Libation Bearers*, are quoted and ridiculed at *Frogs* 1124ff.

Orpheus. A mythical personage, regarded by the Greeks as a supreme singer and musician. "Aischylos" refers in *Frogs* both to the mystery cult of Orpheus and to his supposed role as one of the legendary civilizers of human society, instituting laws against homicide.

Palamedes. One of the Greek heroes who sailed against Troy; a legendary inventor, who in Euripides' tragedy invented writing, which his brother, Oiax, used on oar blades to convey the news of Palamedes' death, treacherously contrived by Odysseus. Their father, Nauplios, found one of the oar blades and avenged his son's death by wrecking much of the returning Greek fleet.

Pallas. A cult title of Athena, of unknown origin and meaning.

Pan. God of flocks and shepherds, lover of music, and inventor of the syrinx ("panpipes"). His grotto was on the northwest side of the Akropolis, not very far from the Propylaia—the entrance gates of the Akropolis, outside which *Lysistrata* is set.

Pantokles. Unknown, except for another reference to his clumsiness in a lost comedy by Eupolis.

Paphos. Town in southwest Cyprus, center of the worship of Aphrodite, who is said to have landed there after her birth from the foam of the waves.

Paralia. The coastal district of Attika.

Paralos. With *Salamis*, one of the two flagship triremes of the Athenian fleet.

Parnassos. The mountain behind Delphi, sacred to Dionysos as well as Apollo.

Patroklos. The heroic companion of Achilleus, killed by Hektor when he fought in Achilleus's armor in the *Iliad* and in Aischylos's Achilleus trilogy.

Pauson. A painter noted for his jokes—and for his poverty; hence the reference at *TWF* 949ff.

Peisandros. At *Lysistrata* 490, Aristophanes prophetically names the political manipulator who had recently arrived back in Athens as the envoy of the oligarchic generals in Samos; he was soon to begin the intrigues that culminated in May in the takeover of Athens by the Four Hundred under his leadership.

Peleus. Son of Aiakos and father of Achilleus. Euripides' lost tragedy may have dramatized his murder of his half brother, Phokos; his first marriage to the daughter of Eurytion, the king of Phthia, whom he involuntarily killed with his spear during the hunt for the Kalydonian boar; or his refuge after that deed in Iolkos and the false accusations against him by Astydamia.

Pelops. Son of Tantalos; founder of the royal house of Argos; father of Atreus and Thyestes, grandfather of Agamemnon and Menelaos.

Penelope. The faithful wife of Odysseus, who resisted the pressure of over a hundred suitors while her husband was absent for twenty years during the ten-year war against Troy and his long-delayed return voyage (see Homer's *Odyssey*).

Persephone. Daughter of Demeter and, during the autumn and winter of each year, wife of Haides.

Perseus. A famous hero, son of Zeus and Danaë. Polydektes, king of the island of Seriphos, sent him on a mission to bring back the head of Medusa, one of the Gorgons. He achieved this by looking at her through a mirror given to him by Athena, since the sight of her would have turned him to stone. He flew with winged sandals given to him by the nymphs and rescued Andromeda before his return to Seriphos.

Phaidra. Wife of Theseus; she fell in love with her stepson, Hippolytos, and brought about his downfall, when he did not requite her love, by accusing him of rape and committing suicide. The second version of Euripides' *Hippolytos*, which dramatizes these events, survives.

Philokles. Nephew of Aischylos, a minor tragic dramatist (though he beat Sophokles in the year when the latter's entry included *Oidipous the King*). His ugliness was due to a misshapen head.

Philoxenos. His son, Erixenos, was a notorious glutton.

Phoibos. Cult title of Apollo, meaning "bright."

Phormio. An Athenian general, celebrated especially for his victory over the Peloponnesians at sea off Naupaktos in 429/98. Aristophanes praised him in several plays.

Phormisios. Another comic poet accused a Phormisios of taking bribes from the Persians, and one of Lysias's speeches (34) was written for a Phormisios, but it is uncertain whether they are the same man or, indeed, whether either of them is the Phormisios reviled by Aristophanes at *Frogs* 965.

Phrynichos. (1) The principal tragic playwright of the generation before Aischylos. (2) A comic poet contemporary with Aristophanes. His *Muses* came second to *Frogs*. (3) Athenian general in 411, who became one of the leaders of the Four Hundred. He was murdered on his return from an unsuccessful embassy that tried to make peace proposals on their behalf to the Spartans.

Phrynondas. A notorious villain.

Phthia. District in southeast Thessaly on the Gulf of Malia, homeland of Achilleus.

Pisa. A town in Elis in the Peloponnese, just east of Olympia.

Plouton. Haides (q.v.), the god of the underworld, or Haides'.

Polybos. King of Korinth, he adopted the infant Oidipous.

Poseidon. Brother of Zeus, god of the sea.

Proteas. Probably a general who commanded two expeditions in the early years of the Peloponnesian War.

Proteus. The recently deceased king of Egypt in Euripides' *Helen*.

Pylos. Town on the west coast of the Peloponnese, in the Spartan territory of Messene. It was the scene of one of the most important victories of the Peloponnesian War, when Demosthenes and Kleon succeeded in isolating and capturing a Spartan force on the adjacent island of Sphakteria (425). The Athenians still occupied it in 411 when *Lys* was performed. Pylos overlooked the narrow northern entrance to the large natural harbor now known as the Bay of Navarino. (Modern Pylos is located at the southern end of the harbor.)

Pythangelos. Unknown.

Salamis. Island in the Saronic Gulf west of Athens; an Athenian territory that was famous for its oarsmen.

Semele. Daughter of Kadmos, king of Thebes; mother of the god Dionysos, fathered by Zeus. Hera contrived her death, but Dionysos afterward removed her from Haides' and immortalized her as Thyone.

Sidon. The chief city of Phoinikia, where Kadmos grew up.

Simois. One of the rivers of the Trojan plain.

Skamander. The other, larger river of Troy.

Skira. A women's festival, chiefly in honor of Demeter.

Sokrates. The great philosopher, caricatured mercilessly by Aristophanes in his earlier play *Clouds*.

Sophokles. The great tragic playwright, c. 496–406. Seven of his tragedies survive, all from his middle and old age, including the famous *Antigone* and *Oidipous the King* and the posthumous *Oidipous at Kolonos*.

Sparta. The leading city of the Peloponnese, situated in the southern district of Lakonia.

Spercheios. River of Thessaly, which flows through Malis and into the Malian Gulf.

Sphinx. A she-monster with a lion's body, an eagle's wings, and a woman's torso; she posed a riddle to the Thebans and murdered all who were unable to guess it. Oidipous solved her riddle and became king of Thebes.

Stenia. A women's festival in honor of Demeter and Persephone.

Sthenoboia. See **Bellerophon**.

Styx. The principal river of the underworld.

Taigetos. The highest mountain range in Lakonia, west and south of Sparta.

Tainaros. The cave, with an exit near the southern point of Lakonia, through which Herakles dragged Kerberos from Haides' to the upper world.

Tantalos. Son of Zeus, father of Pelops, founder of the house of Atreus.

Tartessos. "Tartessian" moray eels were a delicacy. It is unlikely that they were actually imported from Tartessos, which was the name of the southwest part of the Iberian Peninsula.

Telephos. Hero of a tragedy by Euripides, extensively satirized in Aristophanes' *Acharnians* and in the wine-skin hostage scene of *TWF*, he was the king of Mysia in Asia Minor. Achilleus wounded him when the Greeks attacked his country, mistaking it for Troy. In Euripides' play, an oracle told him "your wounder will also be your healer," so he made his way to Argos, where the Greek warlords had gathered, disguised as a Greek beggar. Telephos offered to defend himself with his head on a chopping block and made a speech claiming that "we Greeks" would have counterattacked, like the Mysians, if Greek territory had been invaded. When his identity was discovered, he seized Agamemnon's baby son, Orestes, and took refuge at an altar. Telephos won the case that he argued in defense of himself and his Mysians, and the Greeks learned that they were dependent on him to be their guide if the Trojan expedition was to succeed. It was also revealed that he was of Greek ancestry, the son of Herakles and Auge. Filings from Achilleus's spear cured his wound, and the expedition set off.

Teukros. From Salamis, he was the brother of Aias, one of the great heroes of the *Iliad* and the subject of a surviving tragedy by Sophokles.

Thasos. Island in the north of the Aigeian Sea, off the coast of Thrakia. Thasian was one of the best wine varieties, dark in color and with an aroma reminiscent of apples. Its sale was limited and regulated.

Thebes. Capital of Boiotia, a federation of cities to Athens's north, which was on the Spartan side in the Peloponnesian War.

Theogenes. It is not possible to identify which holder of this common name Aristophanes refers to. The untranslatable puns in *Lysistrata* 63–64 imply that perhaps he was a shipowner.

Theognis. A tragic dramatist, already criticized by Aristophanes for writing boring plays in his first surviving comedy, *Acharnians*. Theognis survived to become one of the junta of thirty installed by the Spartans after the defeat of Athens.

Theonoe. An Egyptian priestess, sister of Theoklymenos in Euripides' *Helen*.

Theramenes. A political survivor who led the establishment in mid-411 of the oligarchy of the Four Hundred. When it divided on factional lines, he led the more democratic side and therefore stayed in favor when democracy was restored. At the battle of Arginousai (the "all-or-nothing" sea battle referred to at *Frogs* 191, when slaves were allowed to serve as sailors), he was supposed to be in charge of the recovery of the dead and wounded, but successfully claimed that bad weather prevented this. He argued that the generals were responsible for the disaster; six of them were executed, but he survived. After *Frogs*, his luck ran out; he negotiated the fall of Athens and became one of the Thirty Tyrants, but was put to death for opposing their ruthless policy of execution and intimidation on the instigation of the tyrants' leader, Kritias.

Theseus. The legendary hero and early king of Athens. In the normal version of the myth, he assisted Pirithoos's unsuccessful attempt to abduct Persephone from the underworld and was imprisoned there until Herakles, descending to Haides' to bring Kerberos up to earth, rescued him.

Thorykion. Not otherwise known.

Thrakia. The country to the north of the Aigeian Sea; there were some Greek colonies along the coastline, which were a scene of hostilities during the Peloponnesian War.

Timon. An archetypal misanthrope, probably a legendary figure rather than a real individual.

Twins. Kastor and Polydeukes, sons of Leda and Tyndareus, a king of Sparta, and therefore brothers of Helen. They were heroes descended from Zeus and were worshiped as gods at Sparta.

Two Goddesses, the. Demeter and **Persephone**, qqv.

Tyndareus. King of Sparta, father of Helen and Klytaimestra.

Xenokles. A tragic playwright, son of Karkinos; he defeated Euripides in 415.

Zakynthos. An island in the Ionian Sea off the coast of Elis, it was part of the Athenian empire.

Zeus. The most powerful god, son of Kronos and Rhea. A sky and weather god, whose weapon is the thunderbolt; he punished several kinds of wrongdoing, especially oath breaking and breaches of the rules of hospitality. However, Zeus did not make the world, and he was not omnipotent or omniscient. Despite his great and wide-ranging powers, both other gods and human beings could defy him (at their own risk), and the ingenious Athenian Peisetairos displaces him as ruler of the world in Aristophanes' *Birds*.

Glossary of Greek Words

Agōn. A formal debate-style contest, usually between the principal character and his or her main opponent.

Chiton. The short tunic worn by Greek males.

Choros. Literally song (and dance); denotes either the group of twenty-four *choros* members or the odes (songs) that they perform.

Daimōn. We would regard a *daimōn* as the personification of an abstract concept, for example, Destruction, Strife, or Reconciliation, but the Greeks regarded such forces as animate beings with a mystic, godlike power.

Eisodos. One of the two entranceways on each side of the *orchēstra*. By a convention reflecting the reality of the theater's location, the *skēnē* left *eisodos* was imagined as leading "downtown" from the place where the action was set (in *Frogs*, back to Athens); the *skēnē* right *eisodos* led to the countryside, the shore, and other cities (in *Frogs*, further into Haides').

Ekkuklēma. The "rolling-out machine," a platform on wheels used in tragedy when the pressure of events inside the building represented by the *skēnē* has such implications for the public forum outside that they must be seen (e.g., when Klytaimestra has murdered Agamemnon and Kassandra in Aischylos's *Agamemnon*). Agathon's entrance and exit in *TWF* parody the use of the *ekkuklēma* in tragedy—doubtless he had employed it in his own work.

Ekstasis. Literally, a state of being outside oneself—the ecstasy felt during celebrations of Dionysos, induced by wine, ceremonies, theatrical and musical performances, or a combination of all three.

Kentaur. A creature with a human head and torso and a horse's body.

Kōmos. Literally revelry—the scene of festive rejoicing that appears at the end of most of Aristophanes' plays and from which the genre of comedy (*kōmoidia*) got its name.

Mechane. The crane used from around 435 B.C.E. to swing into view gods and other characters who are to be imagined as flying into the playing area.

Mimesis. Impersonation, imitation, representation, role playing.

Oikos. The extended family household, which was the basic unit of Greek society.

Orchēstra. The dance floor, almost certainly circular, on which tragedies and comedies were performed.

Parabasis. Literally "stepping forward"; an extended choral ode at the center of an Aristophanic comedy, in which the *choros* moves out of the action of the play to address the audience directly on matters of current political and/or social importance, either in their own character or speaking on behalf of Aristophanes himself.

Parodos. The entry song of the *choros.*

Phallus. The long artificial penis made of leather, worn and protruding under their *chitons* by actors playing male parts in comedy. In the second half of *Lysistrata,* the phalluses of Kinesias, the Spartan Messenger, and the Ambassadors are all erect.

Polis. A city (e.g., Athens, Sparta) that, with its surrounding territory, was also an independent state; the largest social unit in fifth-century Greece.

Prosōpon. Literally "face"; Greek word for the larger-than-life masks, which ensured that the age and gender of characters was visible even to distant members of the audience.

Skēnē. Literally and originally a tent in which the actors changed masks and costumes. By 458 B.C.E. it was a wooden building behind the *orchēstra,* erected for the duration of each festival, with a set of double doors at the center and a practicable roof; it was used to represent, for example, a palace, house, temple, or tent—probably by the addition of painted panels on the front (*skenographia,* "scene painting"). In *Lysistrata* it represents the Propylaia, the entrance doors of the Akropolis; in *The Women's Festival* it represents first the house of Agathon and later a building in the sacred precinct where the Women's Festival (Thesmophoria) takes place; in *Frogs* it represents first the house of Herakles and later that of Plouton and Persephone.

Theatron. The "seeing-place"; the part of the theater in which the audience sat.

BIBLIOGRAPHY

Aristophanes. 2002. *Acharnians.* Edited by S. D. Olson. Oxford: Oxford Univ. Press.

———. 2004. *Thesmophoriazusae.* Edited by C. Austin and S. D. Olson. Oxford: Oxford Univ. Press.

———. 1992. *Lysistrata.* Edited and translated by M. Neuburg. Arlington Heights, Ill.: Harlan Davidson.

Campbell, D. 1984. "The Frogs in *The Frogs.*" *Journal of Hellenic Studies* 104:163–65.

Case, S-E. 1988. *Feminism and Theatre.* Basingstoke: Macmillan.

Czapo, E., and W. Slater. 1995. *The Context of Ancient Drama.* Ann Arbor: Univ. of Michigan Press.

Dale, A. M. 1969. *Collected Papers.* Cambridge: Cambridge Univ. Press.

Dearden, C. W. 1976. *The Stage of Aristophanes.* London: Athlone.

Dover, K., ed. 1993. *Aristophanes: Frogs,* Oxford: Oxford Univ. Press.

English, M. 2005. "Aristophanes' *Frogs*: Brek-kek-kek-kek! on Broadway." *American Journal of Philology* 126:127–33.

Ewans, M., and G. Ley. 1985. "The *Orchestra* as Acting Area in Greek Tragedy." *Ramus* 14.2:75–84.

Ewans, M., ed. and trans. 1995. *Aeschylus: Oresteia,* London: J. M. Dent.

———, ed. and trans. 1996. *Aeschylus: Suppliants and Other Dramas.* London : J. M. Dent.

———, ed. and trans., with G. Ley and G. McCart. 1999. *Sophocles: Four Dramas of Maturity.* London: J. M. Dent.

———, ed. and trans., with G. Ley and G. McCart. 2000. *Sophokles: Three Dramas of Old Age.* London: J. M. Dent.

Foley, H. 1982. "The 'Female Intruder' Reconsidered: Women in Aristophanes' *Lysistrata* and *Ecclesiazusae.*" *Classical Philology* 77:1–21.

Gamel, M. 2002. "From *Thesmophoriazousai* to *The Julie Thesmo Show*: Adaption, Performance, Reception." *American Journal of Philology* 123.3:465–99.

———. 2007. "Sondheim Floats *Frogs.*" In *Aristophanes in Performance 421 BC–AD 2007,* edited by E. Hall and A. Wrigley, 209–30. London: Legenda.

Goette, H. R. 2007. "An Archaeological Appendix." In *The Greek Theatre and Festivals: Documentary Studies,* edited by P. Wilson, 116–21. Oxford: Oxford Univ. Press.

Goldhill, S. 1990. "The Great Dionysia and Civic Ideology." In *Nothing to Do with Dionysos? Athenian Drama in Its Social Context*, edited by J. Winkler and F. Zeitlin, 97–129. Princeton: Princeton Univ. Press.

———. 1997. "The Audience of Athenian Tragedy." In *The Cambridge Companion to Greek Tragedy*, edited by P. Easterling, 54–68. Cambridge: Cambridge Univ. Press.

Halliwell, S., ed. and trans. 1998. *Aristophanes: Birds and Other Plays*. Oxford: Oxford Univ. Press.

Henderson, J. 1975. *The Maculate Muse: Obscene Language in Attic Comedy*. New Haven: Yale Univ. Press.

———, ed. 1987. *Aristophanes: Lysistrata*. Oxford: Oxford Univ. Press.

———. 1991. "Women and the Athenian Dramatic Festivals." *Transactions of the American Philological Association* 121:133–47.

———, trans. 1996. *Three Plays by Aristophanes: Staging Women*. New York: Routledge.

———, ed. and trans. 2000. *Aristophanes: Birds, Lysistrata, Women at the Thesmophoria*. Cambridge, Mass.: Harvard Univ. Press.

———, ed. and trans. 2002. *Aristophanes: Frogs, Assemblywomen, Wealth*. Cambridge, Mass: Harvard Univ. Press.

Holzinger, K. 1928. "Erklärungen umstrittener Stellen des Aristophanes." *SB Wien* 208.5:37ff.

Hubbard, T. 1991. *The Mask of Comedy*. Ithaca, N.Y.: Cornell Univ. Press.

Lada-Richards, I. 1999. *Initiating Dionysus: Ritual and Theatre in Aristophanes' Frogs*. Oxford: Oxford Univ. Press.

Ley, G. 1989. "Agatharchos, Aeschylus and the Construction of a Skēnē." *Maia*, n.s. 1:35–38.

———. 2006. *The Theatricality of Greek Tragedy*. Chicago: Univ. of Chicago Press.

———. 2007. "A Material World: Costume, Properties and Scenic Effects." In *The Cambridge Companion to Greek and Roman Theatre*, edited by M. McDonald and J. M. Walton, 268–87. Cambridge: Cambridge Univ. Press.

McCart, G. 2007. "Masks in Greek and Roman Theatre." In *The Cambridge Companion to Greek and Roman Theatre*, edited by M. McDonald and J. M. Walton, 247–67. Cambridge: Cambridge Univ. Press.

McDonald, M., and J. M. Walton, eds. 2007. *The Cambridge Companion to Greek and Roman Theatre*. Cambridge: Cambridge Univ. Press.

Macdowell, D. 1972. "The Frogs' Chorus." *Classical* Review, n.s. 22:3–5.

———. 1995. *Aristophanes and Athens: An Introduction to the Plays*. New York: Oxford Univ. Press.

McLeish, K. 1980. *The Theatre of Aristophanes.* London: Thames and Hudson.

———, trans. 1993*a*. *Aristophanes: Plays One.* London: Methuen.

———, trans. 1993*b*. *Aristophanes: Plays Two.* London: Methuen.

Moorton, R. 1988. "Aristophanes on Alcibiades." *Greek Roman and Byzantine Studies* 29:345–59.

O'Sullivan, N. 2000. "Poetry from Old Rope: A Neglected Emendation in Aristophanes, *Frogs* 1298." *Classical Quarterly,* n.s. 50.1:297–98.

Rehm, R. 1988. "The Staging of Suppliant Plays." *Greek, Roman & Byzantine Studies* 29:263–307.

———. 1992. *The Greek Tragic Theatre.* London: Routledge.

Revermann, M. 2006. *Comic Business: Theatricality, Dramatic Technique, and Performance Contexts of Aristophanic Comedy.* Oxford: Oxford Univ. Press.

Robson, J. 2008. "Lost in Translation? The Problem of (Aristophanic) Humour." In *A Companion to Classical Receptions,* edited by L. Hardwick and C. Stray, 168–82. Oxford: Oxford Univ. Press.

———. 2009. *Aristophanes: An Introduction.* London: Duckworth.

Seaford, R. 1994. *Reciprocity and Ritual: Homer and Tragedy in the Developing City-State.* Oxford: Oxford Univ. Press.

Silk, M. S. 2000. *Aristophanes and the Definition of Comedy.* Oxford: Oxford Univ. Press.

Sommerstein, A. 1977. "Aristophanes and the Events of 411." *Journal of Hellenic Studies* 97:112–26.

———, ed. and trans. 1990. *Aristophanes: Lysistrata.* Warminster: Aris and Phillips.

———, ed. and trans. 1996. *Aristophanes: Frogs.* Warminster: Aris and Phillips.

———, ed. and trans. 2001. *Aristophanes: The Thesmophoriazusae.* 2nd ed. Warminster: Aris and Phillips.

———, ed. and trans. 2002. *Aristophanes: Lysistrata/The Acharnians/Clouds.* 2nd ed. Harmondsworth: Penguin.

———. 2004. "The Alleged Attempts to Prosecute Aristophanes." In *Free Speech in Classical Antiquity,* edited by I. Sluiter and Rosen, 145–74. Leiden: Brill.

———. 2009. *Talking about Laughter and Other Studies in Greek Comedy.* Oxford: Oxford Univ. Press.

Stanford, W. B. 1983. *Greek Tragedy and the Emotions: An Introductory Study.* London: Routledge and Kegan Paul.

Taaffe, L. 1993. *Aristophanes and Women.* London: Routledge.

Taplin, O. 1977. *The Stagecraft of Aeschylus.* Oxford: Oxford Univ. Press.

————. 1993. *Comic Angels: And Other Approaches to Greek Drama through Vase-Painting.* Oxford: Oxford Univ. Press.

Vaio, J. 1973. "The Manipulation of Theme and Plot in Aristophanes' *Lysistrata.*" *Greek, Roman and Byzantine Studies* 14:369–80.

Walton, J. M. 2006. *Found in Translation: Greek Drama in English.* Cambridge: Cambridge Univ. Press.

Westlake, H. D. 1980. "The *Lysistrata* and the War." *Phoenix* 34:38–54.

Wiles, D. 1997. *Tragedy in Athens: Performance Space and Theatrical Meaning.* Cambridge: Cambridge Univ. Press.

————. 2007. *Mask and Performance in Greek Tragedy: From Ancient Festival to Modern Experimentation.* Cambridge: Cambridge Univ. Press.

Wilson, P. 2000. *The Athenian Institution of the Khoregia: The Chorus, the City, and the Stage.* Cambridge: Cambridge Univ. Press.

Zweig, B. 1992. "The Mute Nude Female Characters in Aristophanes' Plays." In *Pornography and Representation in Greece and Rome,* edited by A. Richlin. New York: Oxford Univ. Press.